Lecture Notes in Computer Science 9361

Commenced Publication in 1973
Founding and Former Series Editors:
Gerhard Goos, Juris Hartmanis, and Jan van Leeuwen

More information about this series at http://www.springer.com/series/7409

Christian Berger · Mohammad Reza Mousavi (Eds.)

Cyber Physical Systems

Design, Modeling, and Evaluation

5th International Workshop, CyPhy 2015
Amsterdam, The Netherlands, October 8, 2015
Proceedings

 Springer

Editors
Christian Berger
University of Gothenburg
Gothenburg
Sweden

Mohammad Reza Mousavi
Centre for Research on Embedded Systems
Halmstad University (CERES)
Halmstad
Sweden

ISSN 0302-9743   ISSN 1611-3349 (electronic)
Lecture Notes in Computer Science
ISBN 978-3-319-25140-0   ISBN 978-3-319-25141-7 (eBook)
DOI 10.1007/978-3-319-25141-7

Library of Congress Control Number: 2015950886

LNCS Sublibrary: SL3 – Information Systems and Applications, incl. Internet/Web, and HCI

Springer Cham Heidelberg New York Dordrecht London

Springer International Publishing AG Switzerland is part of Springer Science+Business Media
(www.springer.com)

Preface

It is with great pleasure that we present the proceedings of the 5th Workshop on Design, Modeling and Evaluation of Cyber Physical Systems (CyPhy 2015). The workshop was organized as part of ESWeek 2015 in Amsterdam, The Netherlands.

Cyber physical systems combine computing and networking power with physical components. They enable innovation in a wide range of domains including robotics; smart homes, vehicles, and buildings; medical implants; and future-generation sensor networks. CyPhy 2015 brought together researchers and practitioners working on modeling, simulation, and evaluation of CPS, based on a broad interpretation of these areas, to collect and exchange expertise from a diverse set of disciplines.

This year the workshop solicited publications in three categories: research papers, position papers, and tool demonstrations. There were submissions in all categories except for tool demonstrations. The full call for papers can be found on the workshop website (www.cyphy.org).

The review process was conducted as follows. First, the international Program Committee (PC) members expressed interest in reviewing specific papers and also declared conflicts of interest. (There were two papers, involving two PC members. Throughout the process, the EasyChair conference system limited those reviewers who declared a conflict with a given paper from access to that paper, its reviews, and from discussions on it.) After collecting preferences and conflicts, papers were assigned to reviewers. Papers received on average three reviews. After the majority of reviews were submitted, there was a week of online PC meeting. Extensive discussions in the PC meeting were conducted for nine papers and a summary thereof was provided to the authors. Out of all 13 submissions, 10 were selected for publication.

We would like to take this opportunity to acknowledge the excellent efforts of the PC, the external reviewers, and the authors. We thank the Steering Committee of the CyPhy workshop series and in particular its chairperson Professor Walid Taha, for their confidence and their advice. We also wish to thank Professor Tulika Mitra (ESWEEK Workshop Chair), Professor Nikil Dutt (member of ESWEEK Steering Committee), and Professor Rolf Ernst (ESWEEK General Chair) for their effort in facilitating this year's workshop.

August 2015

Christian Berger
Mohammad Reza Mousavi

Organization

Program Committee

Jakob Axelsson	Mälardalen University, Sweden
Christian Berger	University of Gothenburg, Sweden
Manuela Bujorianu	University of Leicester, UK
Georgios Fainekos	Arizona State University, USA
Daisuke Ishii	Tokyo Institute of Technology, Japan
Zhiyun Lin	Zhejiang University, China
Wojciech Mostowski	University of Twente, The Netherlands
Mohammad Reza Mousavi	Halmstad University, Sweden
Michel Reniers	Eindhoven University of Technology, The Netherlands
Bernhard Rumpe	RWTH Aachen University, Germany
Maytham Safar	Kuwait University, Kuwait
Bernhard Schaetz	TU München, Germany
Christoph Seidl	Technische Universität Dresden, Germany
Martin Steffen	University of Oslo, Norway
Frits Vaandrager	Radboud University Nijmegen, The Netherlands

Additional Reviewers

Bertram, Vincent	Swartjes, Lennart
Gupta, Pragya Kirti	Tuncali, Cumhur Erkan
Hermerschmidt, Lars	van der Sanden, Bram

Contents

Resource-Aware Control and Dynamic Scheduling in CPS

W.P.M.H. Heemels[(✉)]

Control System Technology Group,
Department of Mechanical Engineering,
Eindhoven University of Technology, Eindhoven, The Netherlands
m.heemels@tue.nl
http://www.heemels.tue.nl

Abstract. Recent developments in computer and communication technologies are leading to an increasingly networked and wireless world. This raises new challenging questions in the context of control for cyber-physical systems (CPS), especially when the computation, communication, energy and actuation resources (for control) of the system are limited and/or shared by multiple control tasks. These limitations obstruct the use of classical design techniques for feedback control algorithms and call for new *resource-aware* control paradigms. These new resource-aware control systems typically have to take both discrete decisions (which task is allowed to use the resource) and continuous decisions (which continuous control input is generated for the task). In this talk two approaches are presented to address this hybrid co-design problem. Both approaches result in control algorithms that exploit real-time measurement information available on the state of the CPS and decide *dynamically* on the actions to take. This leads to the situation that individual control tasks are no longer executed in classical periodic time-triggered patterns, but in aperiodic patterns with varying inter-execution times. By abandoning the periodic scheduling of control tasks, the aim is to realise better trade-offs between the overall performance of the CPS and the required resource utilisation. The approaches are illustrated by various applications. interesting challenges for the future are discussed as well.

1 Introduction

Recent developments in computer and communication technologies are leading to an increasingly networked and wireless world. In the context of control for cyber-physical systems (CPS) this raises new challenging questions, especially when the computation, communication, energy and actuation resources (for control) of the

The work of Maurice Heemels was partially supported by the Dutch Science Foundation (STW) and the Dutch Organization for Scientific Research (NWO) under the VICI grant "Wireless controls systems: A new frontier in automation" (Project number 11382).

© Springer International Publishing Switzerland 2015
C. Berger and M.R. Mousavi (Eds.): CyPhy 2015, LNCS 9361, pp. 1–7, 2015.
DOI: 10.1007/978-3-319-25141-7_1

system are limited and/or shared by multiple control tasks. Examples include limitations in the battery power for wireless sensors, restrictions on actuator moves to avoid strain, multiple actuators sharing the same hardware resource (e.g., several motors sharing one amplifier), many control tasks sharing the same processor and/or communication medium, and so on. Such limitations obstruct the use of classical techniques for the design of feedback control algorithms for CPS and call for new *resource-aware* controller synthesis paradigms.

These new resource-aware control systems typically have to take both discrete and continuous decisions. For instance, in the control of a robot arm in which the motors driving the joints share the same amplifier (and consequently only one joint can be powered at a time), the control system would have to determine based on, e.g., position and velocity information of the robot, which joint (discrete decision) to power and which value of the torque (continuous value) to apply in order that the robot carries out its overall motion task in a desirable manner. Clearly, this a hybrid co-design problem in which both discrete and continuous decisions have to be taken by the resource-aware control algorithm preferably exploiting real-time measurement information available on the physical system.

In this talk two perspectives on this general hybrid co-design problem are discussed.

2   Dynamic Scheduling and Control

The first approach is based on control and scheduling co-design and has similarities to well-known time-sharing solutions. Essentially the time line is divided into specific slots and in each slot one of the (feedback) control tasks is allowed to access the shared resource being, for instance, a computation, communication or actuation device. As an example consider the networked control system (NCS) in Fig. 1 in which we have a physical plant controlled by a feedback controller over a shared communication network. The physical plant is equipped with n_y sensor nodes measuring $y^1, y^2, \ldots, y^{n_y}$, respectively, and there are n_u actuator nodes for which the controller produces the control values $u^1, u^2, \ldots, u^{n_u}$, respectively. As the network is shared among these nodes and communication constraints prohibit that multiple nodes transmit at the same time, at each transmission instant only one of these nodes can transmit its corresponding values (e.g., if sensor node 2 is allowed to communicate at time t then $y^2(t)$ is communicated and $\hat{y}^2(t)$ is updated to this value). Clearly, this calls for a network protocol deciding in which order nodes can communicate (discrete decisions) *and* a feedback controller that based on the received measurement information $\hat{y}^1, \hat{y}^2, \ldots, \hat{y}^{n_y}$ determines the control values $u^1, u^2, \ldots, u^{n_u}$. This is essentially a co-design problem as the choice of network protocol will influence which controller yields optimal performance and behaviour of the overall CPS.

Compared to common scheduling approaches of control loops, which typically use fixed periodic (round robin) schedules, in our solution we strive for *dynamic scheduling* of control tasks based on measured information obtained from the

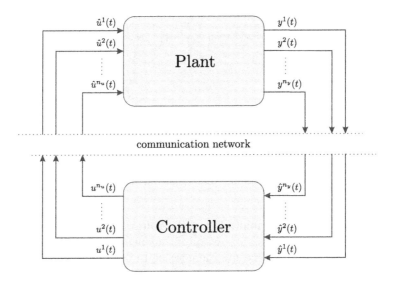

Fig. 1. NCS with a shared communication network.

physical plant to be controlled. By exploiting this information in the decision process improved overall performance of the CPS can be achieved. We discuss a modelling framework and solution strategies for this hybrid co-design problem in which the control and scheduling algorithm has to take both discrete and continuous decisions. In fact, we are able to guarantee that the proposed dynamic scheduling and control method will outperform any given periodic scheduling and control solution in terms of improved overall performance. This part is mainly based on our work in [2–4].

3 Event-Triggered and Self-triggered Control

The first approach takes a rather 'global' view aiming at scheduling *all* tasks such that the resource constraints are adhered to. The second approach, described next, adopts a different point of view as each individual control task aims at only requesting access to a resource when it really has to, i.e., all tasks try to operate under a "minimal attention policy" [7], while still guaranteeing desired overall stability and performance specifications. Consequently, this setup is more self-organising as each task determines locally and independently when to execute. It does not require a global view of the CPS in the design phase and its implementation, although still one has to verify that the overall resource constraints are met.

Before explaining this more self-organising resource-aware control strategy, let us shortly review the conventional method for implementing feedback control tasks. In the majority of digital control applications the execution of control tasks is performed in a periodic time-triggered fashion (connecting conveniently

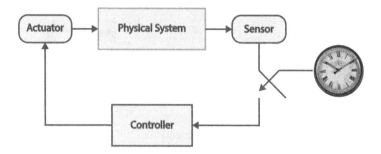

Fig. 2. Periodic time-triggered control.

to the periodic scheduling of multiple tasks). A drawback of the time-triggered paradigm is that control tasks are executed independently of the state of the plant and the actual need to execute these tasks. In fact, the decision of executing a control task is (almost) always taken in an "open-loop" fashion; there is no feedback-based decision mechanism active that determines whether or not it is actually necessary to carry out specific sensing, communication, computation, or actuation (update) tasks in order to realise the desired stability or performance properties. It is only the elapse of a certain time-period (the sampling period) that determines the triggering of the next control task. For instance, in Fig. 2 the communication between the sensor and controller (which is assumed to be a costly and scarce resource in this particular setup) is triggered by a clock resulting in equidistant transmissions along the time axis irrespective of the actual need to communicate certain sensor information. Clearly, periodic execution of control tasks can result in a significant waste of valuable system resources, as tasks are executed even if it is not needed to do so in order to guarantee the stability and performance specifications. As a consequence, one may want to reconsider the classical time-triggered periodic control paradigm in case the resources for executing the control tasks are limited. In such cases, *aperiodic* control strategies that allow the inter-execution times of control tasks to vary in time are potentially better equipped to handle these constraints compared to time-triggered control. In this talk we discuss two aperiodic control strategies being event-triggered and self-triggered control, see [10] for a recent overview.

In *event-triggered control*, see, e.g., [5,6,9,11–13] and the references therein, executions of control tasks are triggered by well-designed events involving the system's state, output, or other available information in an attempt to bring feedback in the sensing, communication, and actuation processes. As an example, in the setup of Fig. 3 the sensor could decide to transmit a measured output to the controller only when the current measurement deviates significantly from the previously transmitted value.

In *self-triggered control*, see, e.g., [1,8,14] and the references therein, the next execution time is precomputed at the current execution time based on predictions using previously received data and knowledge of the system's behaviour. This is illustrated in Fig. 4. The controller determines the next transmission/execution

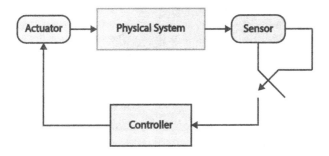

Fig. 3. Event-triggered control.

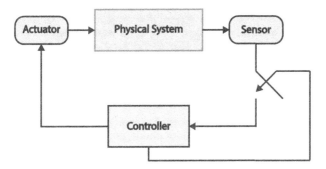

Fig. 4. Self-triggered control.

time for the sensor. Interestingly, in between execution times the sensor and the controller can go to 'sleep'. They only have to wake-up again at the next execution time. Clearly, this is beneficial for saving valuable system's resources, certainly when battery-powered devices such as wireless sensors are used. Note that in both event-triggered and self-triggered control the discrete decision is related to determining whether or not to transmit (at a certain time) and the continuous decisions are related to the selection of the control inputs.

4   Overview

An interesting observation is that both approaches discussed in Sects. 2 and 3 lead to the situation that individual control tasks are no longer executed in a periodic time-triggered fashion, but in an aperiodic execution pattern with varying inter-execution times, see Fig. 5. This feature forms an important distinction

Fig. 5. Paradigm shift: From periodic execution to aperiodic execution of control tasks.

Fig. 6. A platoon of vehicles that communicate wirelessly (photograph courtesy of TNO).

with respect to the conventional periodic time-triggered scheduling of control tasks. By abandoning the periodic scheduling of control tasks, the aim is to realise better trade-offs between the overall performance of the CPS and the required resource utilisation.

For both approaches we discuss some of the main results and illustrate them by various applications in cooperative driving (Fig. 6), robotics, control of inverted pendulums, and fast mixing of polymers. We will also discuss open questions and interesting challenges for the future.

References

1. Anta, A., Tabuada, P.: To sample or not to sample: self-triggered control for nonlinear systems. IEEE Trans. Autom. Control **55**(9), 2030–2042 (2010)
2. Antunes, D., Heemels, W.P.M.H.: Performance analysis of a class of linear quadratic regulators for switched linear systems. In: IEEE Conference on Decision and Control (CDC), pp. 5475–5480, December 2014
3. Antunes, D., Heemels, W.P.M.H.: Rollout event-triggered control: beyond periodic control performance. IEEE Trans. Autom. Control **59**, 3296–3311 (2014)
4. Antunes, D., Heemels, W.P.M.H., Hespanha, J.P., Silvestre, C.: Scheduling measurements and controls over networks - Part II: Rollout strategies for simultaneous protocol and controller design. In: American Control Conference (ACC) 2012, pp. 2042-2047 June 2012
5. Arzén, K.-E.: A simple event-based PID controller. Prepr. IFAC World Conf. **18**, 423–428 (1999)
6. Aström, K.J., Bernhardsson, B.M.: Comparison of periodic and event based sampling for first order stochastic systems. In: Proceedings of IFAC World Conference, pp. 301–306 (1999)

7. Brockett, R.W.: Minimum attention control. In: IEEE Conference on Decision and Control (CDC), pp. 2628–2632 (1997)
8. Gommans, T.M.P., Antunes, D., Donkers, M.C.F., Tabuada, P., Heemels, W.P.M.H.: Self-triggered linear quadratic control. Automatica **50**, 1279–1287 (2014)
9. Heemels, W.P.M.H., Gorter, R.J.A., van Zijl, A., van den Bosch, P.P.J., Weiland, S., Hendrix, W.H.A., Vonder, M.R.: Asynchronous measurement and control: a case study on motor synchronisation. Control Eng. Pract. **7**(12), 1467–1482 (1999)
10. Heemels, W.P.M.H., Johansson, K.H., Tabuada, P.: An introduction to event-triggered and self-triggered control. In: IEEE Conference on Decision and Control (CDC), pp. 3270–3285, December 2012
11. Heemels, W.P.M.H., Sandee, J.H., van den Bosch, P.P.J.: Analysis of event-driven controllers for linear systems. Int. J. Control **81**(4), 571–590 (2008)
12. Lunze, J., Lehmann, D.: A state-feedback approach to event-based control. Automatica **46**, 211–215 (2010)
13. Tabuada, P.: Event-triggered real-time scheduling of stabilizing control tasks. IEEE Trans. Autom. Control **52**, 1680–1685 (2007)
14. Velasco, M., Fuertes, J.M., Marti, P.: The self triggered task model for real-time control systems. In: Proceeding of IEEE Real-Time Systems Symposium, pp. 67–70 (2003)

Current Challenges in the Verification of Hybrid Systems

Stefan Schupp[1][(✉)], Erika Ábrahám[1], Xin Chen[1], Ibtissem Ben Makhlouf[1],
Goran Frehse[2], Sriram Sankaranarayanan[3], and Stefan Kowalewski[1]

[1] RWTH Aachen University, Aachen, Germany
`stefan.schupp@cs.rwth-aachen.de`
[2] Verimag, Gières, France
[3] University of Colorado, Boulder, CO, USA

Abstract. Latest developments brought interesting theoretical results and powerful tools for the reachability analysis of hybrid systems. However, there are still challenging problems to be solved in order to make those technologies applicable to large-scale applications in industrial context. To support this development, in this paper we give a brief overview of available algorithms and tools, and point out some of their individual characteristics regarding various properties which are crucial for the verification of hybrid systems. We present exemplary evaluations on three benchmarks to motivate the need for further development and discuss some of the main challenges for future research in this area.

Keywords: Hybrid systems · Verification · Reachability analysis · Tool support · Benchmarks

1 Introduction

Hybrid systems are systems containing both physical components which evolve continuously over time, as well as discrete components which can influence the continuous dynamics. Also cyber-physical systems can be seen as hybrid systems, where communication between distributed components plays a further important role.

As hybrid systems are often safety critical, in the last two decades much effort was put into the development of efficient algorithms and powerful tools to support their safety analysis. Whereas there is a deep-rooted research for pure continuous and for pure discrete systems, their hybrid combination requires novel methodologies and the adaptation, integration and extension of previous results.

Nowadays, a number of analysis tools for hybrid systems are available, such as ARIADNE [13], CORA [1], DREACH [26], FLOW* [12], HSOLVER [36], HYCREATE [25], ISAT-ODE [15], KEYMAERA [32] and SPACEEX [20]. These tools implement

---

This work was partially supported by the German Research Council (DFG) in the context of the HyPro project.

C. Berger and M.R. Mousavi (Eds.): CyPhy 2015, LNCS 9361, pp. 8–24, 2015.
DOI: 10.1007/978-3-319-25141-7_2

different analysis techniques, leading to individual strength and weaknesses. For further development it is crucial to learn from previous results by evaluating these tools to observe and compare their behaviours, and to identify common obstacles and open problems. Our aim is to support this development by

– describing current analysis techniques, available tools and their individual properties,
– providing exemplary evaluation of a few tools on some benchmarks, and discussing general problems related to tool evaluation and comparison, and
– collecting some important challenges for future research in this area.

The paper is organised as follows: In Sect. 2 we provide some background on hybrid systems, their modelling, and techniques for their reachability analysis. In Sect. 3 we give a brief overview of some tools and discuss their individual properties. On the basis of some evaluations in Sect. 4, we collect challenges and open problems for future research in Sect. 5, and conclude the paper in Sect. 6.

2 Hybrid Systems Modelling and Reachability Analysis

Hybrid systems are systems with combined discrete-continuous behaviour. Typical examples are digitally controlled physical processes, or physical processes with inherent discrete state changes such as phase transitions.

2.1 Modelling

Besides hybrid Petri nets and hybrid programs, a popular modelling formalism for hybrid systems are *hybrid automata* [23,24]. We give a simplified notion of hybrid automata, where we neglect components which are only relevant for their parallel composition.

Definition 1 (Hybrid automata: Syntax [23]**).** *A hybrid automaton is a tuple* $\mathcal{H} = (Loc, Var, Flow, Inv, Edge, Init)$ *consisting of:*

– *A finite set Loc of locations or control modes.*
– *A finite ordered set* $Var = \{x_1, \ldots, x_n\}$ *of real-valued variables; we also use the vector notation* $\boldsymbol{x} = (x_1, \ldots, x_n)$. *The number* n *is called the* dimension *of* $\mathcal{H}$. *By* $\dot{Var}$ *we denote the set* $\{\dot{x}_1, \ldots, \dot{x}_n\}$ *of dotted variables (which represent first derivatives during continuous change), and by* Var' *the set* $\{x'_1, \ldots, x'_n\}$ *of primed variables (which represent values directly after a discrete change). Furthermore,* $Pred_X$ *is the set of all predicates with free variables from* X.
– $Flow : Loc \rightarrow Pred_{Var \cup \dot{Var}}$ *specifies for each location its* flow *or* dynamics.
– $Inv : Loc \rightarrow Pred_{Var}$ *assigns to each location an* invariant.
– $Edge \subseteq Loc \times Pred_{Var} \times Pred_{Var \cup Var'} \times Loc$ *is a finite set of discrete transitions or jumps. For a jump* $(l_1, g, r, l_2) \in Edge$, l_1 *is its source location,* l_2 *is its target location,* g *specifies the jump's guard, and* r *its reset function, where primed variables represent the state after the step.*
– $Init : Loc \rightarrow Pred_{Var}$ *assigns to each location an initial predicate.*

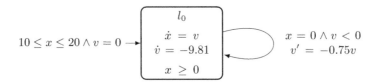

Fig. 1. The hybrid automaton modelling a bouncing ball with height x and velocity v.

Example 1 (Bouncing ball). In the classical *bouncing ball* example, a ball is dropped from some initial height with zero initial velocity. Due to gravity, the ball has an acceleration pointing towards the earth. Therefore the ball falls until it hits the ground, it bounces back into the air, raises until its velocity gets zero, and starts to fall again. Upon bouncing, the ball loses a fraction of its kinetic energy.

An example hybrid automaton model for the bouncing ball is shown graphically in Fig. 1. The dynamics of raising and falling is modelled in a single mode $Loc = \{l_0\}$ using two variables $Var = \{x, v\}$, where x models the vertical position (height) and v the vertical velocity of the ball. The flow $Flow(l_0)$ is specified by the predicate $\dot{x} = v \wedge \dot{v} = -9.81$ with the gravitational force as the only influence on the speed of the ball. The invariant $Inv(l_0)$ is $x \geq 0$, which enforces that the ball bounces when it reaches the ground. This bouncing is represented by the only jump $Edge = \{(l_0, g, r, l_0)\}$ with guard g given by $x = 0 \wedge v < 0$ (that means bouncing only occurs when the ball falls from above and reaches the ground) and reset r specified by $v' = 0.75v$ (i.e., the sign of the velocity gets inverted and the velocity is dampened by a constant factor 0.75). The initial states are described by $Init(l_0) = (10 \leq x \leq 20 \wedge v = 0)$.

The behaviour of a hybrid automaton can be given by an operational semantics. The *states* of an n-dimensional hybrid automaton are pairs $(l, \boldsymbol{v})$, where $l \in Loc$ is the current location and $\boldsymbol{v} \in \mathbb{R}^n$ specifies the current values of the variables. *Initial* states $(l, \boldsymbol{v})$ satisfy both the initial and the invariant conditions of location l. State changes are due to time and discrete steps. A *time step* models the passage of time: while control stays in a location, the values of the variables evolve continuously according to a function which satisfies the flow condition of the current location. Furthermore, the invariant of the location must not be violated during the whole time step. Given a set of states, the states which can be visited from it via time evolution according to the flow in the given location form a *flowpipe*. When flows are described by linear predicates (i.e., linear differential equations) we talk about *linear dynamics*, in the case of polynomial predicates about *non-linear dynamics*. *Discrete steps* follow a jump, moving the control from one location to another, given that the jump's guard is satisfied in the predecessor state. The successor state, resulting from variable resets satisfying the reset condition, must satisfy the invariant of the target location.

Definition 2 (Hybrid automata: Semantics). *The one-step semantics of a hybrid automaton* $\mathcal{H} = (Loc, Var, Flow, Inv, Edge, Init)$ *of dimension* n *is specified by the following operational semantics rules:*

$$\frac{l \in Loc \quad \boldsymbol{v}, \boldsymbol{v}' \in \mathbb{R}^n}{f : [0, \delta] \to \mathbb{R}^n \quad df/dt = \dot{f} : (0, \delta) \to \mathbb{R}^n \quad f(0) = \boldsymbol{v} \quad f(\delta) = \boldsymbol{v}'}{\forall \epsilon \in (0, \delta).\ f(\epsilon), \dot{f}(\epsilon) \models Flow(l) \quad \forall \epsilon \in [0, \delta].\ f(\epsilon) \models Inv(l)}{(l, \boldsymbol{v}) \xrightarrow{\delta} (l, \boldsymbol{v}')} \;Rule\ _{flow}$$

$$\frac{e = (l, g, r, l') \in Edge \quad \boldsymbol{v}, \boldsymbol{v}' \in \mathbb{R}^n \quad \boldsymbol{v} \models g \quad \boldsymbol{v}, \boldsymbol{v}' \models r \quad \boldsymbol{v}' \models Inv(l')}{(l, \boldsymbol{v}) \xrightarrow{e} (l', \boldsymbol{v}')} \;Rule\ _{jump}$$

A path *of* $\mathcal{H}$ *is a (finite or infinite) sequence* $(l_0, \boldsymbol{v}_0) \xrightarrow{\delta_0} (l_1, \boldsymbol{v}_1) \xrightarrow{e_1} (l_2, \boldsymbol{v}_2) \xrightarrow{\delta_2} (l_3, \boldsymbol{v}_3) \xrightarrow{e_3} (l_4, \boldsymbol{v}_4) \xrightarrow{\delta_4} \dots$ *with* $(l_i, \boldsymbol{v}_i)$ *states of* H, $\delta_i \in \mathbb{R}_{\geq 0}$, $e_i \in Edge$, *and* $\boldsymbol{v}_0 \models Init(l_0) \wedge Inv(l_0)$. *A state* $(l, \boldsymbol{v})$ *is* reachable *in* $\mathcal{H}$ *if there is a path* $(l_0, \boldsymbol{v}_0) \xrightarrow{\delta_0} (l_1, \boldsymbol{v}_1) \xrightarrow{e_1} (l_2, \boldsymbol{v}_2) \xrightarrow{\delta_2} \dots$ *of* $\mathcal{H}$ *with* $(l, \boldsymbol{v}) = (l_i, \boldsymbol{v}_i)$ *for some* $i \geq 0$.

2.2   Reachability Analysis

The *reachability problem* for hybrid automata, i.e. the problem to decide whether a given set of states is reachable in a hybrid automaton, is in general undecidable. Nevertheless, there exist subclasses of hybrid automata for which the reachability problem is decidable. For undecidable classes, tools often compute *jump-bounded reachability* (reachability via paths with a limited number of jumps) or *time- and jump-bounded reachability* (where additionally the time step lengths are bounded).

Some of those tools implement *flowpipe-construction-based methods*, which over-approximate the flowpipe over a bounded time horizon by dividing the time horizon into smaller segments (whose length is called the *time-step size*) and over-approximating the flowpipe for each time segment by a single state set. These methods use over-approximative *geometric and/or symbolic representations* [27] of state sets, e.g., by boxes (hyper-rectangles), convex polytopes, zonotopes, ellipsoids, support functions or Taylor models. Given an initial state set, its flowpipe and its discrete successors are computed using efficient operations on such state set representations and safe (over-approximative) conversions between them. User-defined parameters and different techniques for reducing the number of the state sets and the sizes of their representations (on the cost of a stronger over-approximation) allow to find a balance between *efficiency* and *precision* of the computations. These techniques have their strength in a high level of automation and in the possibility to increase efficiency or improve the precision according to the needs of the user. A weakness lies in the fact that, due to over-approximative techniques, only safety (non-reachability) can be proven this way, but not unsafety (reachability).

Some other solutions use *satisfiability checking* algorithms for the reachability analysis, which is based on the formulation of the one-step reachability relation as mixed integer-real arithmetic formulas. Fast SAT-modulo-theories (SMT) solvers can be used if the solutions of the Ordinary Differential Equations (ODEs) in the models are known (e.g., in the case of constant derivatives). When the solutions are not known, the underlying theories in the solvers can also be extended to cope with ODEs. These techniques can efficiently combine a wide range of decision procedures for expressive theories and can theoretically prove both safety and unsafety. However, running times are hard to predict and computations might return inconclusive answers, even for decidable problems, if fast but incomplete solving techniques (e.g., interval constraint propagation) are used.

Last but not least, some other tools are based on *theorem proving* with an embedded theory for hybrid systems. On the one hand, these techniques are very powerful and can handle (at least in theory) a wide range of models using deduction. On the other hand, these approaches are interactive and need experienced users. Predefined and user-defined strategies can be of great help to increase the level of automation and reduce the need for interaction to a minimal level.

3   Tools

The vast variety of tools for hybrid systems verification makes it impossible to rate one particular tool above the others. Each tool brings its strengths and weaknesses, which make it suitable for a certain purpose. Knowing these differences allows users to choose the right tool for their problem requirements. In this section we provide an overview of some of the most popular tools (in alphabetical order) and describe their main capabilities and features; see Table 1 for a short summary.

ARIADNE [13] is a software package implementing functionalities for the reachability analysis of hybrid systems. The package is based on the theory of computable analysis and on a rigorous function calculus with provable approximation bounds on the computations. ARIADNEcan handle expressive models with non-linear differential equations, where state sets can be represented by Taylor models or grid pavings. Besides others, interval arithmetic along with interval solvers and propagation mechanisms are applied in the computations. The support for parallel composition and assume-guarantee reasoning improve scalability.

CORA [1] is an object-oriented MATLAB toolbox which can be used for the fast implementation of different reachability analysis algorithms for continuous and hybrid systems. It implements different state set representation types, conversion algorithms between them, and operations needed for reachability analysis. Additionally to well-known representations such as boxes, polytopes and zonotopes, it provides also non-convex representations (polynomial zonotopes) and representations dedicated to stochastic verification (probabilistic zonotopes). CORAcan be used for the analysis of systems with linear, linear stochastic and non-linear dynamics with uncertain parameters, where non-linear systems are abstracted by linear or polynomial systems.

DREACH [26] is an SMT-based tool performing bounded model checking. Unsafe system runs of bounded length are described by formulas and passed

Table 1. Some hybrid systems reachability analysis tools and their characteristic functionalities.

Tool	
ARIADNE	non-linear ODEs; Taylor models, boxes; interval constraint propagation, deduction
CORA	non-linear ODEs; geometric state set representations; several reachability analysis algorithms, linear abstraction
DREACH	non-linear ODEs; logical state set representation; interval constraint propagation, δ-reachability, bounded model checking
FLOW*	non-linear ODEs; Taylor models; flowpipe computation
HSOLVER	non-linear ODEs; logical state set representation; interval constraint propagation
HYCREATE	non-linear ODEs; boxes; flowpipe computation
ISAT-ODE	non-linear ODEs; logical state set representation; interval constraint propagation, bounded model checking
KEYMAERA	differential dynamic logic; logical state set representation; deduction, computer algebra
SPACEEX	linear ODEs; geometric and symbolic state set representations; flowpipe computation

on to the internal SMT solver DREAL [22], which determines its δ-satisfiability using interval constraint propagation. Due to the generality of interval constraint propagation, DREACH is able to handle non-linear dynamics involving transcendentals. The user can access the SMT calls in SMT-LIB format [5] as well as a witness for the reachability of the set of bad states.

FLOW* is a tool to compute reachable set over-approximations using Taylor-model-based methods. It is able to handle an expressive class of hybrid system models such that the continuous dynamics can be defined by non-linear ODEs with uncertainties, while the jump guards and mode invariants are defined by polynomial inequalities. The basic technique in use is called *Taylor model flow-pipe construction* which is described in [11] and later enhanced by more efficient algorithms [10]. By properly setting the parameters, the tool shows a good scalability on non-linear case studies and succeeds even on large initial sets. Since the tool focuses on non-linear systems, its performance on handling convex guards or invariants is not optimised.

HSOLVER [36] implements classical interval constraint propagation on top of the constraint solving package RSOLVER. Due to its general solving technique, it can handle expressive non-linear ODEs and non-linear jumps. Though HSOLVER uses floating point arithmetic, it uses sound rounding to assure correct results. Besides verification purposes, the tool can also be used to compute abstractions.

HYCREATE [25] is a tool implemented in Java for both time-bounded and unbounded (complete) reachability analysis from an initial state. The tool is designed for low-dimensional models with non-linear, non-deterministic dynamics. It uses box representation and provides error reduction by splitting boxes at the cost of increased complexity. HYCREATE allows further processing of the generated output as well as visualisation via projection on a 2D space.

ISAT-ODE [15] performs, similarly to DREACH, bounded model checking. It is based on the ISAT [17] SMT solver, which tightly integrates interval constraint propagation into a SAT solver. ISAT-ODE extends ISAT with a theory solver module for ODEs to compute validated numerical enclosures for them using the VNODE-LP [31] library. This approach can handle expressive models with non-linear dynamics and transcendental functions. However, despite different embedded optimisation mechanisms, this expressiveness comes at the cost of scalability.

KEYMAERA [32] is an interactive hybrid tool combining deductive, real algebraic, and computer-algebraic prover technologies. Hybrid systems are specified in differential dynamic logic [33] using the notation of hybrid programs, covering non-linear dynamics under uncertainties and non-linear jumps. KEYMAERA tries to prove properties of a given system by finding invariants. On the one hand, this approach is automated but it is still inherently interactive. On the other hand it is flexible, can cope also with infinite time horizons and parametric models, and can provide verified counterexamples. A new re-implementation KEYMAERA X [21] is in its early development phase and it can therefore handle only a restricted model class, but it additionally allows the user to define their own proof search techniques as tactics.

SPACEEX [20] is designed for complex, high-dimensional models with piecewise affine dynamics and non-deterministic inputs. SPACEEX comes with a web-based graphical user interface and a graphical model editor. Its input language facilitates the construction of complex models from automata components using a block-diagram representation. The analysis engine of SPACEEX offers different algorithms (LGG [20,28], STC [18,19]) which combine geometric state set representations (template polyhedra), symbolic state set representations (support functions) and linear programming to achieve maximal scalability while maintaining high accuracy. The prime goal of SPACEEX being scalability, it uses floating-point computations that do not formally guarantee soundness.

4   Benchmarking and Evaluation

Although there are many tools available, their comparative evaluation is problematic. First of all, they do not support the same model classes. The main differences concern the type of the supported ODEs. Though theoretically unspectacular, some tools cannot handle jumps with guard predicate *true*, or unspecified (arbitrary) dynamics. Even if the user identified those tools which can handle a given model class, it is hard to compare their performance: as each algorithm brings its own set of parameters, it requires expertise and knowledge about implementation details to properly instantiate the tool parameters to get optimal results.

Other obstacles are the relatively low number of available benchmarks and missing input language standards. In some other communities, e.g. in SAT and SMT solving or in software verification, the development of such standards

and the organisation of annual competitions gave impressive force and led to
a new sequence of innovations in the given areas. A standardised specification
language for hybrid system models could have a similar positive effect. Currently,
the number of available benchmarks is not satisfactory, even though lately some
improvements were achieved [2,8,16]. The situation is worsened by the fact that
nearly each tool has its own input specification language. To solve this problem,
a CIF 3 standard was proposed [6], however, it is not yet widely established in
the community. Furthermore, some approaches for model conversion were proposed in [4]. A standardisation could drastically improve the situation, enable
the establishment of a competition, give new drive to tool development and thus
contribute to stronger tool functionalities and better efficiency, and ease the
selection of a suitable tool.

To give an impression for the analysis capabilities of available tools and to
motivate some challenges, in the following we give some exemplary verification
results, where we focus on limitations.

Two tanks [8,29]: A two-tank system consists of two connected tanks. The first
is filled with a constant inflow and an additional controlled inflow of a liquid.
A drain at the bottom of the first tank leads to a constant outflow and thus a
constant inflow in the second tank. Conversely, the second tank has a drain which
creates a constant outflow, and a controlled valve which results in an additional
controlled outflow. The hybrid automaton model of this tank system has four
locations, corresponding to the different states of the valves for the controlled in-
and outflows. The dynamics is described by linear differential equations. Initially
both valves are closed, and for the filling levels x_1 and x_2 of the first respectively
the second tank it holds that $x_1 \in [1.5, 2.5]$ and $x_2 = 1$. More details about the
model can be found at [8].

Figure 2 shows the reachability analysis results of SPACEEX/STC (max. iterations: 50, local time horizon: 5, flowpipe tolerance: 0.1) and FLOW* (jump
depth: 2, local time horizon: 5, time-step size: 0.01) on this benchmark. The initial set is located in the upper right of each diagram. As we can see, the results on
this benchmark are comparable, though FLOW* gave a bit more precise results.

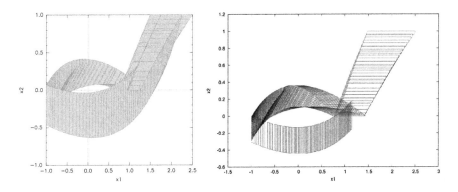

Fig. 2. SPACEEX/STC (left) and FLOW*(right) results for the two-tanks benchmark.

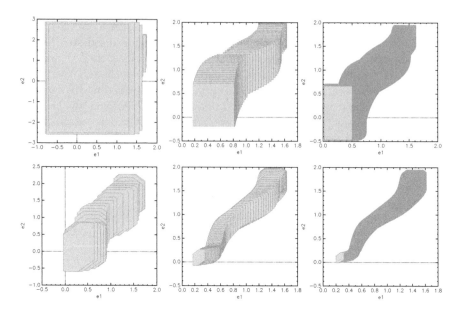

Fig. 3. SPACEEX/LGG results for the three-vehicle platoon benchmark.

Three-vehicle platoon [7,8]: The system consists of a human-driven vehicle and three communicating vehicles following it in a platoon. Two locations are used to model functioning and disrupted communication, respectively. The flows in the locations are described by linear differential equations (without uncertainties). For more details on the model and the initial states see [8].

Some reachability analysis results for this benchmark using SPACEEX/LGG are shown in Fig. 3, using local time horizon 12 and max. iterations 5. The results show the distance e_1 between the human-controlled vehicle and the first following platoon vehicle, and the distance e_2 between the first and the second following platoon vehicles, which are initially $e_1, e_2 \in [0.9, 1.1]$ units. The three results in the first row in Fig. 3 are created using boxes while for the results in the second row octagons are chosen. In the analysis we use time-step sizes 0.3, 0.1 and 0.01 s (from left to right in both rows). We can observe that in general boxes over-approximate more strongly, whereas octagons give more precise results. As expected, for both representations the error can in general be reduced by reducing the time-step size. The error reduction comes at the cost of longer running times: for boxes the computations needed 0.05, 0.1 resp. 0.14 s, whereas in the case of octagons the computational effort has grown from 2.97 over 9.5 to 42.4 s. Note that the plots in the left column use different scales.

Furthermore, an interesting effect can be observed in the top-right plot: the reachable set for precision 0.01 seems to be larger as for time-step size 0.1. However, this fact is *not* due to stronger over-approximation. In contrast to FLOW*, where the user specifies a jump depth (i.e., all paths with this number of jumps are explored), SPACEEX takes the total number of jump successor computations

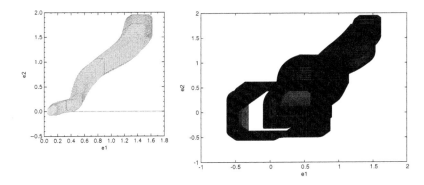

Fig. 4. SPACEEX/LGG (left) and FLOW* (right) results for the three-vehicle platoon benchmark.

in the analysis (in this example 5) as input parameter. Some jumps, which were enabled due to over-approximation with larger step-sizes, are not enabled any more with step size 0.01. Thus the larger reachable set is due to the fact that with the finer precision longer paths can be explored.

Some more results for FLOW* are presented in Fig. 4 (right) in comparison to the octagon setting in SPACEEX/LGG (left). Both tools used a time-step size of 0.01 s and local time horizon 12, max. iterations was set to 5 in SPACEEX, and jump depth to 5 in FLOW*. The computed reachable set is clearly larger for FLOW* than for SPACEEX. This has two reasons. Firstly, in FLOW* all paths with 5 jumps are considered, in contrast to SPACEEX computing a total of 5 jumps. Secondly, the intersection computations for jumps lead to stronger over-approximations in FLOW*, which accumulate in further computation steps. This case illustrates that sometimes tools, which were designed for more expressive model classes (FLOW* was designed for non-linear dynamics), work less optimal on simpler models (here linear dynamics).

Navigation [16]: This benchmark models the movement of an object in a two-dimensional plane. In our case the plane is subdivided into a 3×3 grid structure, whereas other configurations with more cells are also possible. The linear dynamics inside each cell is determined by its position. The corresponding hybrid automaton models each cell by an own location. Jumps between the locations are enabled for all states at the boundaries between the cells; these jumps modify only the location but no other state components. Therefore, this hybrid automaton model exhibits Zeno behaviour, because such switches between the cells can be done back-and-forth infinitely often, without letting time elapse.

This Zeno behaviour can be observed on the reachability analysis results of SPACEEX/LGG (max. iterations: 5, local time horizon: 2, time-step size: 0.001) shown in Fig. 5 (top left). In the zoomed part (top right) the effects of the Zeno behaviour are exposed.

The two plots in the bottom of Fig. 5 show some FLOW* results (jump depth: 1 for bottom left and 2 for bottom right, local time horizon: 2, time-step size: 0.1).

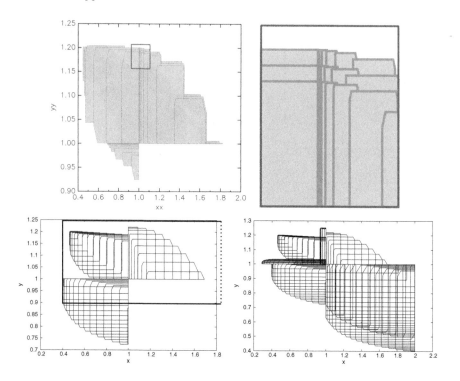

Fig. 5. SPACEEX/LGG results for the navigation benchmark (above), FLOW* results below.

We have chosen a larger time-step size for FLOW*, in order to make the same effect of the Zeno behaviour visible in the plots, however, a similar reachable set is computed also for the smaller time-step size 0.001. For comparability, in the bottom-left plot, we indicate the SPACEEX domain $[0.4, 2.0] \times [0.9, 1.25]$ of the plot above by a rectangle.

5   Further Challenges

The previously described tools cope with a wide range of models and offer powerful technologies for reachability analysis. Nevertheless, there are several challenges still to be addressed in order to increase the applicability and usability of the tools. In this section we discuss some of these challenges.

State set representation: The choice of the state set representation is always a trade-off between computational complexity and precision. There are many different representations usable for the analysis of a hybrid system. Boxes and polytopes are frequently used, also support functions and zonotopes are prominent for models with linear ODEs, whereas Taylor models can be used also for non-linear ODEs. However, none of the representations offers an optimal solution, since they have individual strengths and weaknesses, mainly in the representation size and in the efficiency of certain operations (e.g., union, intersections, Minkowski sum, linear transformation, etc.) needed during the reachability analysis. Although several tools use conversions between representations for certain computations, context-sensitive approaches are still missing. For example, the representation could be adopted to the form of the ODEs in different locations. Also an automated dynamic conversion to reach an optimal trade-off between precision and efficiency during computation using an iterative refinement technique is not yet supported. Furthermore, there is rare support for non-convex representations. Last but not least, most representations are over-approximative, and therefore applicable for safety verification. However, for proving unsafety, novel under-approximative computations would be of help.

Precision: Precision is a crucial component during analysis. For systems, where the distance between the reachable and the unsafe states is small, the used precision can be crucial for the outcome of the reachability analysis. If the outcome is inconclusive (the over-approximation intersects with the unsafe state set), currently the only solution is to re-start the analysis from scratch with new parameters which lead to an error reduction (e.g., reduction of the time-step size in the flowpipe construction). However, since higher precision comes with longer running times, the new parameters must be chosen carefully by the user. An automatic adaptation of the parameters would be not only more user-friendly, but could also be applied dynamically to refine the search only along those paths which led to an intersection with the unsafe state set, instead of executing the whole analysis with high precision.

Fixed-point recognition: Recognising fixed-points in the reachability analysis, i.e., when the whole reachable state set of a hybrid system is already checked for safety, enables the solution of the unbounded reachability problem. However, in order to detect fixed-points, a huge number of state sets need to be stored, and successor sets must be tested for inclusion. As this comes at high costs, current tools use only heuristic checks for fixed-points. A more systematic check would require a highly efficient storage of state sets and fast operations on them - a possible approach could use memory-efficient under-approximations in a representation with fast inclusion and intersection computations (e.g. boxes).

Large uncertainties: Uncertainties can be included in the models when, e.g., some coefficients of the dynamics cannot be fixed precisely, or in the presence of time-varying external inputs like natural forces or users. Though systems with bounded uncertainties can be verified, models with large uncertainties are one more challenge in the verification of hybrid systems. Each uncertainty introduces a bloating factor which is carried onwards and even aggregated during the computation of the reachable set. Although a few approaches were proposed to overcome these limitations (see, e.g., [35]), most tools have problems to find conclusive answers for models with large uncertainties.

Zeno behaviour: Whenever it is possible to execute an infinite number of jumps in a finite amount of time, we observe Zeno behaviour (see the navigation benchmark example and Fig. 5). Naturally, no real system exhibits Zeno behaviour. However, it is hard to avoid Zeno paths in modelling. In [3] the authors distinguish between chattering Zeno (infinite jump sequences with zero dwell time) and genuine Zeno (infinite jump sequences with nonzero dwell time in-between converging to zero) behaviour.

Examples for chattering Zeno behaviours can be found in switching systems, where the state space is divided into grids, each grid having its own dynamics, modelled by an own location. Switching between different grids does not modify the continuous state and is always possible whenever the current state lies at the boundary between two grids. Therefore, infinite back-and-forth switching on boundaries can happen in such models, causing a problem for reachability analysis if the reach-set approximation is not idempotent: Even if no new states are reached, successor states in a sequence of jumps may grow and even diverge as the approximation errors accumulate. If the reach-set computation is exact (such as in HyTech or PHAVer), chattering Zeno has no particularly adverse effect (it may increase the number of image computations necessary to reach a fixed-point).

Genuine Zeno can be problematic for any computation that follows the execution of the system, because any finite number of successor computations may not be able to cover all reachable states. Over-approximations may resolve the problem if they cover the limit points of the sequence. This can be achieved automatically with widening operators [14]; here the difficulty lies in keeping the over-approximation reasonably small [30].

Non-convex invariants: Most tools require that the invariants of the locations are convex sets, mainly for representation reasons. However, similarly to programs which might have disjunctions in loop conditions, also non-convex invariants appear in hybrid system applications. Though one can apply model transformation to eliminate non-convex invariants by splitting the non-convex set into convex subsets and introducing a new location for each convex subset, with this approach the models are extended with Zeno behaviour, hardening their analysis (see Fig. 6). An efficient analysis without such model transformations could be enabled for example by non-convex state set representation techniques.

Urgent transitions: Invariants are one possibility in modelling to force the control to move from one mode to another. Another possibility are urgent transitions, which must be taken as soon as they are enabled. Urgent transitions have the advantage that they make the reason for the mode change more visible (observable), and therefore they are sometimes preferred instead of the usage of invariants. However, most tools do not support urgent transitions, though their analysis would even reduce the computation effort: both the expensive computations of intersections with invariants as well as the computation of flowpipes from those state sets which are included in the guard of an outgoing urgent transition become superfluous.

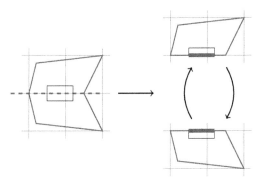

Fig. 6. The split of a location with a non-convex invariant (left) into two locations with convex invariants (right) might introduce Zeno behaviour.

Compositionality: Large systems are usually modelled compositionally as a set of modules running concurrently. Most available tools build the parallel composition of the modules to get a non-compositional model, which can be subsequently analysed. However, the composition results in high-dimensional systems, which pose challenges for the analysis. Compositional analysis techniques would be advantageous, but there is no straightforward way to extend the available techniques to support compositionality. As assume-guarantee methods proved to be useful in program verification, it might also be a promising option in hybrid systems reachability analysis. But when we aim at push-button approaches, suitable assumption-commitment specifications should be derived automatically. Another possibility could be to analyse the concurrent modules simultaneously and communicate between the concurrent analysers on synchronisation-relevant computations using, e.g., partial order reduction techniques.

Counterexamples: Although a few tools, like for example KEYMAERA, can provide counterexamples for unsafe models, most tools do not have this functionality. However, counterexamples are extremely important and provide valuable information for system developers to correct unsafe designs. Furthermore, counterexamples play an important role in counterexample-guided abstraction refinement (CEGAR).

CEGAR: Frequently used in various other research areas, counterexample-guided abstraction refinement is not yet established in the field of hybrid systems. Utilising a relaxed version of the problem can introduce a significant speed up in verification. In case the verification fails, a counterexample path is used to refine relevant components of the model.

Parallelisation: Regarding the efficiency of the reachability analysis of hybrid systems, the current main focus lies on improving the efficiency of sequential algorithms. Approaches for parallelisation are rare and not yet well understood. However, the exploitation of multi-core hardware systems could help to improve the scalability and the applicability of available technologies to large-scale systems.

Modelling language expressiveness: To make hybrid automata as a modelling language more attractive and usable for a wider range of applications, also further extensions regarding expressiveness should be considered. For example, *cyber-physical systems* are distributed hybrid systems, where additionally to discrete and dynamic aspects, also communication plays an important role. Spatio-temporal hybrid automata [37] are a possible extension in this direction, supporting the modelling of communication and other spatial aspects.

Another relevant aspect is *randomised* behaviour, which can affect either the dynamics of a system via stochastic differential equations [9] or the discrete behaviour via probabilistic transitions [38]. The later can involve probabilistic properties regarding the choice between enabled transitions as well as the when to take an enabled transition. A pioneer tool in this area is PROHVER [34], which implements analysis algorithms using a transformation of probabilistic hybrid automata to hybrid automata without probabilistic components.

6   Conclusion

In this paper we gave a brief introduction to state-of-the-art tools for the reachability analysis of hybrid systems, and discussed current challenges for further research. Despite great achievements, there is still a need for efforts to increase applicability and scalability. Standardisation, competitions, and the strengthening of the functionality and the efficiency of techniques and tools may increase visibility and intensify the developments in this relevant research area.

References

1. Althoff, M., Dolan, J.M.: Online verification of automated road vehicles using reachability analysis. IEEE Trans. Robot. **30**(4), 903–918 (2014)
2. Althoff, M., Frehse, G.: Benchmarks of the workshop on applied verification of continuous and hybrid systems (ARCH) (2014). http://cps-vo.org/group/ARCH/benchmarks
3. Ames, A.D., Sastry, S.: Characterization of Zeno behavior in hybrid systems using homological methods. In: Proceedings of ACC 2005, pp. 1160–1165. IEEE Computer Society Press (2005)
4. Bak, S., Bogomolov, S., Johnson, T.T.: HYST: a source transformation and translation tool for hybrid automaton models. In: Proceedings of HSCC 2015, pp. 128–133. ACM (2015)
5. Barrett, C., Stump, A., Tinelli, C.: The satisfiability modulo theories library (SMT-LIB) (2010). http://www.SMT-LIB.org
6. van Beek, D.A., Fokkink, W.J., Hendriks, D., Hofkamp, A., Markovski, J., van de Mortel-Fronczak, J.M., Reniers, M.A.: CIF 3: model-based engineering of supervisory controllers. In: Ábrahám, E., Havelund, K. (eds.) TACAS 2014 (ETAPS). LNCS, vol. 8413, pp. 575–580. Springer, Heidelberg (2014)
7. Ben Makhlouf, I., Diab, H., Kowalewski, S.: Safety verification of a controlled cooperative platoon under loss of communication using zonotopes. In: Proceedings of ADHS 2012, pp. 333–338. IFAC-PapersOnLine (2012)

8. Benchmarks of continuous and hybrid systems. http://ths.rwth-aachen.de/research/hypro/benchmarks-of-continuous-and-hybrid-systems/

9. Bujorianu, M., Lygeros, J.: Toward a general theory of stochastic hybrid systems. In: Blom, H.A.P., Lygeros, J. (eds.) Stochastic Hybrid Systems. LNCIS, vol. 337, pp. 3–30. Springer, Heidelberg (2006)

10. Chen, X.: Reachability Analysis of Non-Linear Hybrid Systems Using Taylor Models. Ph.D. thesis, RWTH Aachen University, Germany (2015)

11. Chen, X., Ábrahám, E., Sankaranarayanan, S.: Taylor model flowpipe construction for non-linear hybrid systems. In: Proceedings of RTSS 2012, pp. 183–192. IEEE Computer Society Press (2012)

12. Chen, X., Ábrahám, E., Sankaranarayanan, S.: Flow*: an analyzer for non-linear hybrid systems. In: Sharygina, N., Veith, H. (eds.) CAV 2013. LNCS, vol. 8044, pp. 258–263. Springer, Heidelberg (2013)

13. Collins, P., Bresolin, D., Geretti, L., Villa, T.: Computing the evolution of hybrid systems using rigorous function calculus. In: Proceedings of ADHS 2012, pp. 284–290. IFAC-PapersOnLine (2012)

14. Cousot, P., Halbwachs, N.: Automatic discovery of linear restraints among variables of a program. In: Proceedings of SIGACT-SIGPLAN, pp. 84–96. ACM (1978)

15. Eggers, A.: Direct Handling of Ordinary Differential Equations in Constraint-solving-based Analysis of Hybrid Systems. Ph.D. thesis, Universität Oldenburg, Germany (2014)

16. Fehnker, A., Ivančić, F.: Benchmarks for hybrid systems verification. In: Alur, R., Pappas, G.J. (eds.) HSCC 2004. LNCS, vol. 2993, pp. 326–341. Springer, Heidelberg (2004)

17. Fränzle, M., Herde, C., Ratschan, S., Schubert, T., Teige, T.: Efficient solving of large non-linear arithmetic constraint systems with complex Boolean structure. J. Satisf. Boolean Model. Comput. **1**, 209–236 (2007)

18. Frehse, G., Kateja, R., Le Guernic, C.: Flowpipe approximation and clustering in space-time. In: Proceedings of HSCC 2013, pp. 203–212. ACM (2013)

19. Frehse, G.: Reachability of hybrid systems in space-time. In: Proceedings of EMSOFT 2015. ACM (2015)

20. Frehse, G., Le Guernic, C., Donzé, A., Cotton, S., Ray, R., Lebeltel, O., Ripado, R., Girard, A., Dang, T., Maler, O.: SpaceEx: scalable verification of hybrid systems. In: Gopalakrishnan, G., Qadeer, S. (eds.) CAV 2011. LNCS, vol. 6806, pp. 379–395. Springer, Heidelberg (2011)

21. Fulton, N., Mitsch, S., Quesel, J.D., Völp, M., Platzer, A.: KeYmaera X: an axiomatic tactical theorem prover for hybrid systems. In: Felty, A.P., Middeldorp, A. (eds.) CADE 2015. LNCS, vol. 9195, pp. 527–538. Springer, Heidelberg (2015)

22. Gao, S., Kong, S., Clarke, E.M.: dReal: an SMT Solver for nonlinear theories over the reals. In: Bonacina, M.P. (ed.) CADE 2013. LNCS, vol. 7898, pp. 208–214. Springer, Heidelberg (2013)

23. Henzinger, T.: The theory of hybrid automata. In: Proceedings of LICS 1996, pp. 278–292. IEEE Computer Society Press (1996)

24. Henzinger, T.A., Kopke, P.W., Puri, A., Varaiya, P.: What's decidable about hybrid automata? J. Comput. Syst. Sci. **57**(1), 94–124 (1998)

25. HyCreate: a tool for overapproximating reachability of hybrid automata. http://stanleybak.com/projects/hycreate/hycreate.html

26. Kong, S., Gao, S., Chen, W., Clarke, E.: dReach: δ-reachability analysis for hybrid systems. In: Baier, C., Tinelli, C. (eds.) TACAS 2015. LNCS, vol. 9035, pp. 200–205. Springer, Heidelberg (2015)

27. Le Guernic, C.: Reachability analysis of hybrid systems with linear continuous dynamics. Ph.D. thesis, Université Joseph-Fourier-Grenoble I, France (2009)
28. Le Guernic, C., Girard, A.: Reachability analysis of linear systems using support functions. Nonlinear Anal. Hybrid Syst. **4**(2), 250–262 (2010)
29. Lygeros, J.: Lecture notes on hybrid systems. In: Notes for the ENSIETA 2004 Workshop (2004)
30. Maka, H., Frehse, G., Krogh, B.H.: Polyhedral domains and widening for verification of numerical programs. In: NSV-II: Second International Workshop on Numerical Software Verification (2009)
31. Nedialkov, N.S.: VNODE-LP - A validated solver for initial value problems in ordinary differential equations. Technical Report CAS-06-06-NN, Department of Computing and Software, McMaster University, Ontario (2006)
32. Platzer, A., Quesel, J.-D.: KeYmaera: a hybrid theorem prover for hybrid systems (system description). In: Armando, A., Baumgartner, P., Dowek, G. (eds.) IJCAR 2008. LNCS (LNAI), vol. 5195, pp. 171–178. Springer, Heidelberg (2008)
33. Platzer, A.: Differential dynamic logic for hybrid systems. J. Autom. Reason. **41**(2), 143–189 (2008)
34. ProHVer: Safety verification for probabilistic hybrid systems. http://depend.cs.uni-sb.de/tools/prohver/
35. Ramdani, N., Meslem, N., Candau, Y.: A hybrid bounding method for computing an over-approximation for the reachable set of uncertain nonlinear systems. IEEE Trans. Autom. Control **54**(10), 2352–2364 (2009)
36. Ratschan, S., She, Z.: Safety verification of hybrid systems by constraint propagation based abstraction refinement. In: Morari, M., Thiele, L. (eds.) HSCC 2005. LNCS, vol. 3414, pp. 573–589. Springer, Heidelberg (2005)
37. Shao, Z., Liu, J.: Spatio-temporal hybrid automata for cyber-physical systems. In: Liu, Z., Woodcock, J., Zhu, H. (eds.) ICTAC 2013. LNCS, vol. 8049, pp. 337–354. Springer, Heidelberg (2013)
38. Sproston, J.: Decidable model checking of probabilistic hybrid automata. In: Joseph, M. (ed.) FTRTFT 2000. LNCS, vol. 1926, p. 31. Springer, Heidelberg (2000)

Constructive Modelling of Parallelized Environmental Models for Structured Testing of Automated Driving Systems

Sebastian Siegl$^{(\boxtimes)}$ and Martin Russer

AUDI AG, Ingolstadt, Germany
{sebastian.siegl,martin.russer}@audi.de

Abstract. In the automotive industry, current activities focus heavily on the development of automated driving systems (ADS). ADS process environmental data from different sensors [10], which are fused to generate a model of the surrounding world. Actors in the generated model are objects, which are e.g., classified as vehicles or pedestrians. The actors run in parallel, as in the real world actions from traffic participants can be taken independently and asynchronously from each other. For verification and validation of these systems a method is required, that allows for a realistic and hence parallel modeling of the system under test's environment. Additionally, the method should allow for structured testing in compliance with international norms such as the ISO 26262 and the first international standard for software testing ISO/IEC/IEEE 29119, published in 2013.

In this paper we present an approach for creating environmental models for structured testing of automated driving systems with a constructive method. One step is the enumeration of all possible sequences, but we first decompose the task into manageable units by input/output dependency analysis. The expected behavior is formalized in temporal logic [4,5]. In doing so, the effort for the creation of the model is feasible in industry. On the other hand, the test model guarantees the representation of all possible scenarios of use, making it a stable basis to derive significant test cases. We applied the method on an embedded system functionality in the automotive industry at AUDI. The system was architectured using the AUTOSAR 3.2 standard and implemented with Matlab Simulink. An existing, previously created test suite was available. This existing test suite served as a benchmark to assess the quality of the new test suite, derived from the environmental models. We compared the reachability of the test cases inside the implementation with code coverage measures and examined the variance of use imposed by the test suites. We present the promising results in this paper.

1 Introduction

Testing is an essential activity for validation and verification in the development of cyber-physical systems. By observing the execution of the system under test,

© Springer International Publishing Switzerland 2015
C. Berger and M.R. Mousavi (Eds.): CyPhy 2015, LNCS 9361, pp. 25–39, 2015.
DOI: 10.1007/978-3-319-25141-7_3

one judges, whether the system behaves as expected. Misbehavior and malfunctions can be identified. As testing provides realistic feedback of the behavior, it is a key activity in industry before releasing a product on the market.

Requirements definition is the first main activity after the decision for the development of a system is made. It also constitutes the first activity in which errors can be made. It is even the most critical activity with regard to faults and defects, because defects discovered in late development phases might have their origin in the initial requirements.

In 2013 the first, second, and third part of the international standard for software testing ISO/IEC/IEEE 29119 were released [3]. The ISO 29119 complements the ISO 26262 [2] w.r.t. the activities for software testing. It states the main purpose of requirements based testing as 'to determine whether the test item meets end-user requirements' [3, Part 1, p. 31]. It should be noted, that in the same section it is highlighted that testing may suffer if the requirements are incomplete or not consistently specified. Following Boris Beizer's bug taxonomy [8, p. 2], the main defects in requirements can be classified into *incorrectness, inconsistency, incompleteness*, and *obsolescence*. In this paper we present an approach, to base the testing activities on a validated, consistent and complete environmental model.

The paper is structured as follows: In Sect. 2 related work is described and the issue of this paper is extrapolated, whereas current approaches are described. In Sect. 3 terminology definitions and foundations of the method are given. In the subsequent Sect. 4 our new approach is presented, followed by a case study and application on an automotive embedded software in Sect. 5. In Sect. 6 we offer the conclusions and an outlook for future work.

2   Related Work

As noted in the introduction, ISO 26262 [2] has a great impact on testing safety critical systems. The standard calls for work products, like a *functional safety concept* and *technical safety concept*, to specify how the system shall reduce risk exposure. To satisfy this claim, it proposes mechanisms to raise fault tolerance by trying to detect and mitigate faults [2, Part 3, 8.2]. Moreover, it proclaims that the effectiveness of such mechanisms controlling random and systematic failures has to be validated [2, Part 4, 9.4.3.2]. For this reason, the ISO 26262 recommends ways of testing a certain functionality of the system based on the assigned Automotive Safety Integrity Level (ASIL). The ASIL is a risk classification determined via hazard analysis and risk assessments based on the severity, the exposure and the controllability of a possible failure. For example, the recommended amount of testing system reliability, called *performance testing*, increases with higher ASIL [2, Part 3, 8.2].

Model-based Testing (MBT) techniques make use of formal descriptions (models) of either the system-under-test (SUT) or the expected usage from the environment of the SUT. UPPAAL is an environment to model the system as networks of timed automata and to simulate and analyze with a model-checker [7].

It provides a complementary method and tooling for the usage oriented approach presented in this paper, in which environmental models are being deduced from the requirements. The environmental model serves as a basis for the subsequent verification and validation activities.

Elaborated techniques are understood to determine dependability measures of the SUT with models. Examples include techniques based on a Bayesian model [16] and on a Markovian Models [11].

The credibility of the dependability measures is up to the quality of the model and the derived testing activities. Sequence-based specification [13] is a constructive requirements engineering method to create an environmental model. In doing so the correctness of the model is ensured by the method of creating it. Sequence-based specification originates from the functional treatment of software by Mills [15]. It is based upon a component-oriented view of software, which is also a main principle of the AUTOSAR methodology [6]. In AUTOSAR, embedded functionality is partitioned into application software components. These components are iteratively developed. Nowadays, AUTOSAR is the prevailing methodology used in the automotive domain for the development of embedded software systems [14]. Also in this paper, we evaluate our approach on an embedded software functionality developed with AUTOSAR, that is presented in Sect. 5.

3   Constructive Requirements Modeling

In this section we introduce foundations of our approach: The elements of the environmental model, and the method to analyze and transform the requirements into the model.

3.1   Modeling Elements

The environmental modeling is done by creating time usage models (TUM). The TUM-representation is the output of the constructive requirements modeling method, that is presented in the following Subsect. 3.2, and the basis for all subsequent activities on the basis of the model. A TUM consists of:

- A set of *states* $S = \{s_1, \ldots, s_n\}$, that represent possible usage states.
- A set of *arcs* A, representing state transitions. An arc from state s_i to state s_j is denoted by a_{ij}.
- A set of *stimuli* Y on the SUT. A stimulus y_j is assigned to each arc.
- The *transition probability* from state i to state j, denoted by p_{ij} for an existing arc a_{ij}. The transition probabilities obey the conditions $0 \leq p_{ij} \leq 1$ and

$$\sum_{j=1}^{n} p_{ij} = 1 \quad \forall i = 1, \ldots, n \tag{1}$$

states that the probabilities of all outgoing arcs from a certain state s_i must sum up to one.

– A probability density function (pdf) t_i to reflect the *sojourn time* is assigned to each state s_i.
– A pdf of the stimulus time t_{ij} is assigned to each arc a_{ij}. This pdf describes the duration of the execution of a stimulus on the SUT.

Test cases can be sampled from the model via a random path using the probabilities p_{ij}. In our approach we focus on the graph abstraction of the model and to apply deterministic and heuristic algorithms for the derivation of test cases. Transitions and states of the model are tagged with information to control the test case generation.

3.2 Foundations of Constructive Requirements Modeling

The method for creating a TUM is the key activity, since the following activities for validation and determination of estimators about the reliability depend on the quality of the model. The method for creating a TUM as the test model follows the principles of sequence-based specification (SBS) [13]. This includes the identification of the system's boundaries as well as the enumeration of all sequences of stimuli, considering their responses over time. Following this procedure one ensures, that the final dynamic model represents the environment completely, consistently, and traceably correct.

Previously uncovered system behavior is identified by this method. Requirements must be derived for it and formulated. The stakeholders who are responsible are invoked to manage this task. They have to derive a new requirement and add it to the existing set of requirements, usually in a document based form. This step allows for linking people with requirements. The model is enhanced with the derived requirements, which are also added to the initial requirements. So this procedure is a technique for analyzing and clarifying the requirements.

4 Leveraging the Environmental Modelling

As described in the previous section, the output of the sequence-based specification is an environmental model for model-based testing.

In practice, environmental models derived from a sequence-based specification can be very complex and confusing. This is due to the growth of required enumerations which result from an increased number of inputs. Additionally, it is challenging to handle requirement changes in a thoroughly correct way. Therefore, it is useful to break away from the traditional way of modelling, in which everything is covered in one enumeration.

4.1 Decomposition of Functional Specification

Applying the sequence-based specification in practice showed some significant improvements in the analysis and modeling of requirements and therefore led to better test suites and more reliable software. With the increase of software

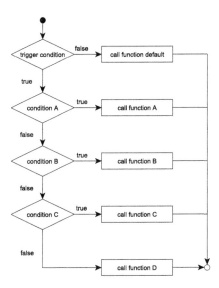

Fig. 1. Function hierarchy

complexity, the feasibility of applying this process is limited to functions with a manageable number of inputs and level of complexity. A safety relevant function with four inputs and simple timing conditions resulted in a TUM containing 35 states. In order to identify the approximately 230 state transitions, more than 600 sequences of stimuli had to be analyzed.

To address this problem of complexity, the analysis of the requirements can help to reduce the necessary effort. These analyses concentrate on dependences between input signals and are influenced by our experiences with sequence-based specification in practice.

Multi-dependencies on Single Values. Often, the processing of a function is active only if a certain trigger condition is met. This can be for many reasons such as saving processing time or power. If such an activation stimulus exists and the output of the respective functionality is independent from the rest of the system, it can be treated in a separate enumeration process. This step can reduce the enumeration effort significantly.

The same principle can be applied to hierarchically structured function calls as well. Figure 1 shows the processing hierarchy with dependences on various conditions. If and only if the trigger condition is met, one of the available functions will be called and the specific return value will be returned. Otherwise, a default or error value is returned. The graph shows the hierarchy inside the module, with function A as the highest order function. If function A is called, its return value is generated and the module step is finished. Depending on the input conditions, only one function is called in one step. The mutual exclusion resulting from the hierarchy allows to simplify the sequence-based enumeration process by dividing it according to the functions. Hence an enumeration process is done for all functions separately. This leads to a larger number of enumerations, yet they are less complex and less time consuming.

Independent Input Values. Another way to reduce the overall complexity of the enumeration process is to identify independent input stimuli. After defining the systems boundaries, the lists of input and output stimuli are defined. If the focus is on low level functionality, it is hard to find independent input values because often one is at a level in which one module implements one feature. Having a look at higher level modules, it's more likely to find independent input signals as these modules encapsulate the underlying modules.

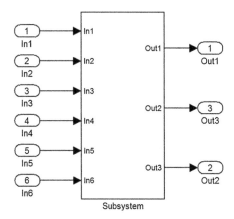

Fig. 2. Software component

Figure 2 shows a software component containing six input signals and three output signals. The subsystem represents the boundaries of the system under test. The internal structure is given in Fig. 3 to get a simpler view on the modules behavior instead of listing the requirements of the example. The analysis of dependent input variables has to certainly be done on the requirements. Figure 3 shows that input one (notation: In1) to four are used to calculate output one (Out1) and two. Output three depends only on input five and six. Thus, In5 and In6 do not affect the outputs calculated by In1 to In4 and vice versa. We propose to split up the enumeration process for the two mentioned groups of inputs. If supported by the testing tool, the test cases derived by the two different enumerations can be run in parallel as the inputs cannot affect each other according to the specification. Sometimes, safety critical functions require the testing of

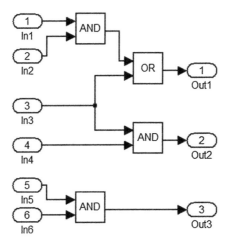

Fig. 3. Internal view of Fig. 2

every possible input combination. In this case, it is still possible to separate the enumeration processes. This leads to two different test suites. Testsuite A runs all the valid sequences developed by enumerating In1 to In4, while the independent stimuli can be stimulated in parallel in the background. The same principle can be applied to Testsuite B, where the enumerated sequences of In5 and In6 can be evaluated together with the combinations of In1 to In4.

4.2   Global Assessments

Instead of defining local assessments, as in the classic sequence-based specification, we define global assessments. These are defined in temporal logic. For leveraging the use in a daily routine we provide patterns [12]. Global assessments can be seen as a global observer checking the output of the SUT. For each enumeration step at least one global assessment and the corresponding requirement must be defined.

4.3   Model Composition

After decomposing the input streams and applying the enumeration separately, the final model consists of different regions. Figure 4 depicts an example of a model. Completely parallel regions are on the top, below are regions with enumerations, which can be run in parallel, but must be synchronized. These regions with synchronization points result from dependencies on trigger conditions.

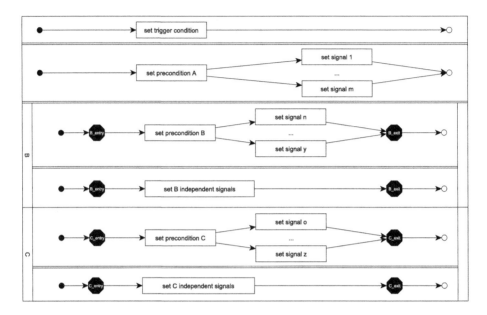

Fig. 4. Requirement and test model structure of embedded system functionality

5   Application on Embedded Body Functionality

After case studies and the elaboration of the theoretical aspects, which were introduced in Sects. 3 and 4 we applied the method in practice on a real implementation in the automotive industry at AUDI. In this section we give a brief introduction to the embedded function and illustrate the methods and processes by means of the example. To gain a evaluation of the results, the derived test model is compared to the existing test suite and presented at the end of this section.

5.1   Application on an Automotive Embedded System

The system controls the timing of various modules in the interior of the car. It was designed in Matlab Simulink [17] and architectured in AUTOSAR [6], as it is done for developing automated driving systems. Depending on the interaction of a human with the car like opening or closing doors as well as the car's environment, the function decides whether to trigger modules and checks the activation, the duration of an activation or the deactivation of a specific timer.

The selected timing-module of the function has a total input of 14 signals, it processes all information in a single step and provides the results by six output signals. Most input signals are described by boolean values and define a certain state of the car, e.g. a signal which gives information whether a door is open(ed) or not. The six output signals give information about the three available timers, two signals for each timer. One describes the running state, a second is true whenever a timer elapses. None of the output signals are returned and used as an input of the module Fig. 5.

The timing behavior is specified by 17 requirements. Timers run in parallel and independently from each other. The timer-related events can be classified into four categories:

- Timer activation:
  Input conditions that cause the start of a timer
- Timer cancellation:
  Input conditions that abort a running timer
- Timer restart:
  Input conditions that lead to a restart of the timer
- Timer elapsed:
  After reaching the timer's threshold value, a timer has to be stopped and the elapsed-signal is transmitted.

The initial requirements seemed to be clear and straightforward. However, Subsect. 5.4 will show that multiple adjustments had to be made to gain a complete and unambiguous module specification, and hence a thorough basis for verification and validation activities.

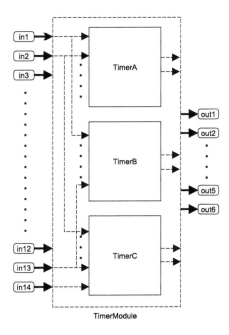

Fig. 5. Architecture of embedded system

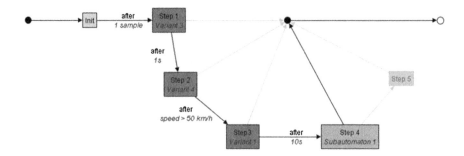

Fig. 6. Detail of a test model in TPT tool

5.2   Tool Framework

Based on the steps and principles described in the previous sections, the modeling framework comprises two tools to perform the two major steps: sequence enumeration and test execution. The sequence-based specification is associated with requirements engineering. As our primary goal was to improve the activities for validation and verification, we implemented it for test case derivation and automated test case execution and assessment. The modeling framework is described below.

Enumeration Tool. It is highly recommended to perform the enumeration with tool support, especially, when changes become necessary in previous sequences during a enumeration. Tools can be found in the Internet such as Protoseq [18], written in Ruby, or REAL [1]. REAL is an Eclipse-based implementation of the sequence-based enumeration with similar features of Protoseq which works faster than the Ruby implementation. Thus, it is more suitable for larger enumerations. Using other software like Excel seems to be justified for very simple examples, but proved to be very error prone when used for more complex functions.

Test Environment. For modeling, test derivation, test execution, and test assessment we used the application TPT (Time Partition Testing) [9]. TPT is a model-based testing tool that provides the required features for the method described in this paper. The tool suited perfectly to our test purpose due to the following reasons [9]:

- Graphical modeling of hybrid, hierarchical, and parallel state charts:
  Models in TPT are decribed by hybrid and parallel automatons with synchronization. Both states and transitions can be mapped on transitions in the underlying automaton. Thus, a complex test model can be visualized with a small number of states. Individual test cases describe different combinations of state sequences, state variants and variations of transition conditions. Figure 6 shows an example test model chart.

- Global and flexible assessment handling with temporal logic:
  TPT offers the implementation of a global assessment library to check the expected behavior. Instead of assigning an expected result to a specific state, one can include global assessments in temporal logic.

5.3   Model of the Embedded System

After defining the test environment, the proposed methods were put into practice. In this subsection, our main focus is on the test model and the derived test cases rather than on the enumeration process, as it was described in detail in Sect. 3. To complement this, we offer information about the enumeration below as well as some details and figures about the decomposition in Table 3.

Before the enumeration, a decomposition of the function took place.

We present the resulting figures of the decomposition in Table 1.

On the top layer, the test model consists of 52 transitions and 26 states and covers all 615 legal sequences gained from the three enumerations. This provides a nice view on the system compared to the overall complexity of the system and model. Furthermore, the visual way of building up the model with preconditions plus stimulus provided a good basis for understanding and discussion between the stakeholders of the project Table 2.

5.4   Results and Evaluation

Prior to applying the decomposed enumeration method, the timer module was tested on basis of the requirements. The existing test suite achieved a code

Table 1. Decomposition details

Timer	Total Number of Inputs	Total Number of Outputs	Decomposed Number of Inputs	Affected Number of Outputs
TimerA			5	2
TimerB	14	6	7	2
TimerC			8	2

Table 2. Requirements clarification measurements

Timer	Initial requirements	Modified requirements	Derived requirements
TimerA	5	4 (80 %)	1
TimerB	6	4 ($\approx$ 67 %)	2
TimerC	6	5 ($\approx$ 83 %)	1
Total	17	13 ($\approx$ 77 %)	4

coverage of 100 %. In this section we show the results of the new test suite and compare it with the existing one.

During the first steps of the sequence-based enumeration, the method quickly discovered the incompleteness of the module's specification. It was notable, that many requirements define an expected result under specific conditions, but make no statement of the expected behavior if the condition is not met. Consequently, there were sequences for which no requirement specified the output of the function. It was therefore necessary to extend six requirements. This conspicuousness occurred at all three different timers.

In addition, inconsistent requirements were discovered. For some sequences, multiple requirements applied and consequently resulted in a contradictory behavior. It is remarkable, that these inconsistencies were discovered only by considering the timing dependent behavior. The explicit consideration of timing aspects eased their discovery (cf. Subsect. 3.1) Additional requirements had to be defined in consultation with the function developer.

All in all, 12 of the 17 existing requirements had to be altered and three additional requirements had to be added. The derived requirements in combination with the enumerated sequences were the basis of the test model. Executing the test cases showed no errors as requirements and implementation had already been corrected during the enumeration process.

The most interesting fact was found when a comparison between the existing and the new test suite was made. The existing test suite turned out to be incomplete w.r.t. the possible legal and expected uses, as only 45 % of the possible operating states and only 9 % of the operational transitions were reached. Table lists some detailed numbers for each of the three timers. Even though, the existing test suite reached a code coverage of 100 %. This finding highlights the importance and significance of a complete and consistent requirements specification, followed by a good test strategy with a suitable stopping criterion. Evidently modern code generators, due to their optimizations for embedded targets, reduce control flow. Code coverage measures catch control flow paths and decisions. In the optimized code decisions are carried out on bit level and with bit shifts, that are not covered by control flow measurements.

An incomplete specification and disputable subsequent test activities give a distorted view of the quality and reliability of the developed system.

Table 3. Original test suite measurements

Timer	Model figures		Original Test Suite Coverage	
	Operational states	Operational state transitions	State coverage	Transition coverage
TimerA	11	83	9 ($\approx 82\%$)	9 ($\approx 11\%$)
TimerB	30	231	6 (20%)	10 ($\approx 4\%$)
TimerC	45	301	24 ($\approx 53\%$)	34 ($\approx 17\%$)
Total	86	615	39 ($\approx 45\%$)	53 ($\approx 9\%$)

With the presented improved method (cf. Subsect. 4.1) it was possible to apply a systematic method for requirements clarification, formalization and structured testing.

6   Conclusion

The development of automated driving systems that process parallel and complex inputs from the environment poses not only a challenge for the test environments, such as virtual simulation, but also for the methods of determining the significant and required test scenarios. International norms like the ISO 26262 state requirements for dealing with such complex systems in its complete life cycle, with a focus on the design and verification and validation activities.

The methods for verification and validation of software were substantiated in 2013, when the first, second, and third parts of the international standard for software testing ISO/IEC/IEEE 29119 were released. It states the main purpose of requirements based testing as 'to determine whether the test item meets end-user requirements' [3, Part 1, p. 31]. In the same section it remarks that testing may suffer if the requirements are incomplete or not consistently specified.

In this paper we presented our approach to facilitate the creation of a complete, traceably correct, and consistent environmental model in industry. Its foundation lies in a separate modeling of the environmental actors with a constructive method. By this approach, the subsequent activities for quality assurance, such as validation and verification, measurement of coverage criteria, and estimators e.g. of the reliability profit from this approach. This improvement heavily relies on a provably correct basis for all the activities mentioned above. Hence, significant test cases can be derived by applying appropriate strategies from the model.

The application of constructive requirements modeling can be hardly feasible for larger systems, because it can result in a rapid growth of the state space. The state space explosion results from the fact, that the method itself requires all possible stimulations to be sequentialized on a certain level of abstraction. To deal with this, we presented techniques, that allow for an early reduction of the modeled state space. Input streams are classified in two categories: completely independent and parallel, and those which can be run in parallel between synchronisation points. The input streams are separately enumerated, which reduces tremendously the state growth. The final complete environmental model is a composition of all models. In doing so, the creation of the model is de-composed into manageable pieces: the creation of the model is feasible for real applications in industry.

We presented the application of this approach on a real automotive embedded functionality in AUTOSAR with timing requirements. A model was created with the method presented in this paper. During the creation of the model, inconsistencies and flaws in the requirements were identified. These were clarified in collaboration with the function owner. In addition, new requirements had to be derived and defined, to obtain a complete specification of the expected behavior.

The functionality was already tested before, with the test stopping criterion of 100 % branch Code Coverage. We mapped the reached operating states for 100 % Code Coverage to the model. The analysis revealed that only 45 % of the operating states from an environmental usage view were reached. This implies that 55 % of all possible use scenarios were untested. Moreover, the stopping criteria such as requirements- or code-coverage did not require testing activities for the omitted scenarios.

We derived a test suite to cover all identified operating states. The test suite revealed a software failure w.r.t. the completed requirement specification. This result affirms the statement of the ISO29119, that testing may suffer if the requirements are not consistent or incomplete [3, Part 1, p. 31].

The determination of dependability estimators is well understood for models created in the classical way. In a next step, we examine how dependability estimators hold for the new composed model, and how they can be computed, respectively.

References

1. REAL Sequence-based Specification Tool (2005)
2. ISO/DIS 26262 - Road Vehicles Functional Safety (2009)
3. Software and Systems Engineering Software Testing Part 1–3. ISO/IEC/IEEE 29119-1-3:2013(E), pp. 1–138 (2013)
4. Alur, R., Henzinger, T.A.: A really temporal logic. J. ACM **41**(1), 181–203 (1994)
5. Alur, R., Henzinger, T.: Modularity for timed and hybrid systems. In: Mazurkiewicz, A. (ed.) CONCUR 1997: Concurrency Theory. Lecture Notes in Computer Science, vol. 1243, pp. 74–88. Springer, Heidelberg (1997)
6. AUTOSAR Munich: AUTOSAR 4.0 (2010)
7. Behrmann, G., David, A., Larsen, K.G.: A tutorial on UPPAAL. In: Bernardo, M., Corradini, F. (eds.) SFM-RT 2004. LNCS, vol. 3185, pp. 200–236. Springer, Heidelberg (2004)
8. Beizer, B., Vinter, O.V.: Bug Taxonomy and Statistics. Technical report, Software Engineering Mentor, 2630 Taastrup (2001)
9. Bringmann, E., Krämer, A.: Systematic testing of the continuous behavior of automotive systems. In: Proceedings of the 2006 International Workshop on Software Engineering for Automotive Systems, SEAS 2006, pp. 13–20. ACM, New York (2006)
10. Gregor, R., Lutzeler, M., Pellkofer, M., Siedersberger, K.H., Dickmanns, E.: Emsvision: a perceptual system for autonomous vehicles. IEEE Trans. Intell. Transp. Syst. **3**(1), 48–59 (2002)
11. Gutjahr, W.J.: Software dependability evaluation based on markov usage models. Perform. Eval. **40**(4), 199–222 (2000)
12. Konrad, S., Cheng, B.H.C.: Real-time specification patterns. In: Proceedings of the 27th International Conference on Software Engineering, ICSE 2005, pp. 372–381. ACM, New York (2005)
13. Lin, L., Prowell, S.J., Poore, J.H.: An axiom system for sequence-based specification. Theor. Comput. Sci. **411**, 360–376 (2010)

14. Michailidis, A., Spieth, U., Ringler, T., Hedenetz, B., Kowalewski, S.: Test front loading in early stages of automotive software development based on AUTOSAR. In: Proceedings of the Conference on Design, Automation and Test in Europe, DATE 2010, pp. 435–440. European Design and Automation Association, Belgium (2010)
15. Mills, H.D.: Stepwise refinement and verification in box-structured systems. Computer **21**(6), 23–36 (1988)
16. Prowell, S., Poore, J.: Computing system reliability using Markov chain usage models. J. Syst. Softw. **73**(2), 219–225 (2004)
17. The Mathworks: MATLAB/Simulink (2010)
18. University of Tennessee: Sequence-based Specification Tool, Protoseq. Software Quality Research Laboratory (2005)

Core Research and Innovation Areas
in Cyber-Physical Systems of Systems
Initial Findings of the CPSoS Project

S. Engell[1], R. Paulen[1], M.A. Reniers[2(✉)], C. Sonntag[3], and H. Thompson[4]

[1] Process Dynamics and Operations, TU Dortmund, Dortmund, Germany
{sebastian.engell,radoslav.paulen}@bci.tu-dortmund.de
[2] Control Systems Technology, Eindhoven University of Technology (TU/e),
Eindhoven, The Netherlands
m.a.reniers@tue.nl
[3] euTeXoo GmbH, Dortmund, Germany
info@eutexoo.de
[4] Haydn Consulting Ltd, Sheffield, UK
info@haydnconsulting.com

Abstract. The CPSoS project is developing a roadmap for future research and innovation in cyber-physical systems of systems. This paper presents preliminary findings and proposals that are put forward as a result of broad consultations with experts from industry and academia, and through analysis of the state of the art in cyber-physical systems of systems.

1 Introduction

Cyber-physical systems of systems (CPSoS) are large physical systems as, *e.g.,* railway systems, the electric grid and production plants that consist of many interacting physical elements and of distributed IT systems for monitoring, control, and optimization and interaction with human operators and managers that are interfaced to the physical system elements and are interconnected via communication networks. These systems are of crucial importance for the welfare of the citizens of Europe as they represent some of the most important infrastructures and the backbone of the European economy.

Characteristic features of cyber-physical systems of systems are:

– Complex dynamics,
– Distributed control, supervision and management,
– Partial autonomy of the subsystems,

This project has received funding from the European Union's Seventh Programme for research, technological development and demonstration under grant agreement No 611115.

C. Berger and M.R. Mousavi (Eds.): CyPhy 2015, LNCS 9361, pp. 40–55, 2015.
DOI: 10.1007/978-3-319-25141-7_4

– Dynamic reconfiguration of the overall system on different timescales,
– Continuous evolution of the overall system during its operation, and
– Possibility of emerging behaviours.

As cyber-physical systems of systems comprise physical elements as well as computing systems that are tightly coupled, the engineering and operation of these systems must build upon theories, tools and knowledge from a large number of domains, from population dynamics and nonlinear systems theory over advanced modelling, simulation, optimisation and signal processing to software engineering, computer networks, validation and verification and user interaction. Knowledge about the physical aspects of the systems as well as about the application domains is indispensable to arrive at solutions that are taken up in the real world. To integrate these diverse research and development communities to realise the opportunities and to respond to the challenges of large-scale, interconnected, distributed synergistic systems and to mitigate the associated risks and challenges is the most crucial aspect for a successful future development of the domain of CPSoS. Relevant theory and tools for CPSoS can only be developed with awareness and in-depth knowledge of application needs and industry trends.

The CPSoS project (www.cpsos.eu) is a Communication and Support Action that acts as an exchange platform for systems of systems (SoS) related projects and communities [10]. One of the main goals of the project is to develop a European research and innovation agenda on CPSoS. To support this process, the project has set up three working groups to capture the views of industry and academia:

– Systems of Systems in Transportation and Logistics, led by Haydn Thompson, Haydn Consulting Ltd, United Kingdom,
– Physically Connected Systems of Systems, led by Sebastian Engell, TU Dortmund, Germany, and
– Tools for Systems of Systems Engineering and Management, led by Michel Reniers, Eindhoven University of Technology, Netherlands.

The working groups currently comprise of 36 members, leading specialists from industry and academia, and include delegates from ongoing EU-funded projects in the area of SoS to ensure that as many views as possible are represented. Information about the composition of these working groups can be found via www.cpsos.eu.

Based on input from the working group members, and extensive consultations with domain experts in three public meetings with over 100 participants, and more than 130 written contributions and interviews, a state of the art document was produced (www.cpsos.eu/state-of-the-art, [5]) and the proposals were synthesized into a first research and innovation agenda (www.cpsos.eu/roadmap, [4]). The agenda describes three main areas of research and development:

1. Distributed, reliable and efficient management of CPSoS,
2. Engineering support for the design-operation continuum of CPSoS, and
3. Cognitive CPSoS.

The contents of this paper is based on documents produced in the context of the CPSoS project [3–5]. An abstract of the research challenges has also been published in [11].

Below, these challenges are explained in more detail. First, Sect. 2 gives an overview of the properties of CPSoS. The specific features and challenges of CPSoS in operation and design are analysed in Sect. 3. Building upon this analysis, the three main areas that have been identified as key challenges for future research and innovation are then outlined in Sect. 4. Section 5 provides a summary of the paper.

2   Cyber-Physical Systems of Systems

The concept of *systems of systems* has been developed to characterize large, distributed systems that consist of interacting and networked, but partially autonomous, elements that together can show emergent behaviour [7,9]. Generic approaches to the analysis, design, management and control of SoS has become an active domain of research in recent years at the interface of various disciplines, such as computer science, systems and control, and systems engineering.

Cyber-physical systems are large complex physical systems that interact with a considerable number of distributed computing elements for monitoring, control and management. Additionally, they can exchange information between themselves and with human users. The elements of the physical system are connected by the exchange of material, energy, or momentum and/or the use of common resources (roads, rail-tracks, air space, waterways) while the elements of the control and management system are connected by communication networks which may impose restrictions on the frequency and speed of information exchange.

The CPSoS project has refined the above definitions into the following definition [3].

Definition 1. Cyber-physical systems of systems *are cyber-physical systems that exhibit the features of SoS:*

– *Large, often spatially distributed physical systems with complex dynamics,*
– *Distributed control, supervision and management,*
– *Partial autonomy of the subsystems,*
– *Dynamic reconfiguration of the overall system on different timescales,*
– *Continuous evolution of the overall system during its operation,*
– *Possibility of emerging behaviours.*

Prominent examples of CPSoS are rail and road transport systems, power plants, large production facilities, gas pipeline networks, container terminals, water systems, and supply chains.

3   Features of CPSoS and Industrial Challenges in Their Development and Operation

In this section the key features that characterise CPSoS are highlighted. This is put into context of real applications to explain the key challenges faced by industrial developers of such systems. Major challenges are in dealing with constantly evolving, highly complex systems with distributed management, a mixture of autonomous and human control interactions, and dynamic reconfiguration to deal with local failure management.

3.1   Size and Distribution

CPSoS comprise a significant number of interacting components that are (partially) physically coupled and together fulfil a certain function, provide a service, or generate products. The components can provide services independently, but the performance of the overall system depends on the "orchestration" of the components. The physical size or geographic distribution of the system are not essential factors to make it a system of systems, but rather is its complexity. A factory with many "stations" and materials handling and transportation systems is structurally not much different from a large rail transportation network that extends over several countries.

A distinguishing feature for a system of systems is that at least some of the components can provide useful services also independently. So a car engine with several controllers that are connected by a communication system is a cyber-physical system, but not a system of systems, as the components only provide a useful function together with the engine, and there is no local autonomy of the subsystems but only a distributed deployment of control functions.

3.2   Control and Management

Owing to the scope and the complexity of the overall system or due to the ownership or management structures, the control and management of CPSoS cannot be performed in a completely centralized or hierarchical top-down manner with one authority tightly controlling and managing all the subsystems. Instead, there is a significant distribution of authority with partial local autonomy, *i.e.,* partially independent decision making.

The distribution of the management and control structure usually follows the physical distribution of the system elements. Large systems are always controlled in a hierarchical and distributed fashion where local "uncertainties", *e.g.,* the effects of non-ideal behaviours of components or of disturbances, are reduced by local control. In CPSoS, there are partly autonomous human or automatic decision makers that steer the subsystems according to local priorities. The "managerial element" of the components of the management and control systems in CPSoS goes beyond classical decentralized control where decentralized controllers control certain variables to externally set reference values.

Communication between the physical sub-systems and the control and management of sub-systems takes place via sensors and actuators and various types of communication channels, from wires to connections over the internet that may be unreliable or have limited bandwidth. The elements of the management and control systems similarly communicate via suitable channels. Internet communication mechanisms and wireless channels have provided a much greater connectivity of distributed system elements and this trend will continue ("Internet of Things"). Research and innovation in CPSoS is about how to use this connectivity for better management and control of the overall SoS. Internet connectivity adds a significant element of flexibility but also of vulnerability to technical systems that can have consequences that go far beyond issues of privacy, as potentially large damages (accidents, power outages, standstills) can be caused. Therefore, security against unauthorized access is a major system issue, and detection of manipulated signals or commands are important aspects of CPSoS design.

For CPSoS, the management of the overall system as well as of its sub-systems will usually not only be driven by technical criteria but rather by economic, social, and ecologic performance indicators, *e.g.,* profitability, acceptance, satisfaction of users, and environmental impact. CPSoS are managed by humans, and many performance criteria concern providing services to human users. Thus, CPSoS have to be addressed as socio-technical systems with the specific feature of a large technical/physical structure that determines and constrains the behaviour of the system to a large extent.

3.3   Partial Autonomy

Partial autonomy of the subsystems both in terms of their independent ability to provide certain services and of partial autonomy of their control and management systems is essential in the definition of CPSoS. Often, the sub-systems can exhibit selfish behaviour with local management, goals, and preferences. The autonomy can in particular result from human users or supervisors taking or influencing the local decisions.

Autonomy is understood as the presence of local goals that cannot be fully controlled on the system of systems level. Rather, incentives or constraints are given to the subsystem control in order to make it contribute to the global system targets. An example is the operation of units of a chemical plant that consume and produce steam as a necessary resource or by-product of their main task. Their operators or managers run their processes autonomously to achieve local goals and meet local targets. The site owner/operator sets mechanisms to negotiate about the steam generation/consumption and in doing so provides suitable incentives so that the global profit of the site is maximized.

Autonomy can lead to self-organizing systems: Consider the flow of cars in a city when there is a new construction site. Due to their autonomous intelligence, the drivers seek new paths, quite predictably, and after a few days each one re-optimizes her or his route to minimize travel time, and a new flow pattern establishes itself. This may not be provably optimal, but the autonomous actions of the "agents" lead to resilience of the overall system.

3.4 Dynamic Reconfiguration

Dynamic reconfiguration, *i.e.,* the frequent addition, modification or removal of components is a widespread phenomenon in CPSoS. This includes systems where components come and go (like in air traffic control) as well as the handling of faults and the change of system structures and management strategies following changes of demands, supplies or regulations.

Fault detection and handling of errors or abnormal behaviours is a key issue in CPSoS design and operation. Due to the large scale and the complexity of CPSoS, failures occur all the time. The average system performance, as well as the degree of satisfaction of the users, is strongly affected by the impact of unforeseen events and outer influences that require non-continuous actions and cannot be compensated on the lower system levels. There is a massive need for detecting such situations quickly and, if possible, preventing them, and for fail-soft mechanisms and resiliency and fault tolerance at the systems level. The handling of faults and abnormal behaviour is challenging from a systems design point of view. In many cases it cannot be done optimally by a design based on separation of concerns but requires a trans-layer design of the reaction to such events.

Living cells with their multiple metabolic pathways are an example of a system that has optimized its ability to reconfigure itself to cope with changing conditions (availability of nutrients and other external factors) by keeping many options (metabolic pathways) intact and being able to switch between them. They may be used as a paradigm for the design of resilient CPSoS that do not operate in a strictly controlled environment.

3.5 Continuous Evolution

CPSoS are large systems that operate and are continuously improved over long periods of time. In many systems, from railways to chemical plants, the hardware (real physical hardware) infrastructure "lives" for 30 or more years, and new functionalities or improved performance have to be realized with only limited changes of many parts of the overall system. Management and control software as well usually has long periods of service, while the computing hardware base and the communication infrastructure change much more rapidly. Components are modified, added, the scope of the system may be extended or its specifications changed. So engineering to a large extent has to be performed at runtime.

The V-model paradigm with consecutive phases: requirements – modelling – model-based design – verification – validation – commissioning – operation – dismantling, is not applicable in its pure form to SoS where the requirements change during operation. There is a need for a scientific foundation to handle multi-layer operations and multiple life-cycle management.

Specification needs to be particularly thorough in the context of SoS, and should be as simply and clearly articulated as possible. Testing also needs to be thorough in the context of real SoS and must include also "mis-use cases". Once rolled out, operating and maintaining a system of systems requires a good knowledge of the "as-deployed-and-configured" system's physical, functional and behavioural configuration. Here the aviation industry has great experience.

When a new system is developed and deployed, the two activities of design and operational management usually can clearly be distinguished and often different groups of people are responsible for them. But later, the distinction is blurred, the experience gained in (day-to-day) management must be taken into account in revisions, extensions etc. The operational management must also take care of the implementation of engineered changes in a running system. Validation and verification has to be done "on the fly". This integration strengthens the role of models in both engineering processes. Up-to-date (because continuously updated) models of the running operation can be used for both purposes. The engineering of system of systems requires methods and tools that can be used seamlessly during design as well as operation (design-operations continuum).

3.6   Possibility of Emerging Behaviours

Emerging behaviours are an issue that is highly disputed. It is a simple and often stated fact that the system as a whole is more than its parts and can provide services that the components cannot provide autonomously. Sometimes the term emerging behaviour is used for the consequences of simple dynamic interactions, *e.g.,* that a feedback loop that consists of stable subsystems may become unstable (and vice versa), or of design flaws due to an insufficient consideration of side-effects. The term emerging behaviour however seems more appropriate for the occurrence of patterns, oscillations or instabilities on a system-wide level, as it may occur in large power systems or in transportation systems, and to self-organization and the formation of structures in large systems.

Emerging behaviour should be distinguished from cascades of failures, like if a traffic jam on one motorway leads to one on the alternative route. However, if faults lead to instabilities and possible breakdowns of a large system due to "long-range interactions" in the system, like in power blackouts, then this can be called emerging behaviour. Emerging behaviour should be addressed both from the side of system analysis under which conditions does emerging behaviour occur and from the side of systems design how can sufficient resiliency be built into the system such that local variations, faults, and problems can be absorbed by the system or be confined to the subsystem affected and its neighbours and do not trigger cascades or waves of problems in the overall system. Formal verification (*e.g.,* assume/guarantee reasoning) as well as dynamic stability analysis for large-scale systems are possible approaches to prove the non-existence of unwanted emerging behaviours.

3.7   Enabling Technologies and Methodologies

In order to build and to operate CPSoS, knowledge and technologies from many domains are needed. We distinguish between enabling technologies that are required to realize CPSoS but are developed independently and for a broad range of purposes, and core technologies that are specific and have to be specifically developed for CPSoS. The following are examples of enabling technologies/methodologies:

- Communication technologies and communication engineering. Standardized protocols, exploiting the Internet of Things, *e.g.,* interactions between phone and car, to provide new functionality/services, LiFi light communications.
- Computing technologies, high-performance and distributed computing. Multicore computing and new computer architectures to deal with more data and provide localised processing, low power processing for ubiquitous installation (with energy harvesting supplies), ability to implement mixed criticality on multicores.
- Sensors, *e.g.,* energy harvesting, Nano NEMs sensors - the next generation beyond MEMs.
- Management and analysis of huge amounts of data ("big data").
- Human-machine interfaces, *e.g.,* head up displays, display glasses, polymer electronics and organic LEDs to display information.
- Dependable computing and communications.
- Security of distributed/cloud computing and of communication systems.

Research and innovation in these areas contributes strongly to the ability to build more efficient and more reliable CPSoS, but have broader applications and includes investigating how to best make use of these technologies and to trigger and jointly perform specific developments related to CPSoS.

4   Key Research and Innovation Challenges in CPSoS

In this section, the identified key research and innovation challenges in the engineering and management of CPSoS are introduced.

4.1   Distributed, Reliable and Efficient Management of CPSoS

Due to the scope and the complexity of CPSoS as well as due to ownership or management structures, the control and management tasks in such systems cannot be performed in a centralized or hierarchical top-down manner with one authority tightly controlling all subsystems. In CPSoS, there is a significant distribution of authority with partial local autonomy. An illustrative example of such a system is a self-organizing automation system for coordinating smart components within the grid as presented in [1]. See Fig. 1 for an illustrative example. The design of such management systems for reliable and efficient management of the overall systems poses a key challenge in the design and operation of CPSoS.

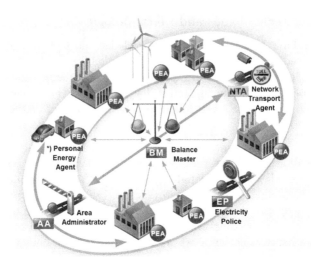

Fig. 1. Self-Organizing energy automation systems: coordinating smart components within the grid, from [1].

The following sub-topics should be addressed:

- Decision structures and system architectures,
- Self-organization, structure formation, and emergent behaviour in technical SoS,
- Real-time monitoring, exception handling, fault detection and mitigation of faults and degradation,
- Adaptation and integration of new components,
- Humans in the loop and collaborative decision making, and
- Trust in large distributed systems.

Decision Structures and System Architectures. The interaction and coordination of dynamic systems with partial autonomy in SoS, possibly with dynamic membership, must be studied broadly. Examples of applicable methods are population dynamics and control and market-based mechanisms for the distribution of constraining resources. The partial autonomy of the components from the overall system of systems perspective leads to uncertainty about the behaviour of the subsystems. Therefore the system-wide coordination must take into account uncertain behaviour and must nonetheless guarantee an acceptable performance of the overall system. Stochastic optimization and risk management must be developed for CPSoS. It must be understood better how the management structure (centralized, hierarchical, distributed, clustered) influences system performance and robustness.

Self-Organization, Structure Formation, and Emergent Behaviour in Technical SoS. Due to local autonomy and dynamic interactions, CPSoS can realize self-organization and exhibit structure formation and system-wide instability, in short, emergent behaviour. The prediction of such system-wide phenomena is an open challenge at the moment. Distributed management and control methods must be designed such that CPSoS do not show undesired emerging behaviour. Inputs from the field of dynamic structure or pattern formation in large systems with uncertain elements must be combined with classical stability analysis and assume-guarantee reasoning. Methods must be developed such that sufficient resiliency is built into the system so that local variations, faults, and problems can be absorbed by the system or be confined to the subsystem affected and its neighbours and no cascades or waves of disturbances are triggered in the overall system.

Real-Time Monitoring, Exception Handling, Fault Detection, and Mitigation of Faults and Degradation. Due to the large scale and the complexity of CPSoS, the occurrence of failures is the norm. Hence there is a strong need for mechanisms for the detection of abnormal states and for fail-soft mechanisms and fault tolerance by suitable mechanisms at the systems level. Advanced monitoring of the state of the system and triggering of preventive maintenance based on its results can make a major contribution to the reduction of the number of unexpected faults and to the reduction of maintenance costs and downtime. Faults may propagate over the different layers of the management and automation hierarchy. Many real-world SoS experience cascading effects of failures of components. These abnormal events must therefore be handled across the layers.

Adaptation and Integration of New or Modified Components. CPSoS are operated and continuously improved over long periods of time. New functionalities or improved performance have to be realized with only limited changes of many parts of the overall system. Components are modified and added, the scope of the system may be extended or its specifications may be changed. So engineering to a large extent has to be performed at runtime. Additions and modifications of system components are much facilitated by plug-and-play capabilities of components that are equipped with their own management and control systems (decentralized intelligence).

Humans in the Loop and Collaborative Decision Making. HMI concepts, *i.e.,* filtering and appropriate presentation of information to human users and operators are crucial for the acceptance of advanced computer-based solutions. Human interventions introduce an additional nonlinearity and uncertainty in the system. Important research issues are the human capacity of attention and how to provide motivation for sufficient attention and consistent decision making. It must be investigated how the capabilities of humans and machines in real-time monitoring and decision making can be combined optimally. Future research on the monitoring of the actions of the users and anticipating their behaviours and modelling their situation awareness is needed. Social phenomena (*e.g.,* the dynamics of user groups) must also be taken into account.

Trust in Large Distributed Systems. Cyber-security is a very important element in CPSoS. A specific challenge is the recognition of obstructive injections of signals or takeovers of components in order to cause malfunctions, suboptimal performance, shutdowns or accidents, *e.g.,* power outages. The detection of such attacks requires taking into account both the behaviour of the physical elements and the computerized monitoring, control and management systems. In the case of the detection of insecure states, suitable isolation procedures and soft (partial) shut-down strategies must be designed.

4.2   Engineering Support for the Design-Operation Continuum of CPSoS

While model-based design methods and tools have been established in recent years in industrial practice for traditional embedded systems, the engineering of CPSoS poses key challenges that go beyond the capabilities of existing methodologies and tools for design, engineering, and validation. These challenges result directly from the constitutive properties of CPSoS:

- CPSoS are continuously evolving which softens, or even completely removes, the traditional separation between the engineering/design phases and the operational stages,
- The high degree of heterogeneity and partial autonomy of CPSoS requires new, fully integrated approaches for their design, validation, and operation,
- CPSoS are highly flexible and thus subject to frequent, dynamic reconfiguration, which must be supported by design support tools to enable efficient engineering,
- Failures, abnormal states, and unexpected/emerging behaviours are the norm in CPSoS, and
- CPSoS are socio-technical systems in which machines and humans interact closely.

The efficient design and operation of such systems requires new design support methodologies and software tools in the following areas:

- Integrated engineering of CPSoS over their full life cycle,
- Modelling, simulation, and optimization of CPSoS,
- Establishing system-wide and key properties of CPSoS.

Integrated Engineering of CPSoS over Their Full Life Cycle. The disappearance of the separation between the design and engineering phases and the operational stage necessitates new engineering frameworks that support the

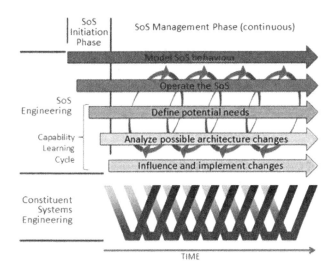

Fig. 2. DANSE system engineering life cycle, from [6].

specification, adaptation, evolution, and maintenance of requirements, structural and behavioural models, and realizations not only during design, but over their complete life cycle.

An example of such a life cycle is the DANSE system engineering life cycle shown in Fig. 2 which features a continuous SoS management phase [6]. The challenges in rolling out SoS are the asynchronous life cycles of the constituent parts and also the fact that many components are developed independently and that legacy systems may only be described insufficiently.

New engineering frameworks must enable the engineers to design fault-resilient management and control architectures by an integrated cross-layer design that spans all levels of the design and of the automation hierarchies, and by providing model-based analysis facilities to detect design errors early and to perform risk management. Such engineering frameworks must be integrated closely with industrial infrastructure (*e.g.*, databases, modelling and simulation tools, execution and runtime systems, ...).

CPSoS usually are not designed and maintained by a single company, but instead many providers of tools and hardware may be involved. Thus, collaborative engineering and runtime environments are essential that enable providers to jointly work on aspects of the CPSoS while competing on others. Integration must be based on open, easy-to-test interfaces and platforms that can be accessed by all component providers. Methods and software tools must provide semantic integration to simplify the interactions of existing systems as well as the deployment of new systems.

The advantages of these new CPSoS technologies may not be immediately apparent to industrial users, in particular in smaller companies. Thus, the demonstration of industrial business cases and application results that clearly illustrate the benefits of these technologies is an important goal.

Modelling, Simulation, and Optimization of CPSoS. Challenges in modelling and simulation are the high cost for building and maintaining models, modelling of human users and operators, simulation and analysis of stochastic behaviour, and setting up models that include failure states and the reaction to abnormal situations for validation and verification purposes. Key for the adaptation of models during the life cycle of a system and for reduced modelling cost are methodologies and software tools for model management and for the integration of models from different domains. Such model management requires meta-models.

Efficient simulation algorithms are needed to enable the system-wide simulation of large heterogeneous models of CPSoS, including dynamic on-the-fly reconfiguration of the simulation models that represent the reconfiguration of the underlying CPSoS. For performance and risk analysis, global high-level modelling and simulation of CPSoS is necessary including stochastic phenomena and the occurrence of abnormal states.

The model-based development of SoS necessitates collaborative environments for competing companies and the integration of legacy systems simulation as well as open approaches for tight and efficient integration and consolidation of data, models, engineering tools, and other information across different platforms. New business models may lead to a situation where for potential system components simulation models are delivered such that the overall system can be designed based on these models.

The real potential of model-based design is only realized if the models can be coupled to optimization algorithms. Single-criterion optimization of complex systems, including dynamic systems that are described by equation-based models has progressed tremendously in the recent decade. The next steps will be to develop efficient optimization tools for heterogeneous models, to progress towards global optimization and to use multi-criterion optimization in order to explore the design space.

Establishing System-Wide and Key Properties of CPSoS. Establishment, validation, and verification of key properties of CPSoS is an important challenge. New approaches are needed for dynamic requirements management during the continuous evolution of a CPSoS, ensuring correctness by design during its evolution, and for verification especially on the system of systems level. New algorithms and tools should enable the automatic analysis of complete, large-scale, dynamically varying and evolving CPSoS. This includes formal languages and verification techniques for heterogeneous distributed hybrid systems including communication systems, theory for successive refinements and abstractions of continuous and discrete systems so that validation and verification at different levels of abstraction are correlated, and the joint use of assume-guarantee reasoning and simulation-based (Monte Carlo) and exhaustive (model checking) verification techniques.

4.3   Cognitive CPSoS

SoS by their very nature are large, distributed and extremely complex presenting a myriad of operational challenges. To cope with these challenges there is a need for improved situational awareness [2,8]. Gaining an overview of the entire SoS is inherently complicated by the presence of decentralized management and control. The introduction of cognitive features to aid both operators and users of complex CPSoS is seen as a key requirement for the future to reduce the complexity management burden from increased interconnectivity and the data deluge presented by increasing levels of data acquisition. This requires research in a number of supporting areas to allow vertical integration from the sensor level to supporting algorithms for information extraction, decision support, automated and self-learning control, dynamic reconfiguration features and consideration of the socio-technical interactions with operators and users. The following key subtopics have been identified as being necessary to support a move to cognitive CPSoS.

- Situation awareness in large distributed systems with decentralized management and control
- Handling large amounts of data in real time to monitor the system performance and to detect faults and degradation
- Learning good operation patterns from past examples, auto-reconfiguration and adaptation
- Analysis of user behaviour and detection of needs and anomalies

Situation Awareness in Large Distributed Systems with Decentralized Management and Control. In order to operate a system of systems efficiently and robustly there is a need to detect changes in demands and operational conditions (both of the equipment and outer factors) and to deal with anomalies and failures within the system. This can only be achieved via the introduction of much greater levels of data acquisition throughout the CPSoS and the use of this data for optimization, decision support and control. Here a key enabler is the introduction of novel, easy to install, low cost, sensor technologies and monitoring concepts. If wireless monitoring is to be used there is also a need for ultra-low power electronics and energy harvesting technologies to avoid the need for, and associated maintenance costs of, battery change. An increase in data gathering will also require robust wired and wireless communication protocols that can deal with efficient transmission of individual data values from a multitude of sensors to streaming of data at high data rates, *e.g.*, for vibration and video monitoring.

Handling Large Amounts of Data in Real Time to Monitor the System Performance and to Detect Faults and Degradation. A challenge for the future will be the physical system integration of highly complex data acquisition systems and the management of the data deluge from the plethora of installed sensors and the fusion of this with other information sources. This will require analysis of large amounts of data in real time to monitor system performance and to detect faults or degradation. Here there is a need for visualization tools to manage the complexity of the data produced allowing managers to understand the "real world in real time", manage risk and make informed decisions on how to control and optimize the system.

Learning Good Operation Patterns from Past Examples, Auto-Reconfiguration, and Adaptation. There is a great opportunity to aid system operators by incorporating learning capabilities within decision support tools to identify good operational patterns from past examples. Additionally, to deal with the complexity of managing system faults, which is a major burden for CPSoS operators, auto-reconfiguration and adaptation features can be built into the system.

Analysis of User Behaviour and Detection of Needs and Anomalies. CPSoS are socio-technical systems and as such humans are an integral element of the system. SoS thus need to be resilient to the effects of the natural unpredictable behaviour of humans. There is thus a need to continuously analyse user behaviour and its impact upon the system to ensure that this does not result in system disruption.

The end result of combining real world, real-time information for decision support with autonomous control and learning features will be to provide cognitive CPSoS that will support both users and operators, providing situational awareness and automated features to manage complexity that will allow them to meet the challenges of the future.

5 Summary

After a thorough investigation of the state of the art in the domains of transportation and logistics, electrical grids, processing plants, smart buildings, distribution networks and methods and tools for the engineering and management of CPSoS and discussions and consultations with stakeholders in the domains from industry and from academia, the project CPSoS has identified three core research and innovation areas for the next decade:

1. Distributed, reliable and efficient management of CPSoS,
2. Engineering support for the design-operation continuum of CPSoS, and
3. Cognitive CPSoS.

Important long-term research topics in these domains have been described above. CPSoS will continue to raise awareness about cyber-physical systems of systems and their importance for the welfare of Europe and will propose also shorter term research and innovation topics for national and European research and innovation funding.

References

1. Böse, C., Hoffmann, C., Kern, C., M., M.: New principles of operating electrical distribution networks with a high degree of decentralized generation. In: 20th International Conference on Electricity Distribution, Prague (2009)
2. Broy, M., Cengarle, M.V., Geisberger, E.: Cyber-physical systems: imminent challenges. In: Calinescu, R., Garlan, D. (eds.) Monterey Workshop 2012. LNCS, vol. 7539, pp. 1–28. Springer, Heidelberg (2012)
3. CPSoS Consortium: Cyber-Physical Systems of Systems – definition and core research and innovation areas (2014). http://www.cpsos.eu/wp-content/uploads/2015/07/CPSoS-Scope-paper-vOct-26-2014.pdf
4. CPSoS Consortium: Cyber-Physical Systems of Systems: Research and innovation priorities (2015). http://www.cpsos.eu/roadmap
5. CPSoS Consortium: D2.4 Analysis of the state-of-the-art and future challenges in Cyber-physical Systems of Systems (2015). http://www.cpsos.eu/state-of-the-art
6. DANSE project: Deliverable D4.4 DANSE methodology V03 (2015)
7. Jamshidi, M. (ed.): Systems of Systems Engineering: Principles and Applications. CRC Press, Boca Raton (2008)
8. van de Laar, P., Tretmans, J., Birth, M. (eds.): Situation Awareness with Systems of Systems. Springer, Heidelberg (2013)
9. Maier, M.W.: Architecting principles for system of systems. Syst. Eng. 1(4), 267–284 (1998)
10. Reniers, M.A., Engell, S.: A European roadmap on cyber-physical systems of systems. ERCIM News 2014(97), 21–22 (2014)
11. Reniers, M.A., Engell, S., Thompson, H.: Core research and innovation areas in cyber-physical systems of systems. ERCIM News 2015(102) (2015)

A Parametric Dataflow Model for the Speed and Distance Monitoring in Novel Train Control Systems

Benjamin Beichler[(✉)], Thorsten Schulz, Christian Haubelt,
and Frank Golatowski

Institute of Applied Microelectronics and CE,
University of Rostock, Rostock, Germany
{Benjamin.Beichler,Thorsten.Schulz,Christian.Haubelt,
Golatowski}@uni-rostock.de

Abstract. The Speed and Distance Monitoring (SaDM) in a train control system is a cyber physical system, which constantly has to process information about the train and its environment. The specification of such systems, however, is often done in an informal way, hindering formal analysis and optimization. In this paper, we propose to use Parametric Synchronous Dataflow Graphs (PSDF) to formally specify the SaDM. For this purpose, the information about the environment is modeled via piecewise constant functions, where each discontinuity corresponds to a physical location. As the number of relevant locations depends on the actual track side and, thus, is unknown a priori, we use parameters to construct consistent PSDF models. Based on our formal model, we have implemented the SaDM using *SCADE*.

1 Introduction

Model-based system engineering has proven to be a well-suited methodology to develop embedded systems and especially safety-critical cyber-physical systems. Model-based approaches are widely used in the automotive and avionics domain but are still uncommon in the railway sector. The increasing complexity of software in locomotive on-board units renders software development and verification with traditional methods nearly impossible. We propose model-based engineering techniques as a means to ease this process. However, finding the right model for a model-based engineering approach is a challenging task.

The modeling formalism of *synchronous dataflow models* (SDF) and its extensions like *parametric synchronous dataflow* (PSDF) are well-suited for streaming applications e.g. from the domain of multimedia. The big advantages like well-developed formal methods for analysis and optimization could enhance the development process of safety-relevant applications in other domains as e.g. the railway sector.

In this paper, we propose to use PSDF for modeling parts of the train control system, which constantly interacts with its physical environment. Train control

© Springer International Publishing Switzerland 2015
C. Berger and M.R. Mousavi (Eds.): CyPhy 2015, LNCS 9361, pp. 56–66, 2015.
DOI: 10.1007/978-3-319-25141-7_5

systems (or respectively automatic train protection systems) have been developed since the very beginning of railway operation. Consequently, trains operated by different countries mostly use non-interoperable train control systems. Especially in the converging European Union this leads to a problem: all trains that need to cross borders also need to be equipped with several expensive train control systems.

The European Train Control System (ETCS), designed in the 1990s, is the designated solution to overcome this problem. ETCS includes a set of modern concepts for train control to achieve high speed and high utilization of the rail network. Besides this, ETCS aims to be flexible to address all requirements of national railway operators. The resulting ETCS standard became rather complex and difficult to implement, since the standard is currently only available as a natural, non-formal language document. This leads to high development costs and incompatible implementations by different vendors caused by ambiguities of the specification.

In this environment, the openETCS project was created with to implement an open source version of the on-board unit software. To achieve this, model-based systems engineering methods are employed. In this paper we present our efforts to model and implement the Speed and Distance Monitoring (SaDM) component using PSDF, which is part of the ETCS standard.

2   Related Work

Since the first release of the ETCS standard, several publications examined different aspects of the ETCS specification. Many of them deal with real-time properties and reliability of the communication link between train and trackside equipment. In [10–12,17] Petri net extensions are used to investigate the functional properties and stochastic guarantees of the communication. Modeling and calculation of SaDM of ETCS were covered in [8,14,16]. These focus on the functional properties of the computation and use of an application-specific modeling methodology. Other publications in the ETCS context focus on formalization and safety analysis. The authors in [7] show in three case studies how formal languages can ease the verification process of safety-critical systems. They show how the SPARK language and its toolset can be integrated into the existing development process to decrease the effort of system certification in the railway domain. However none of these publications deal with the modeling of the tight interaction with the physical environment.

In the last decades, the formalism of dataflow graph models as a refinement of process networks, have evolved to a valuable approach to develop streaming application like multimedia processing. The specialized type of *synchronous dataflow graphs* (SDF graphs) were presented in [13]. Due to their static nature, many analysis and optimization methods are available for SDF graphs. Since the expressiveness of SDF graphs is limited, many adoptions to increase their computational power have been proposed. Examples are *Boolean Dataflow Graphs* [6] and *cyclo-static dataflow graphs*[5]. *Parametric synchronous dataflow graphs*

(PSDF graphs) extend the modeling features towards even more dynamic behavior, which allows reconfiguration of subgraphs based on a set of parameters. The computation of these parameters could be done by a configuration dataflow model or a parent model, where this subgraph is embedded. The applications of PSDF graphs described in research are mostly limited to applications in the area of de-/encoding data. An exception is [9], which discusses an approach to integrate the timing of cyber physical systems into process networks, but it lacks of other physical constrains as locations. In this paper, we propose to model the physical environment by a set of piecewise constant function, where each discontinuity corresponds to a physical location. As the number of discontinuities is not known a priori, we use the PSDF model to construct a consistent model.

3   Parametric Synchronous Dataflow

The basic formalism for PSDF graphs are SDF graphs. A SDF graph $G = (V, E, cons, prod, D)$ consists of a set of Vertices V, a set of edges $E \subseteq V \to V$, token consumption rates $cons : E \to \mathbb{N}$, token production rates $prod : E \to \mathbb{N}$, and a delay function $D : E \to \mathbb{N}_0$. The vertices are actors communicating data tokens over unbounded channels represented by edges, so every channel is annotated with the number $d(e)$ of tokens on it. In SDF graphs the consumption and production rates need to be static. An actor $v \in V$ can be fired if $\forall e = (\widetilde{v}, v) \in E : d(e) \geq cons(e)$. If actor v fires, it consumes $cons(e)$ token from each incoming edge $e = (\widetilde{v}, v) \in E$ and produces $prod(e)$ token on each outgoing edge $e = (v, \widetilde{v}) \in E$ A SDF graph is called consistent, if a non-trivial repetition vector γ could be found, which describes the number of activations (firings) of every actor to get into the same state (count of tokens on the channels) as in the initial situation. In PSDF graphs this description is extended by configurable consumption and production rates are specified by parameters, which represent a runtime determined integer consumption or production rate.

4   ETCS - Speed and Distance Monitoring

To illustrate our proposed modeling approach, we use the speed and distance monitoring (SaDM) from the European Train Control System (ETCS). The SaDM is described next.

One of the main tasks of ETCS is to supervise the speed and position of a train to ensure that the train stays in the permitted speed ranges. Because of the low friction between steel wheels and rail and the relatively high mass of the train, the braking distance is very large compared to, e.g., automobiles. As a consequence driving on sight is limited to relative low speeds and for higher speeds technical assistant is needed.

An established approach to ensure the safe track operation cascaded signals and mutual exclusive track usage is used. The size of the track segments significantly effects the utilization and possible throughput and therefore the profitability of a track. Since the signal equipment is fixed at the track side, a

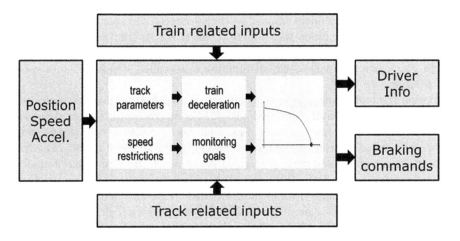

Fig. 1. Simplified overview of the ETCS SaDM extracted from [15]

customization for different rolling stock is effectively impossible. This becomes a serious problem if trains with significantly different maximum speeds and braking abilities are used on a track.

To prevent a human failure of the perception of safety-critical information, all modern train control systems must have an automatic intervention possibility for dangerous situations. More sophisticated train control systems like ETCS make usage of customized signaling with displays within the train cab. This "cab signaling" helps to customize the speed and distance limits for every train. The challenge of a calculation on the on-board unit of the train control system is to ensure the safe operation of the train. This includes the functional safety and the time-critical aspects of the calculation of speed and distance limits.

4.1   Overview

An overview SaDM is shown in Fig. 1. The tasks of SaDM are defined within the System Requirements Specification [15]. The main output of the SaDM comprises information for the driver, e.g., the currently permitted speed or monitoring targets. For critical situations, the SaDM issues automatic braking commands. In order to determine this information, SaDM needs several inputs such as dynamic values of the current position, speed and acceleration of the train. Moreover, a certain number of other train and track related inputs are needed which have lower dynamics as position or speed.

The most important train related inputs are the braking abilities of a train. Modern trains have multiple sets of brakes which have different operating principles and are used in several combinations according to various conditions. Thus, the applicable braking deceleration in a dangerous situation needs to be defined for all possible combinations. Other important characteristics such as curve tilt abilities, maximum train speed or the train length also need to be considered to calculate the train dependent impact on the speed and distance limits. All train related inputs are combined to a function called A_{safe}, that assigns a braking acceleration to the two independent parameters of speed and location on track. Hence, A_{safe} is a piecewise constant function or so-called step function of speed and position.

Beside the train characteristics, the track related information are important input data as well. A train equipped with ETCS receives information about the track properties while moving on it. This includes a profile of track slopes and a set of static speed restrictions which are caused by the shape of a track. Furthermore, dynamic speed restrictions (e.g., in areas which are under maintenance) are transmitted to the train. This collection of location-based speed restrictions is compressed to a single data structure called *Most Restrictive Speed Profile* (MRSP) which contains a single speed limit for every position on the track ahead. Again, the MRSP can be modeled by a piecewise constant function where every discontinuity corresponds to a location on the trackside.

From this profile the particular targets for the supervision are derived by getting all points with a decreasing allowed speed. An additional special target is derived from the limited permission of a train to move on the track. This *End of Authority* results from the *Movement Authority* which is transmitted by the chief of operation to the train. All of the described supervision targets are forwarded to the calculation of the target-specific braking curve. To predict the behavior of the train in an emergency case the *Emergency Brake Deceleration* (EBD) curve is one of the most important calculations. It is therefore in the focus of the following sections.

4.2   Emergency Brake Deceleration Curve Calculation

The Emergency Brake Deceleration curve (EBD) represents the reliably expected braking behavior in case of emergency. The system has to use all available and allowed brakes to reach zero speed at a concrete location. In addition, there exist several constraints, e.g., there is a slippery track which leads to a reduced braking performance, or the system is unable to use all brakes but only a specific combination. The system has to calculate the position of brake initiation to stop before the target position under any circumstances. As shown in Fig. 2 the braking performance influences the braking distance and as a consequence the maximum allowed speed for a constant deceleration value a at a given position s is described by the formula $v_{max} = \sqrt{2 \times a \times (s - s_0) + v_0^2}$, where s_0 and v_0 are a known point on the parabola. Since the deceleration value is only piecewise constant for a given speed and location range, several arcs of the form of the latter function are needed to describe the maximum allowed speed for a bigger part of the track. If the stop location and the braking performance on each section of the track are known, the latest point for brake initiation can be calculated to stop at the desired position. Hence, there is a need of a backward calculation algorithm which starts its calculation from the target location and calculates backwards to at least the current front end position of the train on the track as Fig. 3 shows.

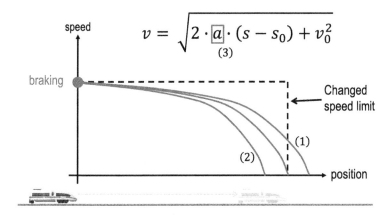

$$v = \sqrt{2 \cdot \boxed{a} \cdot (s - s_0) + v_0^2}$$
(3)

Fig. 2. Braking performance and its influence on the braking distance

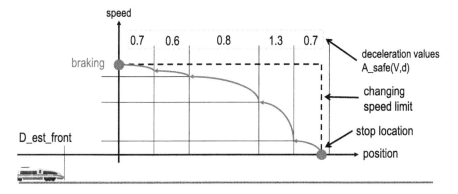

Fig. 3. Backward calculation of brake initiation depending on braking performance

The result of this algorithm is the maximum speed of the train on a specific position on the track. By exceeding this speed limit the train will fail to stop at the desired location. This information is known as EBD. After determining the maximum speed in comparison to the current speed, the ETCS on-board computer can intervene and brake automatically.

5   Parametric Dataflow Modeling of the EBD Calculation

For a formalized representation of the EBD calculation several analyses were done. The first step was the construction of the program flowchart in Fig. 4 to describe the algorithm. The calculation starts for every speed reduction location (supervised target) at the first known data point on the curve of allowed maximum speed. This is essentially the position of the supervised target itself and its associated speed limit. The initialization phase also includes a look-up into the two-dimensional array A_safe(V,d) containing information about deceleration values of the train depending on the on-track location and speed. These three values lead into a first arc of the EBD. Afterwards, the iteration checks whether the current iteration point is behind the current real front end position of the train. This condition serves as a fast exit of the algorithm which is specified in [15] because the information behind the current real front end is irrelevant. Following model shows that for the worst case analysis and a static memory allocation this condition could be substituted by a static parameter-based condition.

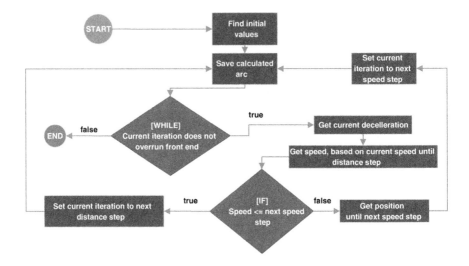

Fig. 4. Algorithm of the EBD curve calculation

The next step of the calculation determines the current acceleration of the A_safe(V,d) function and calculates the speed which the train would have at the next speed step if constantly accelerated from the current speed starting at the current position. This derived speed is compared to the speed of the next speed step of A_safe(V,d). If it is lower, the arc is valid and stored. Derived speed and position are updated to the end of the new arc. In the other case, the arc is only continuous until the speed of the next speed step of A_safe(V,d) so that the position where this speed step is passed needs to be determined. These three values make up the following arc and the current iteration values are updated.

For clarification it is noted that – seen from the absolute position – the calculated arc parameters are the end point of an arc and describe the parabolic before this position until the next point with other parameters is reached.

Table 1 illustrates an example of an iteration through a simplified A_safe(V,d). As already indicated by the parameter of the function, the table consists of a location and a velocity dimension. While iterating over this function, a diagonal path through this table is taken. The only possible directions are the cell at the left or the bottom cell. Special conditions could also allow a diagonal jump, but this could be safely approximated by two arcs, where the first one would start and end at the same point.

Table 1. Iteration through `A_safe(V,d)`

s[m] v[m/s]	0	1000	3000	4400
0	1.0	1.2	1,3————————0.7	
40	0.8	0,6————————0.8		0.9
80	0.7————————0.7		0.6	0.8
120	0.6	0.8	0.6	0.7

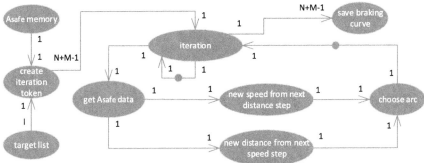

Fig. 5. Parametric synchronous dataflow of braking curve calculation

When we choose the parameter N to describe the number of position steps and the parameter M as the number of speed steps, the worst case of needed iteration steps is from the right uppermost corner to the left lowermost corner which will lead into a count of $N+M-1$ iterations. Most safety-relevant software designs inhibit dynamical memory allocation. Thus, a result array with $N+M-1$ arcs entries needs to be reserved.

With this parameter model a parametric synchronous dataflow was implemented, which is shown in Fig. 5. The $N+M-1$ factor is taken from the physical environment. Note that the exact value is depending on the track side and is unknown at compile time. Here a parametric model is needed. An additional aspect present in the parametric model, which was unmentioned in the previous model, is the effect of multiple targets. Since every supervision target needs its own adjusted emergency braking curve, the calculation has to be repeated for every target. Therefore, for every target $N+M-1$ tokens are generated with the data of `A_safe(V,d)` and the specific target to match the number of iterations for every curve. Afterwards, the iteration node consumes one token from this edge and compares its value to the last iteration which is saved in the self-edge.

If they differ, a new braking curve is calculated and the first arc based on the target data is saved. In this case the token from **choose arc** is discarded, as it is a dummy trailing token of the last braking curve.

As in the program flow before (see Fig. 4), the cycle in the graph determines the end point of the next arc with its parameters. Because of the data dependency of each arc on the last iteration, low parallelism can be achieved, except the parallel calculation of the two possible cases. Until the $N + M - 1$-th iteration, every result of the `choose arc` node is used as a new end point of an arc. But for the next braking curve a dummy token needs to be generated. In general, if the path through `A_safe` is shorter than $N + M - 1$, e.g., if the supervised target is located before the upper right corner, the last significant arc is in the left lower corner and all arcs to fill up the structure are copies of this arc. Therefore, the trailing token of the last iteration is such a copy as well.

Because of the sequential characteristics of this PSDF graph, the values of the repetition vector of the cyclic subgraph are $N + M - 1$ firings for every target. If the count of targets is considered, the factor l needs to be multiplied. The spatial dimensions change slowly – only when the train receives new information from the track-side. Since every change requires a recalculation of all curves, the parameters are of the static type described in [4]. But the parameters N and M also met the requirements for the dynamic type of [4], because the subgraph fulfill the local synchrony condition defined in [4].

6   Implementation

The realization of the parametric SDF graph was done as part of the ecosystem of the openETCS project. Therefore, the integration into the existing modeling framework *SCADE-Suite* was used. *SCADE-Suite* is a widely used model development tool which is used to generate safety-critical software with the requirements of, e.g., *ISO 26262* or *EN 50128*. *SCADE-Suite* bases on the synchronous reactive language *scade*, a successor of the *esterel* language (first mentioned in [1], see [2,3] for further details). The translation of the given PSDF graph needs some adaptation, caused by the different models of computation. But the changes are minimal due to the nature of applying the PSDF graph. Since the cyclic subgraph of the computation only consists of edges which are obviously bounded to a capacity of 1, they could be easily translated into connections in *scade*. Moreover, synchronous reactive languages do forbid direct feedback loops. The loop of the calculation needs to be cut and feedbacked through a memory element or other elements. In the case of our graph, the feedback is solved by the iteration scheme `foldwi` operator which virtually performs a sequential instantiation of every iteration, where every iteration is connected through an accumulator connection. In Fig. 6 the top operator with the `foldwi` is shown. A special constraint of the virtual inflation of the `foldwi` operator is the fact that every input needs to have the dimensions of the iteration count, so they are inflated to `cMAX_BC_ARCS` which is equal to the former defined $N + M - 1$ parameter.

Fig. 7 shows the inner part of the `foldwi` operator which defines the calculation cycle. The left side comprises the part of choosing the acceleration values according to the next distance step (upper part) and the next speed step (bottom part). Afterwards, the two cases are calculated in the boxes `FormularNewSpeed` and `FormularNewPosition`. The selection of the result of the two cases is broken up into several switches which are controlled by the Boolean expression in the upper right corner. The result is passed to the `newArc` output and saved in a higher stage.

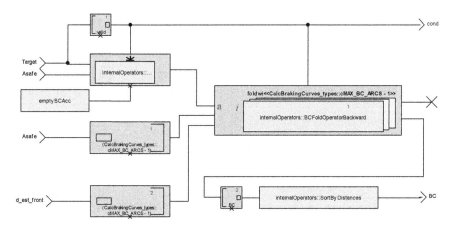

Fig. 6. Top operator of calculation subgraph

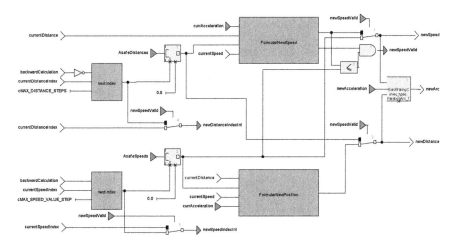

Fig. 7. Subgraph for inner operator calculation

What is unmentioned here is the operator to execute the braking curve calculation for every target of the target list. But again, this is only a `foldwi` operator with the target list as input.

7   Conclusion

This paper has presented a PSDF graph model of a real world safety-critical application of a cyber-physical system in the railway domain. The PSDF graph have proven the ability to reflect the spatial dimension parameters of the track side layout in the form of piecewise constant function, which were extensively used in ETCS. The created model of the calculation of the emergency brake deceleration curve have been implemented in the development environment

SCADE-Suite, which encourage the goals of the openETCS project to get a formalized specification of the ETCS norm.

Acknowledgement. This work was funded by the German Federal Ministry of Education and Research (Grant No. 01IS12021) in the context of the ITEA2 project open-ETCS.

References

1. Berry, G., Moisan, S., Rigault, J.: Towards a synchronous and semantically sound high level language for real-time applications. In: IEEE Real Time Systems Symposium, pp. 30–40 (1983)
2. Berry, G.: The esterel v5 language primer version v5 91 (2000). ftp://ftp.inrialpes.fr/pub/synalp/reports/esterel-primer.pdf.gz
3. Berry, G., Gonthier, G.: The esterel synchronous programming language: Design, semantics, implementation. Sci. Comput. Program. **19**(2), 87–152 (1992)
4. Bhattacharya, B., Bhattacharyya, S.: Parameterized dataflow modeling for DSP systems. IEEE Trans. Sig. Process. **49**(10), 2408–2421 (2001)
5. Bilsen, G., Engels, M., Lauwereins, R., Peperstraete, J.: Cycle-static dataflow. IEEE Trans. Sig. Process. **44**(2), 397–408 (1996)
6. Buck, J., Lee, E.: Scheduling dynamic dataflow graphs with bounded memory using the token flow model. In: 1993 IEEE International Conference on Acoustics, Speech, and Signal Processing, ICASSP-1993, vol. 1, pp. 429–432, April 1993
7. Dross, C., Efstathopoulos, P., Lesens, D., Mentré, D., Moy, Y.: Rail, space, security: three case studies for SPARK 2014. In: ERTS, Toulouse, February 2014
8. Friman, B.: An algorithm for braking curve calculations in ERTMS train protection systems. In: Advanced Train Control Systems, p. 65 (2010)
9. Grimm, C., Ou, J.: Unifying process networks for design of cyber physical systems. In: Electronic System Level Synthesis Conference (ESLsyn), June 2011
10. Hermanns, H., Jansen, D., Usenko, Y.: A comparative reliability analysis of etcs train radio communications, aVACS Technical report No. 2, February 2005
11. zu Hörste, M., Hungar, H., Schnieder, E.: Modelling functionality of train control systems using petri nets. In: Towards a Formal Methods Body of Knowledge for Railway Control and Safety Systems, p. 46 (2013)
12. Jansen, L., zu Hörste, M., Schnieder, E.: Technical issues in modelling the european train control system. In: Proceedings of the Workshop on Practical Use of Coloured Petri Nets and Design /CPN 1998, pp. 103–115 (1998)
13. Lee, E., Messerschmitt, D.: Synchronous data flow. Proc. IEEE **75**(9), 1235–1245 (1987)
14. Nitsch, A., Beichler, B., Golatowski, F., Haubelt, C.: Model-based systems engineering with matlab/simulink in the railway sector. In: Proceeding of Methoden und Beschreibungssprachen zur Modellierung und Verifikation von Schaltungen und Systemen (MBMV), Chemnitz, Germany (2015)
15. UNISIG: SUBSET-026 - System Requirements Specification. SRS 3.3.0, ERA (2012)
16. Vincze, B., Tarnai, G.: Development and analysis of train brake curve calculation methods with complex simulation. Adv. Electr. Electron. Eng. **5**(1–2), 174–177 (2011)
17. Zimmermann, A., Hommel, G.: Towards modeling and evaluation of etcs real-time communication and operation. J. Syst. Softw. **77**(1), 47–54 (2005)

A Modelling Framework for Cyber-Physical System Resilience

Manuela L. Bujorianu$^{(\boxtimes)}$ and Nir Piterman

Department of Computer Science, University of Leicester, Leicester, UK
{lb312,Nir.Piterman}@le.ac.uk

Abstract. Resilience engineering is a recent paradigm for the development, analysis and control of systems that interact with their environment and are subject to perturbances or part failures. Resilience engineering has many facets, some of them being well studied in control engineering like fault tolerance or robust control. In this paper, we propose a mathematical model that considers the following aspects relevant to resilience engineering: uncertainty, autonomy, and system-environment interaction. The model extends stochastic hybrid systems with Markov decision processes to capture system autonomy, and game theory to capture the system-environment interaction. For this model, we consider the state-constrained reachability problem as defined for stochastic hybrid systems. We give a characterization of the solutions of this problem in terms of the value function of an ergodic stochastic game.

Keywords: Resilience · Autonomous stochastic hybrid systems · Stochastic reachability · Markov models · Zero-sum stochastic games · Average payoff criteria

1 Introduction

Resilience engineering offers a new perspective on system safety [11]. If the risk analysis is more concerned with the computation of various probabilities of failure, resilience engineering has a different approach. The major concerns are the prevention of failures, or recovery following a failure.

Resilience engineering has been developed mostly in application areas like psychology and social sciences. Examples include: the resilience of the brain against stress, the resilience of a community in the face of natural or industrial disasters, or the resilience of a business organization in conditions of economic crisis [18].

For engineering systems [16], the resilience has been studied mostly in the form of fault tolerant and/or robust control. Recently, a new discipline of resilient control has been investigated for uncertain dynamical systems [15]. Resilience is also an important feature of VLSI [2] and nano circuits. Complex networked systems [19] also demand resilience as an essential feature. Resilience is a major necessary condition for aerospace and air traffic control systems [7]. For example, for a flight, beyond all performance criteria, the most important goal is to

C. Berger and M.R. Mousavi (Eds.): CyPhy 2015, LNCS 9361, pp. 67–82, 2015.
DOI: 10.1007/978-3-319-25141-7_6

land safely despite adverse weather influence, or the failure of a physical part. Other examples can be easily found when considering the deployment of systems in their physical environment. Such examples constitute cyber-physical systems (CPS) with formally proved correctness of design or safe behaviour. This correctness might no longer be ensured when the system is deployed in a physical environment, or when facing the failure of a physical part.

In this paper, we propose a mathematical model that can be used for the resilience engineering of cyber-physical systems. The paper is structured as follows. In the first section, we explain the key ideas of the modelling framework: what are the main features of a CPS model such that we can define indicators for resilience? In the Sect. 3, we develop a multi-scale modelling framework (that is constructed by adding autonomy and reactivity features to the 'classical' models of stochastic hybrid systems) suitable for CPS resilience. The result is a type of hybrid Markov decision process. The interaction with the environment is modeled via a zero-sum stochastic hybrid game. In the Sect. 4, we model resilience in the form of state-constrained stochastic reachability, for the model developed in the previous section. We give a characterization of this stochastic reachability in terms of the value function with respect to an appropriate payoff function of the stochastic hybrid game that describes the interaction system-environment. The paper ends with some conclusions.

2   Problem Formulation

In this paper, we address resilience modelling in cyber-physical systems. Resilience—in the contex of CPS—is the ability of a system to perform adequately, not only in standard situations, but also to manage unexpected events. A resilient system is able to anticipate and to adapt to potentially unexpected situations, faults/failures and to cope with uncertainty. Traditionally, fault analysis is just simple cause-and-effect analysis; hence this analysis is not able to capture unforeseen failings. Qualitative, decisional and quantitative models are necessary to capture CPS interdependencies and hierarchical structures. We propose a multi-scale model-based formalism for CPS, where different layers like hybridicity, uncertainty, and decision are encapsulated in a hierarchical structure.

A model for resilient cyber-physical systems should be flexible enough to accommodate with some important CPS features:

(i) *Autonomy:* The mathematics of autonomous systems are very diverse. Markov decision processes are able to capture the decisional activity of autonomous agents quite adroitly.
(ii) *Hybrid dynamics:* Hybrid discrete continuous models have proven very well-suited in modelling CPS. Highly interdisciplinary methods have been developed for safety verification, and control.
(iii) *Reactivity:* A well known mathematical framework for reactive systems is provided by game theory.
(iv) *Randomness:* The theory of Markov processes is by far the most developed framework for understanding and modelling the uncertainty.

Therefore, CPS resilience requires a modelling framework that integrates stochastic models, hybrid systems, and Markov decision processes.

The aim of resilience analysis is to develop methods to quantify the resilience of a given CPS towards unpredictable scenarios (hazards or rare events). A hazard is understood as any kind of exogeneous or endogenous condition, event or circumstance that has a potentially negative impact on the performance measure. This includes malicious attacks, faults, disturbances, changes in the system architecture or system parameters. The performance measure of the system might be defined as the probability of reaching a safe state/mode. One way to quantify resilience is to use state-constrained reachability analysis and to see resilience as the ability of the system to transit from a bad state (where the system was subject to hazards) to a good state (where the system is in an operational mode).

There are many ways to connect reachability analysis with resilience. In this paper, we present just the first steps of a research program. First, we construct such an integrated hierarchical model and then we quantify resilience as a reachability problem.

3   Integrating Models of Hybrid Systems and Autonomic Control

Hierarchical hybrid systems (HHS) [14] have been introduced with the primary scope of modeling multi-agent hybrid systems. An HHS has two controllers organized in two layers. At the basic layer, a controller is responsible with the mode change that ensures the standard system behaviour. Usually, this controller is specified by the guards (Boolean formulas) for the discrete transitions. At the top layer, an additional controller ensures satisfaction of additional control constraints such as keeping a safe distance from another agent, execution of collaboration activities, and so on. At this layer, a discrete abstraction (like time automaton) of the underlying hybrid system is used. In our approach, HHSs are defined such that the top level controller is responsible for safety analysis, adaptive control and autonomic behavior. For this purpose, the top controller operates at the mode switching level, the hierarchical controller being realized by introducing priorities or constraints over the controlled transitions. In our setting, the top controller is specified by a Markov decision process.

It is known that a stochastic hybrid dynamical system can be thought of as a continuous space stochastic process with discrete or continuous transitions, which are governed by two different types of controllers. We adopt the perspective of dynamical system theory (used in mathematics and control engineering) that models a system as the collection of all its possible trajectories. Therefore a controller is identified by the corresponding set of (discrete) transitions it can govern. One controller is responsible for those mode changes necessary for the basic system operation. The corresponding transitions are called forced transitions. The other controller is responsible for some mode changes that ensure near optimal behaviour. The corresponding transitions are called supervised transitions.

Stochastic Hybrid Systems. For the purposes of this paper, we consider here with a simplified version of the general model of stochastic hybrid systems (SHS) presented in [3]. Usually, a stochastic hybrid process is defined on an appropriate state space $\mathbf{S}$ (which is a subset of an Euclidean space $\mathbb{R}^p$), partitioned into a boundary $\mathbf{S}_\delta$ and interior $\mathbf{S}_o$, although the state space might be something more general as we have seen [3]. Its Borel σ-algebra, denoted by $\mathcal{B}(\mathbf{S})$, is the σ-algebra generated by the open sets. By convention, by "measurable" sets/functions we mean "Borel measurable" sets/functions.

Let $\mathcal{P}(\mathbf{S})$ be the space of probability measures (equipped with the topology of weak convergence) on the measurable space $(\mathbf{S}, \mathcal{B})$.

If $\mathbf{S}$ and $\mathbf{U}$ are nonempty topological spaces, a stochastic kernel on $\mathbf{S}$ given $\mathbf{U}$ is a function $R(\cdot, \cdot)$, $R : \mathbf{U} \times \mathcal{B}(\mathbf{S}) \to [0, 1]$, or $R : \mathbf{U} \to \mathcal{P}(\mathbf{S})$, such that $R(u, \cdot)$ is a probability measure on $\mathbf{S}$ for each fixed $u \in \mathbf{U}$, and $R(\cdot, B)$ is a measurable function on $\mathbf{U}$ for each fixed $B \in \mathcal{B}(\mathbf{S})$.

If $\mathbf{S}$ and $\mathbf{U}$ coincide, R is called stochastic kernel on $\mathbf{S}$.

Under standard assumptions an SHS can be uniquely characterized by

- a vector field: $b : \mathbf{S} \to \mathbb{R}^p$,
- a matrix: $\sigma : \mathbf{S} \to \mathbb{R}^{p \times m}$ that is a $\mathbb{R}^p$-valued matrix, $m \in \mathbb{N}$,
- a rate function: $\lambda : \mathbf{S} \to \mathbb{R}_+$, and
- stochastic kernels: $R_o : \mathbf{S}_o \to \mathcal{P}(\mathbf{S})$, and $R_\delta : \mathbf{S}_\delta \to \mathcal{P}(\mathbf{S})$.

Between discrete transitions the SHS dynamics obeys to the stochastic differential equation

$$dz(t) = b(z(t))dt + \sigma(z(t))dW_t.$$

In the interior of the state space $\mathbf{S}_o$, the process may have discrete transitions with the rate $\lambda(x)$ when the process is at state x, independently of the process history. Then the process is transferred immediately to a new state randomly according to the stochastic kernel $R_o(x|dx)$. This type of discrete transition is called *supervised transition*. If the process reaches the boundary at $x \in \mathbf{S}_\delta$, the process has a discrete transition to a new random state given by $R_\delta(x|dx)$. This type of discrete transition is called *forced transition*.

Always, we assume that $R_o(x, \mathbf{S}_o) = 1$ and $R_\delta(x, \mathbf{S}_o) = 1$.

A *controlled SHS* is defined when the tuple $(b, \sigma, \lambda, R_o, R_\delta)$ is allowed to depend on a control parameter u.

Markov Decision Processes. *Markov decision processes* (MDP) represent an automata theoretic concept used in formal methods and AI. An MDP is a five-tuple $(\mathbf{Q}, \mathcal{A}, \{\mathcal{A}(x)|x \in \mathbf{Q}\}, R, r\}$ consisting of

- *state space:* $\mathbf{Q}$ - a nonempty Borel space,
- *control* or *action set:* $\mathcal{A}$ - a nonempty Borel space,
- *feasible controls* or actions: $\{\mathcal{A}(x)|x \in \mathbf{Q}\}$ - a family of nonempty measurable subsets $\mathcal{A}(x)$ of $\mathcal{A}$, such that the set $\mathbb{K} := \{(x, a)|x \in \mathbf{Q}, a \in \mathcal{A}(x)\}$ of feasible state-action pairs is a measurable subset of $\mathbf{Q} \times \mathcal{A}$;
- *transition law:* R - a stochastic kernel on $\mathbf{Q}$ given $\mathbb{K}$; and
- *reward per-stage function:* $r : \mathbb{K} \to \mathbb{R}$ - a measurable function.

Autonomous Hybrid Systems. *Autonomous hybrid systems* (AHS) are open hybrid systems that are partially driven by a controller of complexity similar to that of a hybrid automaton. This means that an AHS is partially self-managed (autonomous behavior) and potentially controlled from outside (supervised autonomy). A simple example is the human bipedal walking: it may be learned, it can be performed autonomously if necessary, and it can be also controlled to a large extent. An increased complexity of the controller means more *system autonomy* in the form of agile or adaptive behaviors, or performing complex tasks via effectors. Sometimes, AHS can change their environment and consequently affect their own future behavior. In fact, AHS can be very diverse and they can be described using different modeling paradigms. Autonomous hybrid systems raise plenty of research issues: learning, adaptive behavior, and optimization under uncertainty are such examples. An important class of AHSs is given by multi-agent systems where a single AHS agent may be influenced not only by the environment, but also by the other agents. In this case, additional topics appear like concurrency, communication, coordination, collaboration, security, and so on.

In this paper, we present the foundations of an interdisciplinary modelling paradigm for CPS thought of as AHS deployed in continuous dynamic and random environments. For such systems, we introduce the problem of *probabilistic verification* known as *stochastic reachability analysis* in control engineering. Moreover, the stochastic reachability problem will be treated in game theoretic framework.

3.1   Autonomous Stochastic Hybrid Systems

In the following we present one way to model *Autonomous Stochastic Hybrid Systems*. We integrate the dynamical system viewpoint and the automata theoretic viewpoint into a new model that combines the advantages of both approaches. The autonomy of an SHS is obtained adding a decision maker modeled by a Markov Decision Process (MDP).

Assumption 1. *The elements of an SHS:* $\lambda : \mathbf{S} \to \mathbb{R}_+$ *(the stochastic rate) and* R_o, R_δ *(stochastic kernels on* $\mathbf{S}_o$*-interior of* $\mathbf{S}$*, respectively* $\mathbf{S}_\delta$*-boundary of* $\mathbf{S}$*) are assumed to be Borel measurable functions.*

Let I_T be the time interval $[0, T]$ if $T < \infty$ and $[0, \infty)$ if $T = \infty$. Let $\mathcal{A}$ be an *action space* consisting of a family of continuous trajectories $\omega : I_T \to \mathbb{R}^p$ with $\omega(0) = \mathbf{0}$, i.e.

$$\mathcal{A} := \{\omega \in C_{\mathbb{R}^p}(I_T) | \omega(0) = \mathbf{0}\}.$$

The action space $\mathcal{A}$ can be described in different ways. Its elements may be sample paths of some diffusion processes, continuous flows that represent solutions of some ordinary differential equations (continuous dynamical systems), or can be described by some algebraic functions. Moreover, these trajectories can be associated with some continuous random dynamical systems. We may consider only deterministic trajectories, and study the additional noise later for solving different practical problems.

Formally, $\mathcal{A}$ is a compact metric space in which convergence implies pointwise convergence.

For each $x \in \mathbf{S}$, let $\mathcal{A}_x \subset \mathcal{A}$ be the set of those continuous trajectories from $\mathcal{A}$ that are available at state x. We can also consider a disjoint partition of the action space $\mathcal{A}$ over the operational modes of a given SHS H, i.e.

$$\mathcal{A} = \cup_{q \in Q} \mathcal{A}_q, \; \mathcal{A}_q \cap \mathcal{A}_{q'} = \emptyset, \text{ if } q \neq q'.$$

In this case, for a hybrid state space $\mathbf{x} = (q, z) \in \{q\} \times X_q$, it is necessary that $\mathcal{A}_x \subset \mathcal{A}_q$.

For any trajectory $\omega_x(t) = x + \omega(t)$, we consider its *first hitting time* of the boundary defined as

$$t^*(\omega_x) = \inf\{t \in I_T : \omega_x(t) \in \mathbf{S}_\delta\},$$

and define its *final time*

$$t^f(\omega_x) = \inf\{T, t^*(\omega_x)\}$$

with the convention that $\inf \emptyset = \infty$.

For each $x \in \mathbf{S}$, we define the state-action space

$$\Gamma := \{\omega_x | x \in \mathbf{S}, \omega \in \mathcal{A}_x\}$$

that can be identified with a subset of $\mathbf{S} \times \mathcal{A}$. The following assumption needs to be in force:

Assumption 2. *For all $\omega_x \in \Gamma$, we assume:*

(i) Invariance of $\mathbf{S}$: $\omega_x(t) \in \mathbf{S}, \forall t \leq t^f(\omega_x)$;
(ii) "Killing" besides of hitting times of the boundary: $\omega_x(t) = \omega_x(t^*(\omega_x))$, for all $t \geq t^*(\omega_x)$ when $t^*(\omega_x) < \infty$.

The Assumption 2 implies that $\omega_x(t^*(\omega_x)) \in \mathbf{S}_\delta$ for all $\omega_x \in \Gamma$ and for any boundary point the only admissible action is $\omega \equiv \mathbf{0}$.

An autonomous stochastic hybrid systems (ASHS) will be defined as a hybrid decision process whose skeleton (discrete states) is given by the discrete modes of the given SHS, and the action space has been described above. The continuous dynamics of an ASHS is packed in the action space. The semantics of this ASHS will be described using the embedded (discrete time) decision process

$$\{\widehat{\omega}_n = (\omega_n)_{\widehat{x}_n} \in \Gamma | n \geq 0\}$$

with the associated time sequence for the discrete transitions $(T_n)_{n \geq 0}$.

This ASHS can be defined iteratively as follows. Suppose that we have a hybrid state $\widehat{x}_n \in \mathbf{S}_o$ for which we have chosen a decision $\omega_n \in \mathcal{A}_{\widehat{x}_n}$ and time T_n. Then the process follows the trajectory $\widehat{\omega}_n(t) = \widehat{x}_n + \omega_n(t - T_n), t \geq T_n$, until time

$T_n + t^f((\omega_n)_{\widehat{x}_n})$, unless a supervised discrete transition appears at a time $t' \in (T_n, T_n + t^f((\omega_n)_{\widehat{x}_n}))$. These supervised discrete transitions occur at rate $\lambda(x)$ when the process is in state $x \in \mathbf{S}_o$, independently of the process history. If such a discrete transition appears at state x' , then the post discrete transition location $\widehat{x}_{n+1} \in \mathbf{S}_o$ is chosen randomly accordingly with the distribution $R_o(x', dx)$, and we set $T_{n+1} := t'$. If no supervised discrete transition occurs, before reaching the boundary, we set $T_{n+1} := T_n + t^f((\omega_n)_{\widehat{x}_n})$. In this case, if $t^*((\omega_n)_{\widehat{x}_n}) < \infty$, and the process has reached the boundary at state $x' \in \mathbf{S}_\delta$, then the post discrete transition state $\widehat{x}_{n+1} \in \mathbf{S}_o$ is given by $R_\delta(x', dx)$. Otherwise, if the end of the trajectory piece ω_n has been reached before the boundary, i.e. $t^*((\omega_n)_{\widehat{x}_n}) = \infty$, $T < \infty$, then set

$$\widehat{x}_{n+1} = \widehat{x}_n + \omega_n(T_{n+1} - T_n).$$

A new decision $\omega_{n+1} \in \mathcal{A}_{\widehat{x}_{n+1}}$ is then made.

An initial state $\widehat{x}_0$ and initial decision ω_0 are specified with $T_0 = 0$. If $\widehat{x}_0 \in \mathbf{S}_\delta$, then we set $T_1 = T_0 = 0$, $\omega_0 \equiv 0$ and the next post discrete transition location $\widehat{x}_1 \in \mathbf{S}_o$ is given by $R_\delta(\widehat{x}_0, dx)$. Consequently, each $\widehat{x}_m \in \mathbf{S}_o$, for $m \geq 1$. The initial state $\widehat{x}_0$ can be chosen accordingly with an initial probability distribution $Init \in \mathcal{P}(\mathbf{S})$.

The ASHS realization is defined in the style of a revival process [3] or a Markov string. The embedded discrete decision process $(\widehat{x}_n, \omega_n)$ will be characterized by its transition measure $R : \Gamma \times \mathcal{B}(\mathbf{S}) \to [0, 1]$, where $R(x, \omega, K)$ is the probability that $\widehat{x}_{n+1} \in K$ given that trajectory $\omega_n = \omega$ is selected at state $\widehat{x}_n = x$.

The overall structure of the model can be easily described, as follows. An abstract SHS model is used by a double nested feedback controller for continuous modelling and control of a multi-modal CPS. One feedback is used to update the knowledge about the environment, and it is called perturbation evaluation. Another feedback, called state update, uses measurements (from a sensor network deployed on the CPS) and tests them against the SHS model to identify the current mode of the CPS. The parameters of the Gaussian perturbations from the environment are statistically checked and used to update the model (the perturbation evaluation feedback). Then a control policy is chosen and the corresponding commands are transmitted to the CPS.

Example 1. (The Titan Aerobot Mission [6]): A proposed mission to Titan consists of a satellite orbiting Titan that would release an aerobot probe. It will use wind currents to explore Titan. The environment of this ASHS is remarkable for its atmosphere—which is comprised of almost 95 % nitrogen. The aerobot's forced transitions are responsible for localizing and mapping the surface of Titan while maintaining a safe altitude above Titan's surface. The supervised transitions are responsible for detecting spontaneous events such as cloud formation, precipitation, and cryo-volcanism. The system must be highly autonomous sas there are long communication latencies between the aerobot and the Earth-based supervisor due to a significant time delay of about 2.5 hours. Some operating modes of the aerobot are: "flight" towards a constrained area; "station keeping" where the current position is maintained; and "float" where drifting is executed without position control. This, however, is a CPS based on two agents. The satellite and the aerobot can collaborate on reducing uncertainty of the moon map. An abstract model for multi-agent based CPS has been proposed in [5] in the form of a colored SHS. That construction can be easily adapted to the current model.

The ASHS model makes possible to combine the verification methods developed for SHS, like reachability analysis and model checking, with the optimization methods available for MDP. Moreover, from the integration process gives rise to new emergent and useful features like adaptive and autonomic behavior.

3.2 Probabilistic Hybrid Games

We model the interaction between the autonomous CPS (modeled as a stochastic hybrid decision process) and the environment (modeled as another decision process) as a probabilistic two-player hybrid game.

A hybrid multi-player game is a game in which the players have both discrete and continuous dynamics [14]. Each player controls a set of real-valued variables. The game takes place in a sequence of steps. In each step, every player either updates some of its variables (a discrete transition) according with a probability law, or chooses a law that will govern the dynamics of its variables together with a probability distribution for the duration of the round (a continuous dynamics). If some player chooses a discrete transition, then the variables are updated instantaneously. If all players choose continuous (stochastic) dynamics, then the variables evolve according to the selected laws until the minimum jumping time occurs.

We consider a two-player zero-sum Markov hybrid game that describes the interaction system-environment. The mathematical model for such a game is a tuple:
$$H_G := (\mathbf{S}, \mathcal{A}, \mathcal{A}^e, \omega, \omega^e, \mathbb{D}, R, r)$$
of the following meaning:

- $\mathbf{S}$ is a nonempty Borel space called the (common) *state space of the game,*
- $\mathcal{A}, \mathcal{A}^e$ are nonempty Borel spaces that represent *action sets* of the two players, respectively,
- α (resp. α^e) is a measurable multivalued mapping from $\mathbf{S}$ into nonempty measurable of $\mathcal{A}$ (resp. $\mathcal{A}^e$). For each $x \in \mathbf{S}$, $\mathcal{A}_x := \alpha(x)$ (resp. $\mathcal{A}_x^e := \alpha^e(x)$) represents the set of actions available to player I (resp. II) in state x.
- We assume that the set of feasible state-action tuples

$$\mathbb{D} := \{(x, \omega, \omega^e) | x \in \mathbf{S}, \omega \in \mathcal{A}_x, \omega^e \in \mathcal{A}_x^e\}$$

  is a measurable subset of $\mathbf{S} \times \mathcal{A} \times \mathcal{A}^e$;
- R is a stochastic kernel on $\mathbf{S}$ given $\mathbb{D}$ called the *transition law*; and
- $r : \mathbb{D} \to \mathbb{R}$ is a measurable function called the *payoff function* (called also *reward function* for player I, and *cost function* for player II).

If x is a state at some stage of the game and the players select $(\omega, \omega^e) \in \mathcal{A}_x \times \mathcal{A}_x^e$ then the first player receives the immediate payoff $r(x, \omega, \omega^e)$ and the second player receives $-r(x, \omega, \omega^e)$. A new state y for the game is selected according to the probability distribution $R((x, \omega, \omega^e), \cdot)$.

We have to consider also the sequence of decision times, or discrete transition times (T_n) where $T_0 := 0$ and $T_n := T_{n-1} + \delta_n$. δ_n represents the time between the $(n-1)^{th}$ and the nth decision epoch. Note that these sojourn times between decisions may be either exponentially distributed, or hitting times of some active boundaries. Then their direct distributions cannot be used when defining the payoff function.

The hybridicity of the game arises from the fact that the continuous dynamics are encoded in the action spaces. Each player is an ASHS defined in the style presented in the previous subsection. The actions of the environment represent the 'disturbances' exerted towards the trajectories of the underlying system. These can be thought of as the effect of the 'noise' produced by the environment over the continuous trajectories usually governed by some deterministic equations. We may have 'small' or 'large' perturbations that can be modelled by the Gaussian noise multiplied by a parameter $\epsilon > 0$ that represents the magnitude of the deviation from the prescribed trajectory. Therefore, we can consider that the environment actions are also paths of the underlying system with a certain degree of randomness (small/large deviations of the prescribed trajectories). In other words, if the controller chooses a certain action (path) for the system then the environment tries to perturb/randomize this path.

Each space of action $\mathcal{A}$ (resp. $\mathcal{A}^e$) is endowed with $\mathcal{P}(\mathcal{A})$ (resp. $\mathcal{P}(\mathcal{A}^e)$) that represents the set of all probability measures. Such spaces will be equipped with the weak* topologies based on bounded continuous functions. The Borel σ-algebra of $\mathcal{P}(\mathcal{A})$ will be the smallest σ-algebra such that the functions $p \mapsto p(X)$ is measurable for each Borel measurable set of actions X of $\mathcal{A}$. Further, $\mathcal{P}(\mathcal{A})$ is a Borel space. For $x \in \mathbf{S}$, we consider $\mathcal{P}(\mathcal{A}_x)$ as the set of probability measures on $\mathcal{A}$ with support in $\mathcal{A}_x$. Then

$$\mathbb{K} := \{(x, \lambda, \mu) | \lambda \in \mathcal{P}(\mathcal{A}_x), \mu \in \mathcal{P}(\mathcal{A}_x^e)\}$$

is a measurable subset of $\mathbf{S} \times \mathcal{P}(\mathcal{A}) \times \mathcal{P}(\mathcal{A}^e)$.

We write $H_1 := \mathbf{S}$; $H_{n+1} := \mathbb{D} \times H_n$, for $n \in \mathbb{N}$ and $H_\infty := \mathbb{D}^\infty$. These are the history spaces. A strategy for player I is a measurable mapping (transition probability) which associates with each given finite history H_n of the game a probability distribution on the set $\mathcal{A}$ of actions available to him, i.e. $\pi = (\pi_n)$

$$\pi_n : H_n \to \mathcal{P}(\mathcal{A})$$

such that $\pi_n(h) \in \mathcal{P}(\mathcal{A}_{x_n})$ for any $h = (x, \omega, \omega^e, ..., x_n) \in H_n$. Let Δ be the set of all strategies for the player I. Denote by F the set of all measurable functions $f : \mathbf{S} \to \mathcal{P}(\mathcal{A})$ such that $f(x) \in \mathcal{P}(\mathcal{A}_x)$. A stationary strategy for player I is a mapping which associates with each state $x \in \mathbf{S}$ a probability distribution on the set $\mathcal{A}_x$, independent of the history that led to the state x. Formally, a stationary strategy is a strategy $(f_n) \in F^\infty$ such that $f_n = f$ independent of n. Such a policy will be denoted shortly by f. In a similar way, for the player II, we define the set of all strategies Σ and the set of stationary strategies G.

Given an initial distribution $\gamma \in \mathcal{P}(\mathbf{S})$ and a pair of strategies $(\pi_1, \pi_2) \in \Delta \times \Sigma$, the corresponding state and action processes $\{x_k\}, \{\omega_k\}, \{\omega_k^e\}$ are stochastic processes defined on the canonical space $(H_\infty, \mathcal{B}(H_\infty), \mathbb{P}_\gamma^{\pi_1,\pi_2})$ (where $\mathcal{B}(H_\infty)$ is the Borel σ-algebra of H_∞) via the projections on the space H_∞, where $\mathbb{P}_\gamma^{\pi_1,\pi_2}$ is uniquely defined probability measure by π_1, π_2, and γ by the Ionescu Tulcea's theorem. When $\gamma = \delta_x$, $x \in \mathbf{S}$, we simply write $\mathbb{E}_x^{\pi_1,\pi_2}$.

The agent is interested in maximizing its expected return in the minimax sense, that is, assuming the worst case of an optimal opponent. Since the underlying rewards are zero-sum, we can suppose that the opponent is acting to minimize the agents return. Therefore, the state value function for the zero-sum Markov game can be defined in similar way like the value function for MDPs. The n-stage payoff function is

$$V_n(x, f, g) := \mathbb{E}_x^{fg} \sum_{k=0}^{n} r(x_k, \omega_k, \omega_k^e)$$

$\mathbb{E}_x^{fg}$ represents the conditional expectation given that player I and II have chosen the stationary strategies f and g, respectively, and the system starts in $x \in \mathbf{S}$. Here, x_k; ω_k and ω_k^e represent the state and the actions for players I and I, respectively, at the kth decision epoch. The *average payoff per unit time* is defined as:

$$V(x, f, g) := \liminf_{n \to \infty} \frac{1}{n} \mathbb{E}_x^{fg} \sum_{k=0}^{n-1} r(x_k, \omega_k, \omega_k^e)$$

In a usual way, we define the lower value and the upper value, respectively, of the (expected) average payoff game as follows

$$L(x) := \sup_f \inf_g V(x, f, g) \quad U(x) := \inf_g \sup_f V(x, f, g)$$

In general, it is clear that $L(\cdot) \leq U(\cdot)$. The zero-sum Markov game has a value if

$$L(x) = U(x).$$

We now introduce the following notations (bilinear extensions of r and R):

$$\widehat{r}(x, \lambda, \mu) := \int r(x, \omega, \omega^e) \lambda(d\omega) \mu(d\omega^e);$$

$$\widehat{R}(x, \lambda, \mu, dy) := \int R(x, \omega, \omega^e, dy) \lambda(d\omega) \mu(d\omega^e).$$

Let $\mathbf{B}(\mathbf{S})$ be the set of all bounded measurable functions on $\mathbf{S}$. Then the isotone operators L, L_{fg}, and U are well defined on $\mathbf{B}(\mathbf{S})$:

$$\mathbf{H}u(x, \lambda, \mu) := \widehat{r}(x, \lambda, \mu) + \int u(y) \widehat{R}(x, \lambda, \mu, dy); \tag{1}$$

$$\mathbf{H}_{fg}u(x) := \mathbf{H}u(x, f(x), g(y)) = r_{fg}(x) + \widehat{R}_{fg}u(x); \qquad (2)$$
$$Tu(x) := \sup_\lambda \inf_\mu \mathbf{H}u(x, \lambda, \mu), \ x \in \mathbf{S}.$$

A pair of stationary strategies $(f, g) \in F \times G$ is called stable if the corresponding state process $\{x_k\}$ is *ergodic*, i.e. it has a unique invariant measure denoted by $\eta[f, g] \in \mathcal{P}(\mathbf{S})$ such that

$$\frac{1}{n} \sum_{k=0}^{n-1} \widehat{R}_n(x, f(x), g(y), \cdot) \to \eta[f, g]$$

in $\mathcal{P}(\mathbf{S})$ as $n \to \infty$ for any $x \in \mathbf{S}$, where $\widehat{R}_n(x, f(x), g(y), \cdot)$ denotes the n-step transition function under (f, g).

4   Resilience Analysis

We will quantify the resilience of a CPS using stochastic reachability indicators. A CPS is resilient if these indicators remain in some predefined safety intervals. For SHSs, the problem of safety verification is dealt with stochastic reachability. In the presence of random environments, reachability can thought of as characterizing the probability of the state reaching certain (desirable/unsafe) set of states. If control inputs are available, one may want to select a control policy to maximize or minimize this probability. The difficulty arises from the interaction between discrete/continuous dynamics and the active boundaries.

For an SHS, given a target set (measurable set in the state space), stochastic reachability problem aims to compute the probability (or upper/lower bounds of this probability) of the trajectories that start in a given initial state (eventually chosen with a given probability distribution) and reach in finite/infinite horizon time $T > 0$ the target set.

For a CPS modelled as an ASHS, the formulation of the stochastic reachability has also to consider a measurable set of destination states $E \subset \mathbf{S}$. Usually, we consider that E is a subset of the (given) invariant open set S_p associated to a discrete mode p.

The new elements that have to be considered for defining reachability of ASHS are:

(i) *running cost functions* that associate with each mode q and each action ω (continuous path) the cost $c(q, \omega)$;
(ii) *reachability cost function*

$$\int_0^{T_E(\omega)} [g(\omega(t))] dt$$

in the mode S_p, where T_E is the first hitting time of E along the trajectory ω in the mode S_p and g is a cost function defined along the trajectories.

Then stochastic reachability analysis for ASHS is twofold into two subproblems:

(i) the stochastic shortest path problem (see [1] for more details) for the embedded MDP (i.e. find the minimum cost path for reaching the mode p);
(ii) the local optimal control problem for the mode p that aims to minimize the reachability cost function over the actions available for the mode p.

The use of an embedded decision process makes also possible the study of the mode/state constrained reachability problem for ASHS. That means computing the min/max cost for reaching a target set whilst avoiding another dangerous state set or mode. It is clear that as soon as a strategy is chosen, the stochastic reachability analysis becomes the "classical" reachability that has been studied elsewhere.

In the remaining of this section, we present the problem of state-constrained reachability for hybrid games. Suppose that H_G is a hybrid game as we defined earlier in this paper. Remember that the two-player structure of H_G is given by the player I, which is an ASHS H, and the player II, which is the environment. The stochastic reachability problem will be defined with respect to the player I.

Let $E \in \mathcal{B}(\mathbf{S})$ be a set of goal states, and $O \in \mathcal{B}(\mathbf{S})$ be a set of obstacle states. The 'controller' wins if it can keep the system from entering the interior of the set O and drive the system towards E. Conversely, the environment wins if it can drive the system into the interior of O. The reachability problem is depicted in the Fig. 1

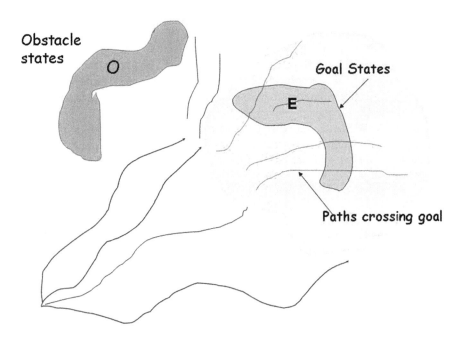

Fig. 1. Reachability for ASHS.

For safety reasons, we consider an "invariant set" $\mho$ outside of O (i.e. $\mho \subset \mathbf{S}\backslash O$) with a 'large enough' distance between $\mho$ and O, i.e.

$$dist(\mho, O) := \inf\{d(x,y)|x \in \mho \wedge y \in O\} \leq \epsilon$$

where $\epsilon > 0$ is the maximum allowed deviation magnitude and $d(x,y)$ is the Euclidean distance between x and y. Then we can define a set of "good actions" (such that 'disturbed trajectories' from $\mho$ to not 'touch' ∂O) for player I as follows

$$\mathcal{A}(O^-) := \{\omega \in \mathcal{A}|\omega \subset \mho\}. \tag{3}$$

and the "targeted actions" are

$$\mathcal{A}(O^-, E) := \{\omega \in \mathcal{A}|\omega \in \mathcal{A}(O^-), \omega \cap E \neq \emptyset\}.$$

Then the "neuter actions" are

$$\mathcal{A}(O^-, E^-) := \mathcal{A}(O^-)\backslash\mathcal{A}(O^-, E)$$

Since the "hybrid trajectories" of the player I are obtained by concatenation of actions (elements of $\mathcal{A}$), then the set of 'safe hybrid trajectories' that arrive at the destination E is:

$$Reach(E) : = \{\omega_1 * \omega_2 * ... * \omega_n|$$
$$\omega_1, \omega_2, ..., \omega_{n-1} \in \mathcal{A}(O^-, E^-), \omega_n \in \mathcal{A}(O^-, E)\}.$$

To set up the stochastic reachability analysis in the game theoretic framework, we need to specify the reward function r that should illustrate the cost of obstacle avoidance.

Let f and g be arbitrary stationary strategies for the system and its environment, respectively. Clearly, for any state $x \in \mathbf{S}$, a good strategy f should be chosen such that any $\lambda = f(x)$ is a probability distribution supported in the subset of $\mathcal{A}_x$ of the actions that do not intersect the obstacle. O. Formally, if we define

$$\mathcal{A}_x(O^-) := \{\omega \in \mathcal{A}_x|\omega \subset \mho\}. \tag{4}$$

then $supp\lambda \subset \mathcal{A}_x(O^-)$.

The natural choice for the reward function r is to take the value 0 for all actions that do not intersect the obstacle O. Value 1 can be attributed to r for all "targeted actions" that do not intersect the obstacle O, but intersect E. For the "bad actions", the player I will be penalized with $(-\infty)$. Formally, $r : \mathbb{D} \to \mathbb{R}$

$$r(x, \omega, \omega^e) := \begin{cases} 1, & \text{if } \omega \in \mathcal{A}(O^-, E); dev(\omega^e) \leq \epsilon \\ 0, & \text{if } \omega \in \mathcal{A}(O^-, E^-); dev(\omega^e) \leq \epsilon \\ -\infty, \text{otherwise.} \end{cases} \tag{5}$$

where $dev(\omega^e)$ represents the magnitude of the deviation of ω^e from the prescribed path ω. Clearly, the actions of the environment that produce large deviations have a very "negative effect" towards the payoff function r.

It is easy to see that the underlying ASHS will evolve safe for all stationary strategies for which the value function of the average payoff game with respect to the 'reachability reward' r is nonnegative. Since we consider the average payoff criterion with respect to a non-continuous unbounded reward function of a zero-sum stochastic hybrid game, we need to impose the 'right assumptions' that will ensure the existence of the game value function and stationary optimal strategies for each player.

For zero-sum stochastic games with general state space, conditions for the existence of the value function have been studied starting with Nowak's seminal work (see [17], and the references therein). Since then, other authors have investigated this problem assuming different types of hypotheses according with various practical applications [10,12,13], and so on. In the context of the stochastic reachability analysis of the hybrid processes studied in this paper, we consider that the ergodic payoff criterion and the ergodicity assumptions of [9] are more appropriate with the theoretical foundations we have proposed. We can not impose Feller transition probabilities like in [13], since the stochastic hybrid processes allow predictable jumps (governed by some guard conditions), or continuity conditions for the reward function like in [12], since our reachability reward may not fullfil such conditions.

In the following, we briefly recall the ergodicity assumption from [9].

Assumption 3 (Ergodicity). *(i) There exists $\alpha < 1$ such that*

$$\sup ||\widehat{R}(x, \lambda, \mu, \cdot) - \widehat{R}(x', \lambda', \mu', \cdot)||_{TV} \leq 2\alpha,$$

where the supremum is over all $x, x' \in \mathbf{S}$, $\lambda, \lambda' \in \mathcal{P}(\mathcal{A})$, $\mu, \mu' \in \mathcal{P}(\mathcal{A}^e)$, and $||\cdot||_{TV}$ denotes the total variation norm.
(ii) For $x \in \mathbf{S}$, $\omega \in \mathcal{A}$, $\omega^e \in \mathcal{A}^e$, $R(x, \omega, \omega^e, A) > 0$, for any open set $A \subset \mathbf{S}$.

Under this ergodicity assumption, all pairs of stationary strategies $(f, g) \in F \times G$ will be stable [9]. Then we can define

$$\rho(f, g) := \int_{\mathbf{S}} \widehat{r}(x, f(x), g(x)) \eta[f, g](dx).$$

Under such a condition, we have

$$V(x, f, g) = \rho(f, g)$$

for any $x \in \mathbf{S}$.

Usually, the existence of a value and the optimal strategies are obtained as solutions of appropriate dynamic programming equations:

$$\begin{aligned}
\rho + u(x) &= \min_{\mu \in \mathcal{P}(\mathcal{A}^e)} \max_{\lambda \in \mathcal{P}(\mathcal{A})} \mathbf{H}u(x, \lambda, \mu) \\
&= \min_{\lambda \in \mathcal{P}(\mathcal{A})} \max_{\mu \in \mathcal{P}(\mathcal{A}^e)} \mathbf{H}u(x, \lambda, \mu)
\end{aligned} \tag{6}$$

where $\mathbf{H}$ is given by (1). A solution to (6) is a pair (ρ, u) satisfying (6), where ρ is a scalar and $u \in \mathbf{B}(\mathbf{S})$.

Proposition 1. *[9] Let $(\rho^*, u^*) \in \mathbb{R} \times \mathbf{B}(\mathbf{S})$ be a solution of (6). Then:*
(i) ρ^* is the value of the game.
(ii) Let $(f^*, g^*) \in F \times G$ be such that for each $x \in \mathbf{S}$

$$
\begin{aligned}
\rho^* + u^*(x) &= \min_{\mu \in \mathcal{P}(\mathcal{A}^e)} \mathbf{H}u^*(x, f^*, \mu) \\
&= \max_{\lambda \in \mathcal{P}(\mathcal{A}^e)} \mathbf{H}u^*(x, \lambda, g^*),
\end{aligned}
$$

then f^* is a stationary strategy for player I, and g^* is a stationary strategy for player II. Under our assumption such f^*, g^* always exist.

Under the ergodicity assumption, a solution of (6) always exists. A uniform approximation of ρ^* can be obtained using the value iteration scheme (see [9]).

Regarding the safe evolution of the underlying stochastic hybrid system, we can derive now the following result.

Theorem 1. *Under the ergodicity Assumption 3, the ASHS H (player I of H_G) will evolve in safety conditions (in the invariant set $\eth$) if and only if the game value ρ^* with respect to the average payoff criterion defined with respect to the reachability reward r given by (5) satisfies the following condition $\rho^* \geq 0$.*

5   Conclusions

Recent developments in cyber-physical systems raised a new discipline called resilience engineering. So far, this discipline has been investigated mostly for social organizations and in psychology. A rigorous approach to resilience engineering of CPS will start by constructing a suitable mathematical model. We have identified four major features for such a model: autonomy, hybridicity, reactivity, and uncertainty. We have described a guided construction of such a model by starting with a stochastic hybrid system model, and integrating it with other concepts like Markov decision processes and stochastic games. Furthermore, we have studied resilience through reachability analysis for this model.

The future developments of this model will include more features that will allow us to model interdependencies/interconnections in networked cyber-physical systems (like intelligent transportation systems). These will consider both quantitative and qualitative connections. Most likely, we will have to introduce multi-layered networked cyber-physical systems. Also, more resilience indicators (e.g. fault-tolerance, physical and cyber security, or recovery) will be added. Tools will be developed to enable the assessment and improvement of resilience.

Acknowledgments. This work was funded by the EPSRC project EP/L007177/1.

References

1. de Alfaro, L.: Computing minimum and maximum reachability times in probabilistic systems. In: Baeten, J.C.M., Mauw, S. (eds.) CONCUR 1999. LNCS, vol. 1664, pp. 66–81. Springer, Heidelberg (1999)
2. Garg, R., Kathri, S.P.: Analysis and Design of Resilient VLSI Circuits: Mitigating Soft Errors and Process Variations. Springer, New York (2009)
3. Bujorianu, M.L., Lygeros, J.: Towards modelling of general stochastic hybrid systems. Stochastic Hybrid Systems: Theory and Safety Critical Applications. LNCIS, vol. 337, pp. 3–30. Springer, Heidelberg (2006)
4. Bujorianu, M.L., Bujorianu, M.C.: State constrained reachability for stochastic hybrid systems. J. Nonlinear Anal. Hybrid Syst. **5**(2), 320–342, Elsevier Press (2011)
5. Bujorianu, M.C., Bujorianu, M.L., Barringer, H.: A formal framework for user centric control of probabilistic multi-agent cyber-physical systems. In: Fisher, M., Sadri, F., Thielscher, M. (eds.) CLIMA IX. LNCS, vol. 5405, pp. 97–116. Springer, Heidelberg (2009)
6. Elfes, A., et al.: Autonomous flight control for a titan exploration aerobot. In: Proceedings of Robotics Science and Systems (2005)
7. Eurocontrol: A White Paper on Resilience Engineering for ATM (2010)
8. Feng, Z., Dearden, R., Meuleau, N., Washington, R.: Hybrid Discrete-Continuous Markov Decision Processes. NASA Technical Report 20040010791 (2003)
9. Ghosh, M.K., Bagchi, A.: Stochastic games with average payoff criterion. Appl. Math. Optim. **38**, 283–301 (1998)
10. Hernandez-Lerma, O., Lasserre, J.B.: Zero-sum stochastic games in borel spaces: average payoff criteria. SIAM J. Control Optim. **39**(5), 1520–1539 (2001)
11. Hollnagel, E., Woods, D.D., Leveson, N.: Resilience Engineering: Concepts and Precepts. Ashgate, Aldershot (2006)
12. Jaskiewicz, A., Nowak, A.S.: On the optimality equation for zero-sum ergodic stochastic games. Math. Methods Oper. Res. **54**, 291–301 (2001)
13. Jaskiewicz, A., Nowak, A.S.: Zero-sum Ergodic Stochastic Games with Feller Transition Probabilities. SIAM J. Control Optim. **45**(3), 773–789 (2006)
14. Lygeros, J.: Hierarchical, Hybrid Control of Large Scale Systems, Ph.D. thesis (1996)
15. Mahmoud, M.S.: Resilient Control of Uncertain Dynamical Systems. Lecture Notes in Control and Information Sciences, vol. 303. Springer, Heidelberg (2004)
16. Mitchell, S.M., Mannan, M.S.: Designing resilient engineered systems. Chem. Eng. Prog. **102**(4), 39–45 (2006)
17. Nowak, A.S.: Zero-sum average payoff stochastic games with general state space. Games Econ. Behav. **7**, 221–232 (1994)
18. Proceedings of the 1st International Symposium on Resilient Control Systems, Idaho Falls, ID (2008)
19. Rieger, C.G., Gertman, D.I., McQueen, M.A.: Resilient control systems: next generation design research. In: 2nd IEEE Conference on Human System Interaction (2009)
20. Tomlin, C., Lygeros, J., Sastry, S.: A game theoretic approach to controller design for hybrid systems. Proc. IEEE **88**(7), 949–970 (2000)

Recharging Probably Keeps Batteries Alive

Holger Hermanns, Jan Krčál, and Gilles Nies$^{(\boxtimes)}$

Computer Science, Saarland University, Saarbrücken, Germany
{hermanns,krcal,nies}@cs.uni-saarland.de

Abstract. Battery powered systems are a major area of cyber physical system innovation. This paper develops a kinetic battery model with bounded capacity in the context of piecewise constant yet random charging and discharging. The resulting model enables a faithful time-dependent evaluation of the risk of a mission failure due to battery depletion. This is exemplified in a power dependability study of a nano satellite mission currently in orbit.

1 Introduction

More and more cyber physical systems are operating at hard-to-reach locations and are exposed to hostile environment conditions such as extreme temperatures [20]. Many are battery-operated and include energy harvesting technology, combined with self-adaption concepts. For this, the systems have to keep track and control their power budget. This induces the need to conduct power-aware scheduling [3,26] of tasks rather than to simply monitor the remaining power budget so as to guarantee successful operation.

A prime example of a cyber physical system exhibiting these features is a satellite system, typically drawing its energy from a built-in battery which in turn is charged by solar panels, unless in eclipse. Especially low-earth orbiting nano satellites are gaining popularity [11,18]. Since the battery is physically inaccessible after launch, the mission planning in turn depends crucially on a model of the battery that is as accurate as possible, while still being abstract and easy-to-handle.

The *kinetic battery model* (KiBaM) is a popular representation of the dynamic behaviour of the *state-of-charge* (SoC) of a conventional rechargeable battery [27,28]. Given a constant load, it characterizes the battery SoC by two coupled differential equations. Empirical evaluations show that this model provides a good approximation of the SoC across various battery types [23,24], especially because it can capture two important real phenomena; the *rate capacity effect* (the higher the discharge rate, the smaller the fraction of the batteries nominal capacity that can be used) and the *recovery effect* (the battery recovers to some extent during periods of no or little discharge). The original KiBaM however does not take capacity bounds into considerations, it can thus be interpreted as assuming infinite capacity. Reality is unfortunately different. When studying the KiBaM operating with capacity bounds, it becomes apparent that

C. Berger and M.R. Mousavi (Eds.): CyPhy 2015, LNCS 9361, pp. 83–98, 2015.
DOI: 10.1007/978-3-319-25141-7_7

charging and discharging are *not* dual to each other. In contrast to the discharging process, the charging process near capacity bounds has not received dedicated attention in the literature. That problem is attacked in the present paper.

Furthermore, real of-the-shelf batteries exhibit considerable variances in actual performance [7], rooted in manufacturing and wear differences. This observation asks for a stochastic re-interpretation of the classical KiBaM to take the observed SoC variances into account on the model level, and this is what the present paper develops – in a setting with capacity bounds. It views the KiBaM as a transformer of the continuous probability distribution describing the SoC at any real time point, thereby also supporting uncertainty and noise in the load process.

The approach presented not only enables the treatment of randomness with respect to the battery itself, but also makes it possible to determine the SoC distribution after a sequence of piecewise constant, yet *random* charge or discharge loads. We develop the approach in a setting with continuous randomness so as to directly support normal (i.e. Gaussian), Weibull or exponential distributions.

The resulting battery model can be viewed as a particular stochastic hybrid system [1,2,4,6,30], developed without discretising time. It is similar in nature, yet somewhat orthogonal to *Piecewise Deterministic Markov Processes* (PDMPs) [10]. Instead of having Markovian jump times as in PDMPs, jump times are considered deterministic while the randomness is present in the evolution of the system given by ODEs over continuously distributed SoC and load. It can (for instance) for any given real time point provide probabilistic guarantees about the battery never being depleted before. We apply our abstract findings to a concrete case study inspired by a nano satellite currently orbiting the earth [18], for which we need to superpose it with a periodic charge load, representing the infeed from on-board solar panels.

2   Battery Kinetics

The kinetic battery model (KiBaM) approximates the ion density throughout a battery by dividing the stored charge into two parts, the *available* charge and the *bound* charge. When the battery is strained only the available charge is consumed instantly, while the bound charge is slowly converted to available charge by diffusion. In contrast to the simpler and widely used linear model, the KiBaM captures well the recovery effect and the rate capacity effect, rooted in the relatively slow conversion of bound charge into available charge. This *diffusion* between available and bound charge can take place in either direction depending on the amount of both types of energy stored in the battery.

The KiBaM is often depicted as two wells holding liquid, interconnected by a pipe that represents the diffusion of the two types of charge, as depicted on the right. The available charge well is exposed directly to the load I and connected to the

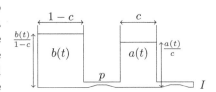

bound charge well by a pipe of width p. Value $c \in [0, 1]$ corresponds to the width of the available charge well, and $1 - c$ is the width of the bound charge well. Formally, the KiBaM is characterized by two coupled differential equations,

$$\dot{a}(t) \;=\; -I + p\left(\frac{b(t)}{1-c} - \frac{a(t)}{c}\right), \qquad \dot{b}(t) \;=\; p\left(\frac{a(t)}{c} - \frac{b(t)}{1-c}\right). \quad (1)$$

[The functions $a(t)$ and $b(t)$ describe how the available and bound charge respectively, evolve over time. Intuitively, $a(t)/c$ and $b(t)/(1-c)$ are the level of the fluid stored in the available charge well and the bound charge well, respectively.]

Example 1. We illustrate the evolution of the state of charge as time passes (top) with the battery strained by a piecewise-constant load (bottom). The initially available charge decreases heavily due to the load 400 but the limited diffusion makes the bound charge decrease only slowly up to time 10; after that the battery undergoes a mild recharge, and so on. At all times the

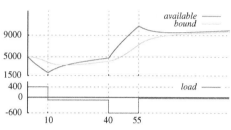

bound charge approaches the available charge by a speed proportional to the difference of the two values.

By Laplace transforms, we arrive at a solution of the ODEs at time t when applying load I expressed as a vector-valued linear mapping taking the initial available and bound charge a_0 and b_0 as argument:

$$\mathbf{K}_{t,I}\begin{bmatrix} a_0 \\ b_0 \end{bmatrix} = \begin{bmatrix} q_a & r_a & s_a \\ q_b & r_b & s_b \end{bmatrix} \cdot \begin{bmatrix} a_0 \\ b_0 \\ I \end{bmatrix} \quad \text{where} \quad \begin{aligned} q_a &= (1-c)e^{-kt} + c, \\ r_a &= -c\,e^{-kt} + c, \\ s_a &= \frac{(1-c)(e^{-kt}-1)}{k} - t \cdot c \end{aligned}$$

and $q_b = 1 - q_a$, $r_b = 1 - r_a$, $s_b = -t - s_a$ and finally $k = p/c(1 - c)$.

In the following we use $[a; b]$ to denote column vectors inline. Whenever $[a_0; b_0]$ and I are clear from context, we denote the SoC $\mathbf{K}_{t,I}[a_0; b_0]$ at time t also simply by $[a_t; b_t]$. When comparing vectors, as in $[a; b] \leq [a'; b']$, we use component-wise comparison.

Powering a Task. A standard problem in battery modelling and evaluation is to find out whether a task can be performed with a given initial state of charge without depleting the battery. A task is a pair (T, I) with T being the task execution time, and I representing the load, imposed for duration T. For an execution time T and a load I, we say that a battery with a SoC $[a_0; b_0] > [0; 0]$ *powers a task* (T, I) iff $\forall 0 < t \leq T : a_t > 0$.

It is worthwhile to mention that the SoC of the battery as presented evolves in negative numbers in the same way as in positive numbers. Furthermore, it is not monotonous with respect to time. We however observe that the KiBaM is monotonous with respect to *crossing a bound* κ when both tanks start below (or above) this bound.

Lemma 1. *For any* $I \in \mathbb{R}$, $\kappa \in \mathbb{R}$, $\prec \in \{<, >\}$, $[a_0; b_0] \prec [c\kappa; (1 - c)\kappa]$ *and for* $t \in \mathbb{R}_{>0}$ *such that* $a_t = c\kappa$ *we have*

- $b_t \prec (1 - c)\kappa$ *(available charge is always the first to cross a bound);*
- $a_T \not\prec c\kappa$ *for all* $T > t$ *(available charge never crosses back for a given load).*

As a consequence of Lemma 1, we can decide the task powering problem by evaluating the SoC after task execution: a battery with a SoC $[a_0; b_0] > [0; 0]$ powers a task (T, I) if and only if $a_T > 0$, i.e. the SoC *at the end* of the task execution is positive.

3 Random Battery Kinetics

In order to consider the KiBaM as a stochastic object, it appears natural to consider the vector $[a_0; b_0; I]$ as being random. This reflects the perturbations of the load and of the initial SoC of the batteries. The latter is a notorious real phenomenon, rooted in wear and manufacturing variances [7]. We thus assume the initial SoC to be random variables A_0, B_0 jointly distributed according to a density function f_0, while the load on the battery is a random variable I independent of the SoC, endowed with a probability density function g.

Example 2. Instead of a single (Dirac) SoC, we now consider that the joint density f_0 of the charge is, say, uniform over the area $[4, 6.5] \times [4, 6.5]$. We shall illustrate how the SoC distribution evolves as the time passes on this particular example, using illustrations as depicted on the right.

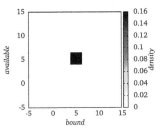

Evolution Over Time. We are interested in the random vector expressing the SoC after some time T for a *constant* (but random) load I. This is given by

$$[A_T; B_T] = \mathbf{K}_{T,I}[A_0; B_0] \tag{2}$$

The core tool for studying the joint density of $[A_T; B_T]$ is the transformation law for random variables, which enables the construction of unknown density functions from known ones if given the relation between the corresponding random variables. Formally, for every d-dimensional random vector $\mathbf{X}$ and every injective and continuously differentiable function $g : \mathbb{R}^d \to \mathbb{R}^d$, we can express the density function of $\mathbf{Y} := g(\mathbf{X})$ at value y in the range of g as

$$f_Y(y) = f_X\left(g^{-1}(y)\right) \cdot \left|\det\left(J_{g^{-1}}(y)\right)\right| \tag{3}$$

where $J_{g^{-1}}(y)$ denotes the *Jacobian* of g^{-1} evaluated at y. However, the mapping (2) is not invertible, thus we cannot directly apply the transformation law. Instead, we express the joint density conditioned by the random load I attaining some arbitrary but fixed value i. For this fixed i, we can exploit the specific structure of the KiBaM to express the transformation using an invertible linear mapping

$$\mathbf{K}_{T,i}\begin{bmatrix} A_0 \\ B_0 \end{bmatrix} = \begin{bmatrix} q_a\ r_a \\ q_b\ r_b \end{bmatrix} \cdot \begin{bmatrix} A_0 \\ B_0 \end{bmatrix} + \begin{bmatrix} s_a \\ s_b \end{bmatrix} \cdot i.$$

A straightforward inversion of the mapping results in

$$\mathbf{K}_{T,i}^{-1}\begin{bmatrix} a \\ b \end{bmatrix} = e^{kT}\begin{bmatrix} r_b & -r_a & r_a s_b - r_b s_a \\ -q_b & q_a & q_b s_a - q_a s_b \end{bmatrix} \cdot \begin{bmatrix} a \\ b \\ i \end{bmatrix}.$$

Applying (3) we arrive at the joint density of $[A_T; B_T]$ conditioned by $I = i$

$$f_T(a, b \mid i) = f_0\left(\mathbf{K}_{T,i}^{-1}[a; b]\right) \cdot \left|e^{kt}\right|$$

where e^{kT} is the determinant of the Jacobian of $\mathbf{K}_{T,i}^{-1}$. Interestingly, it is constant in a, b and i, it only depends on T. It is also non-negative for $T \geq 0$ as $k > 0$.

Finally we get rid of the conditional $I = i$ by marginalizing the variable $[A_T; B_T]$. Intuitively, this averages the conditional densities over the distribution g of I. It corresponds to integration over the support of I:

$$f_T(a, b) = \int_{-\infty}^{\infty} f_0\left(\mathbf{K}_{T,i}^{-1}[a; b]\right) \cdot e^{kT} \cdot g(i)\ \mathrm{d}i.$$

Example 3 (Cont.). We return to our example assuming the density g of the load being uniform between $[-0.1, 0.1]$. We can compute the SoC of the battery after task $(20, g)$, displayed on the left, and $(60, g)$, displayed on the right. Here, we arbitrarily chose the parameters $c = 0.5$ and $p = 0.002$.

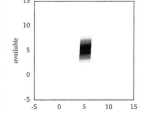
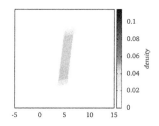

Probability of Powering a Task. We are now in the position to transfer the problem of powering a task to the stochastic setting. We say that a density f_0 is *positive* if it does not support any negative points, i.e. for any a, b such that either $a \leq 0$ or $b \leq 0$ we have $f_0(a, b) = 0$. For an execution time $T > 0$ and a load density g, we say that the battery (with positive initial SoC f_0) *powers* a task (T, g) *with probability (at least)* $p > 0$ if

$$\mathbf{Pr}\left[\forall 0 \leq t \leq T : A_t > 0\right] \geq p.$$

Due to the monotonicity of the KiBaM from Lemma 1, this is equivalent to observing the probability of being empty *only* at time T. We obtain that a battery with SoC f_0 powers with probability $p > 0$ a task (T, g) if and only if

$$\int_0^\infty \int_0^\infty f_T(a, b) \, \mathrm{d}b \, \mathrm{d}a \geq p.$$

Example 4 (Cont.). It suffices to perform the integration on the densities displayed in the above plots in this running example. The probability to power the tasks $(20, g)$ is 1, while for the task $(60, g)$ it is just ≈ 0.968 (note that the axes are labelled starting from -5).

4 Bounded Recharging

Both charging and discharging are well supported by the theory developed so far, as charging has occurred in our examples in the form of negative loads. What is not treated in the theory yet is a capacity bound. This however is an obvious real constraint in applications employing rechargeable batteries. To the best of our knowledge, charging in KiBaM while respecting its capacity restrictions has not been addressed even in the deterministic case. This is what we are going to develop first, and then extend to the randomized setting. We assume that the battery has capacity d divided into capacity $a_{\max} = c \cdot d$ of the available charge well and capacity $b_{\max} = (1 - c) \cdot d$ of the bound charge well.

Deterministic KiBaM with Lower and Upper Bounds. Charging and discharging are not fully symmetric: A battery with empty available charge can no longer power its task, contrary to a battery with full available charge that *continues to operate*. We thus need to consider its further charging behaviour.

When the available charge is at its capacity $a_{\max} = c \cdot d$ and is still further charged by a *sufficiently* high charging current, its value stays constant and only the bound charge increases due to diffusion. Hence, for any $t \geq 0$ we have $a(t) = c \cdot d$ and thus $\dot{a}(t) = 0$ and the equation for the bound charge from (1) is modified to an ODE

$$\dot{b}(t) = p\left(d - \frac{b(t)}{1 - c}\right) \tag{1a}$$

with the solution at point T given by $\bar{b}_T := e^{-ckT}\bar{b}_0 + \left(1 - e^{-ckT}\right) \cdot b_{\text{max}}$. Here we write $\bar{b}$ instead of b to distinguish the solution of (1a) from the solution of (1). Let us point out that for a fixed $\bar{b}_0$, the curve of $T \mapsto \bar{b}_T$ is a negative exponential starting from the point $\bar{b}_0$ with the full capacity b_{max} of the bound charge being its limit. Thus, the bound charge in finite time never gets full and there is no need to discuss this situation. Finally, similarly to $\mathbf{K}_{T,I}$, we define a mapping $\bar{\mathbf{K}}_T \left[a_{\text{max}}; \bar{b}_0\right] := [a_{\text{max}}; \bar{b}_T]$.

Staying at the Upper Bound. The differential equation above describes the behaviour of the battery at time t only if the incoming current to available charge tank is *sufficient* to compensate the diffusion, i.e. $-I \geq \dot{b}(t)$. Since I is constant and the diffusion is decreasing over time, the charging current is sufficient at all times if and only if it is sufficient at time 0, i.e. $-I \geq \dot{b}(0)$. Using (1a), one can express the condition equivalently as

$$b(0) \geq b_{\text{tresh}}(I) := b_{\text{max}} + I \cdot \frac{1-c}{p}, \tag{4}$$

which requires the initial bound charge to be close enough to the maximum capacity so that the charging current overcomes the diffusion.

Hitting the Upper Bound. When charging with a given constant load I, we have two types of behaviour of the battery: (*i*) *before* the available charge hits a_{max} and (*ii*) *after* it hits (and stays at) a_{max}. The remaining question is *when* it hits that capacity limit. For a given initial state $[a_0; b_0] < [a_{\text{max}}; b_{\text{max}}]$ and a load I, this amounts to finding $\bar{t} \in \mathbb{R}_{>0}$ such that $a_{\bar{t}} = a_{\text{max}}$. This induces an equation with $\bar{t}$ appearing in an exponential as well as in a linear term, which is characteristic for a non-elementary function called *product logarithm*. The solution can be expressed as

$$\bar{t} = -\mathcal{W}\left(\frac{u}{v} \cdot e^{-\frac{w}{v}}\right) - \frac{w}{v} \tag{5}$$

where $\mathcal{W}$ is the product logarithm function, $u = a_0\left(1 - c\right) - b_0 c + (c+1) \cdot I/k$, $v = -Ic$, and $w = cd - a_0 c - b_0 c - (1 - c) \cdot I/k$. The product log function can approximated by numerical methods [9].

Integrating Lower and Upper Bounds into KiBaM. All the previous building blocks allow us to express easily the SoC of a deterministic KiBaM after powering a given task (T, I) when considering battery bounds. We define it as

$$\mathbf{K}^{\square}_{T,I}[a_0; b_0] = \begin{cases} \mathbf{K}_{T,I}[a_0; b_0] & \text{if } a_0 > 0 \wedge 0 < a_T \leq a_{\text{max}}, \\ \bar{\mathbf{K}}_t \circ \mathbf{K}_{\bar{t},I}[a_0; b_0] & \text{if } a_0 > 0 \wedge \quad\quad a_T > a_{\text{max}}, \\ [0; 0] & \text{if } a_0 = 0 \vee 0 \geq a_T \end{cases}$$

where $\bar{t}$ is the largest solution of (5) and $t = T - \bar{t}$.

The first two cases in $\mathbf{K}^{\square}_{T,I}$ match the behaviour explained earlier thanks to Lemma 1. Whenever the upper bound is hit, it will never be crossed back with the given I and thus also I is sufficient according to (4).

Example 5 (Cont.). If we put an upper
bound of 9000 to the previous scenario,
the battery ends up with a slightly
smaller charge at time 100. The computation of the final SoC changes only
in the interval $[40, 55]$. Here, instead of
$\mathbf{K}_{15,-600}$, we apply $\mathbf{K}_{\bar{t},-600}$ for the first
$\bar{t} \approx 7.8$ time units, followed by $\bar{\mathbf{K}}_{15-\bar{t}}$.

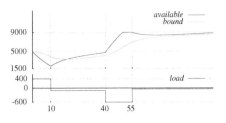

Efficient Approximation. For our application later, we need the computation of
bounded KiBaM to be as *efficient* as possible. The problematic part is the computation of the time point $\bar{t}$, the solution of (5). An efficient and less cumbersome
alternative to numerical approximation can be developed as follows: If $[a_0; b_0]$,
T and I is fixed, we can check whether $a_T > a_{max}$. If it is the case, we solve
the equation $a_T = a_{max}$ for load I instead of time t, determining the charging
current $\bar{I}$ (which is a weaker charging current than I) for which the available
charge hits the upper bound *exactly* after T time units, i.e. $a_T = a_{max}$ when
applying $\bar{I}$ instead of I. The load $\bar{I}$ can be expressed much simpler than $\bar{t}$ by

$$\bar{I} = -\frac{q_a}{s_a} \cdot a_0 - \frac{r_a}{s_a} \cdot b_0 + \frac{a_{max}}{s_a}.$$

Based on this observation, we define an operator $\mathbf{K}_{T,I}^{\approx\square}$ by

$$\mathbf{K}_{T,I}^{\approx\square}[a_0; b_0] = \begin{cases} \mathbf{K}_{T,I}[a_0; b_0] & \text{if } a_0 > 0 \wedge 0 < a_T \leq a_{max}, \\ \mathbf{K}_{T,\bar{I}}[a_0; b_0] & \text{if } a_0 > 0 \wedge \qquad a_T > a_{max}, \\ [0; 0] & \text{if } a_0 = 0 \vee 0 \geq a_T. \end{cases}$$

This is a conservative under-approximation of $\mathbf{K}_{T,I}^{\square}$ as for any $[a_0; b_0]$, T and I,
we have $\mathbf{K}_{T,I}^{\approx\square}[a; b] \leq \mathbf{K}_{T,I}^{\square}[a; b]$.

This remains true, by a transitivity argument, along sequences of tasks, as
KiBaM preserves order, meaning: for any $[a; b]$, $[a'; b']$, T and I, we have

$$[a; b] \leq [a'; b'] \implies \mathbf{K}_{T,I}^{\square}[a; b] \leq \mathbf{K}_{T,I}^{\square}[a'; b'].$$

In other words, from the moment we used $\mathbf{K}^{\approx\square}$ first, we will never overshoot
the exact behaviour $\mathbf{K}^{\square}$.

Example 6 (Cont.). Let us apply $\mathbf{K}^{\approx\square}$
to the same situation as before. In the
interval $[40, 55]$, we apply $\bar{I} \approx -432.49$
instead of $I = -600$ so that the available
charge reaches 9000 exactly at $t = 55$.
From here on, the SoC is in both components (slightly) smaller than the SoC
from the previous figure.

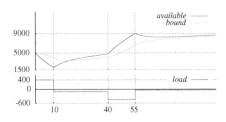

Random KiBaM with Lower and Upper Bounds. We now turn our attention to the challenge of assuming that the random variables (A_t, B_t) evolve according to $\mathbf{K}_{T,I}^{\square}$. We first observe that the joint distribution of (A_T, B_T) may not be absolutely continuous, because positive probability may accumulate in the point $(0,0)$ where the battery is empty as well as on the line $\{(a_{\max}, b) \mid 0 < b < b_{\max}\}$ where the available charge is full. Hence, we represent each (A_t, B_t) by a triple $\langle f_t, \bar{f}_t, z_t \rangle$ where

- f_t is the joint density describing the distribution in the "inner" area $(0, a_{\max}) \times (0, b_{\max})$,
- $\bar{f}_t$ is the density over bound charge describing the distribution on the upper line $\{a_{\max}\} \times (0, b_{\max})$, and
- $z_t \in [0, 1]$ is the probability of being empty.

For a technical discussion concerning measurability as well as derivations of how SoC distributions $\langle f_t, \bar{f}_t, z_t \rangle$ evolve over time, we refer to [21]. While being technically non-trivial, the ideas of the $\mathbf{K}_{T,I}^{\approx\square}$ operator can basically be lifted to SoC distributions. For the remainder it is however enough to assume that we can express such $\langle f_T, \bar{f}_T, z_T \rangle$ for any task (T, g) given an initial SoC distribution.

Example 7 (Cont.). We illustrate the transformation of the SoC distribution from our second running example for *battery bounds* $[0, 10]$. We consider the same tasks, $(20, g)$ on the left and $(60, g)$ on the right. The bounded area of the joint density f_T is depicted by the large box in the middle. In the smaller box above we display the density $\bar{f}_T$ at the capacity limit.

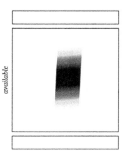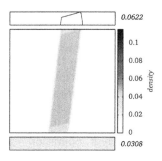

The numbers next to the smaller boxes are the probabilities of available charge being full and empty, respectively (the color encodes the probability).

5   Random Charging and Discharging in Practice

We apply the results established in the previous sections to a concrete scenario. The problem is inspired by experiments and evaluations currently being carried out with the earth orbiting nano satellite GoMX–1, as part of the European FET project SENSATION [29]. The empirical studies carried out with GoMX–1 serve as a source for parameter values and form the base line of our modelling efforts. The case study described below is derived from a number of detailed observations and well-justified assumptions. We refer to [21] for details.

Markov Task Process. To faithfully represent the load imposed by the satellite, we use a discrete-time Markov model which randomly generates representative charging and discharging tasks: A *Markov task process (MTP)* is a tuple $\mathcal{M} = (S, P, \pi, \Delta, \mathbf{g})$ where S is a finite set of states, $P : S \times S \to [0,1]$ is a probability transition matrix, π is an initial probability distribution over S, $\Delta : S \to \mathbb{N}$ assigns to each state an integer time duration, and $\mathbf{g}$ assigns to each state a probability density function of the load. A pictorial representation of an MTP is provided below.

For a given $T \in \mathbb{R}_{\geq 0}$, the SoC of the battery w.r.t. an MTP at time T is expressed by random variables A_T, B_T. We are then interested in the probability *to power an MTP for time T*, which corresponds to determining $\mathbf{Pr}\left[A_T > 0\right]$. To arrive there, intuitively we can propagate a SoC distribution along the paths of an MTP by splitting and scaling it into subdistributions and assigning them to MTP states according to its probabilistic branching. Subdistributions can be merged again once they are assigned to the same MTP state at the same time. For a detailed development of a procedure to (under-)approximate the probability that an MTP is powered for a given time we refer to [21].

Satellite Model. Induced by the specific earth orbiting characteristics, the load on the satellite is the superposition of two piecewise constant loads: (*i*) a strictly periodic charge load alternating between 66 minutes at -400 mA, and the remaining 33 minutes of the orbit at 0 mA (reflecting solar infeed), and (*ii*) a probabilistic load reflecting the different operation modes, mod-

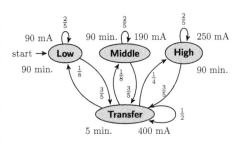

elled by the MTP depicted on the right, where all load distributions are normal with mean depicted next to the states and with standard deviation 5. One can easily express the solar infeed as a second independent Markov task process (where all probabilities are 1) and consider the combined loads generated by these two processes in parallel, the analysis methods adapt straightforwardly to this setting.

The KiBaM in our model is parameterised with $c = 1/2$ (artificially chosen value as parameters fitted by experiments on similar batteries strongly vary [24,32]); and a diffusion rate of $p = 0.0006$ (we decreased the value reported by experiments [24] by a factor of 4 because of the low average temperature in orbit, $3.5°C$, and the influence of the Arrhenius equation [25]).

Computational Aspects. We implemented the continuous solution developed in the previous sections in the high-level computational language Octave. This turned out to be practical only up to sequences of a handful of tasks. Therefore, we implemented a solution over a discretised abstraction of the stochastic process induced by the MTP and the battery. By discretising the battery state space into $K \in \mathbb{N}$ bins along both dimensions we can represent SoC densities by an array and a matrix of dimension K and $K \times K$ respectively. Every cell is represented by the smallest battery state still contained in the cell (i.e. the the lower left corner). Whenever, by transforming the densities, a SoC is mapped into a cell, the target SoC will instead be under approximated by the representative of that cell. Thus, the probability of the battery powering the satellite is under approximated as well.

The continuous methods introduced before are easily adapted to this discrete setting, basically replacing integrals by finite sums. We do not have any prior error bound, but one can make the results arbitrarily precise by increasing K, at the price of quadratic cost increase.

Our implementation is done in C++, we used $K = 1200, 600, 300$ and 150 for the experiments with the batteries of capacity 5000, 2500, 1250 and 625 mAh, respectively to guarantee equal relative precision. All the experiments have been performed on a machine equipped with an Intel Core i5-2520 M CPU @ 2.50 GHz and 4GB RAM. All values occurring are represented and calculated with standard IEEE 754 double-precision binary floating-point format except for the values related to the battery being depleted where we use arbitrary precision arithmetic (as to this number, we keep adding values from the inner area that are of much lower order of magnitude).

Model Evaluation. We performed various experiments with this model, to explore the random KiBaM technology. We here report four distinct evaluations, demonstrating that valuable insight into the model can be obtained. Each instance of the experiments took no longer than 7 hours of computation.

(1) The 5000 mAh battery in the real satellite is known to be over-dimensioned. Our aim was to find out how much. Hence, we performed a sequence of experiments, decreasing the size of the battery exponentially. The results are displayed in Fig. 1. We found out that 1/4 of the capacity still provides sufficient guarantees to power the satellite for 1 year while 1/8 of the capacity, 625 mAh, does not. The smaller the battery, the more crucial is the

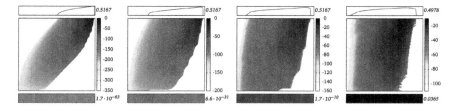

Fig. 1. SoC of the satellite after 1 year for battery capacity 5000, 2500, 1250, and 625 mAh (Actually it is after 364 days, as this is in the middle of the charging phase. After 365 days the satellite is in eclipse and no density is exhibited in the upper diagram). Density values are depicted on a log scale, labels of the color bar indicate orders of magnitude.

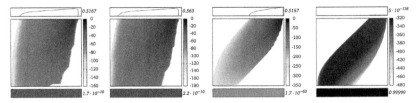

(a) SoC for 1250 mAh with Dirac loads (left) compared to noisy loads (right).   (b) SoC for 5000 mAh battery with 9 (left), respectively 6 solar panels (right).

Fig. 2. SoC after 1 year with noisy loads and with reduced solar input.

distinction of available and bound charge as a larger area of the plots is filled with non-trivial density.

(2) We compared our results with a simple linear battery model of the same capacity. This linear model is not uncommon in the satellite domain, it has for instance been used in the *Envisat* and *CryoSat* missions [16]. The depletion probabilities are displayed on the right. We can see that the linear model turns out to be surprisingly (and likely unjustifiably) optimistic, especially for the 625 mAh battery.

capacity	linear	KiBaM
5000 mAh	$1.86 \cdot 10^{-84}$	$1.7 \cdot 10^{-63}$
625 mAh	$2.94 \cdot 10^{-8}$	0.0365

(3) We (computationally) simplified the two experiments above by assuming Dirac loads (thus showing zero variance). To analyse the effect of white noise, we compared the Dirac loads with the noisy loads, explained earlier, on the 1250 mAh battery. As expected, the noise (a) smoothes out the distribution and (b) pushes more of the distribution to full and empty states, see Fig. 2a.

(4) Our reference satellite is a two-unit satellite, i.e. is built from two cubes, each 10 cm per side. In the current design, 9 of the 10 external sides are covered by solar panels, the remaining one is used for both radio antenna and camera. We thus analysed whether a one-unit design with only 5 solar panels is possible. The answer is negative, the system runs out of energy rapidly with high probability. Figure 2b displays that even for 6 panels the charge level is highly insufficient to sustain the load.

6   Related Work and Analysis Alternatives

Haverkort and Jongerden [23] review broad research on various battery models. The problem of capacity bounds does not get dqedicated attention. The latter has been addressed by Boker et al. [5], with respect to a discretised, unbounded KiBaM together with a possibly non-deterministic and cyclic load process, synthesizing initial capacity bounds to power the process safely. Hence, capacity is here understood as an over-dimensioned initial condition and not as a limiting charging bound.

Random discharge loads have been studied in the context of continuous-time Markov approximations of the KiBaM [8,28]. That setting views available and bound charge levels as two types of *accumulated reward* in a reward-inhomogeneous Markov reward model. Since charging would correspond to accumulation of negative reward, the solution techniques do not easily extend to cover charging.

An extension of the KiBaM to battery scheduling problems has been considered [22], where optimal schedules for multiple batteries are computed in a discretized setting with only discharging. This has been taken up and improved using techniques from the planning domain [13].

While the theoretical basis of the present paper is developed in continuous time, the results reported for the experimental evaluation are obtained from a discretized abstraction of the stochastic process induced by the MTP and the battery, solved numerically and with high-precision arithmetic where needed. One could instead consider estimating the probability z_t of the battery depletion using ordinary simulation techniques [17]. Considering a battery of capacity 5000 mAh, this would mean that about 10^{63} simulations traces are needed on average to observe the rare event of a depleted battery at least once. This seems prohibitive, also if resorting to massively parallel simulation, which may reduce the exponent by a small constant at most. A possible way out of this might lie in the use of rare event simulation techniques to speed up simulation [31].

The behaviour of KiBaM with capacity bounds can be expressed as a relatively simple *hybrid automaton* model [19]. Similarly, the random KiBaM with capacity bounds can be regarded as an instance of a *stochastic hybrid system* (SHS) [1,2,4,6,10,30]. This observation opens some further evaluation avenues, since there are multiple tools available publicly for checking reachability properties of SHS. In particular, FAUST[2] [12], SiSAT [15] and PROHVER [14,33] appear adequate at first sight. Our experiments with FAUST[2] however were unsuccessful, basically due to a model mismatch: The tool thus far assumes stochasticity in all dimensions, because it operates on stochastic kernels, while our model is non-stochastic in the bound charge dimension. With SiSAT, we so far failed to encode the MTP (or its effect) into an input accepted by the tool. The MTP can be considered as a compact description of an otherwise intricate semi-Markov process running on a discrete time line. This is in principle supported by SiSAT, yet we effectively failed to provide a compact encoding. Our PROHVER experiments failed for a different reason, namely the sheer size of the problem. All the above tools have not been optimized for dealing with very low probabilities as they appear in the satellite case.

7   Conclusion

Inspired by the needs of an earth-orbiting satellite mission, we extended in this paper the theory of kinetic battery models in two independent dimensions; adding capacity bounds and casting the theory into a stochastic setting. We provided a symbolic solution for a random initial SoC and a sequence of piece-wise constant random loads. These sequences can be generated by a stochastic process representing an abstract and averaged behavioural model of a nano satellite operating in earth orbit, superposed with a deterministic representation of the solar infeed in orbit. We illustrated the approach by several experiments performed on the model, especially varying the size of the battery, but also the number of solar panels.

We showed how the random KiBaM can help quantify the risk of premature depletion for the various battery dimensions at hand, highlighting the inadequacy of the simpler linear battery model as a side result.

The approach enables a sophisticated exploration of the design space of a cyber-physical battery powered system with respect to optimal use of weight and space budget. For a particular satellite mission, one can apply the technology offered by us for optimal online task scheduling by branching into several distributions and determining which of them is best according to some metric. Taking inspiration from [32], this can be combined with statistical model checking so as to find the optimal task schedule of a given set of tasks. Computing optimal schedules using the methods presented in this paper will indeed play a major role in the upcoming GOMX–3 CubeSat mission which is faced with a much tighter energy budget.

As further work, extensions regarding temperature dependency should be integrated into the model, as temperature is known to influence both the diffusion rate of the KiBaM as well as the solar panel efficiency. Another challenge manifests when lifting the restriction of the load being piecewise constant. This would void Lemma 1. An extension particularly important for long lasting missions, is incorporating a model of battery wearout, typically manifesting by decreasing the capacity over time.

Acknowledgements. The authors are grateful for inspiring discussions with Peter Bak and Morten Bisgaard (GomSpace ApS), Erik R. Wognsen (Aalborg University), and other members of the SENSATION consortium, as well as with Pascal Gilles (ESA Centre for Earth Observation), Xavier Bossoreille (Deutsches Zentrum für Luft- und Raumfahrt) and Marc Bouissou (Électricité de France S.A., École Centrale Paris - LGI).

This work is supported by the EU 7th Framework Programme under grant agreements 295261 (MEALS) and 318490 (SENSATION), by the DFG as part of SFB/TR 14 AVACS, by the Czech Science Foundation under grant agreement P202/12/G061, by the CAS/SAFEA International Partnership Program for Creative Research Teams, and by the CDZ project CAP (GZ 1023).

References

1. Abate, A., Prandini, M., Lygeros, J., Sastry, S.: Probabilistic reachability and safety for controlled discrete time stochastic hybrid systems. Automatica **44**(11), 2724–2734 (2008)
2. Altman, E., Gaitsgory, V.: Asymptotic optimization of a nonlinear hybrid system governed by a markov decision process. SIAM J. Control Optim. **35**(6), 2070–2085 (1997)

3. Aydin, H., Mejía-Alvarez, P., Mossé, D., Melhem, R.G.: Dynamic and aggressive scheduling techniques for power-aware real-time systems. IEEE RTSS **2001**, 95–105 (2001)
4. Blom, H.A., Lygeros, J., Everdij, M., Loizou, S., Kyriakopoulos, K.: Stochastic Hybrid Systems: Theory and Safety Critical Applications. LNCS, vol. 337. Springer, Heidelberg (2006)
5. Boker, U., Henzinger, T.A., Radhakrishna, A.: Battery transition systems. In: POPL, pp. 595–606. ACM (2014)
6. Bujorianu, M.L., Lygeros, J., Bujorianu, M.C.: Bisimulation for general stochastic hybrid systems. In: Morari, M., Thiele, L. (eds.) HSCC 2005. LNCS, vol. 3414, pp. 198–214. Springer, Heidelberg (2005)
7. Cao, J., Schofield, N., Emadi, A.: Battery balancing methods: a comprehensive review. In: Vehicle Power and Propulsion Conference, VPPC 2008, pp. 1–6. IEEE, September 2008
8. Cloth, L., Jongerden, M.R., Haverkort, B.R.: Computing battery lifetime distributions. In: DSN, pp. 780–789. IEEE Computer Society (2007)
9. Corless, R.M., Gonnet, G.H., Hare, D.E.G., Jeffrey, D.J., Knuth, D.E.: On the lambertW function. Adv. Comput. Math. **5**(1), 329–359 (1996)
10. Davis, M.H.: Piecewise-deterministic markov processes: a general class of non-diffusion stochastic models. J. Roy. Stat. Soc. Ser. B (Methodol.) **46**, 353–388 (1984)
11. Esa: Esa cubesat program, October 2014. http://www.esa.int/Education/CubeSats
12. Soudjani, S.E.Z., Gevaerts, C., Abate, A.: Faust2: formal abstractions of uncountable-state stochastic processes. In: Baier, C., Tinelli, C. (eds.) TACAS 2015. LNCS, vol. 9035, pp. 272–286. Springer, Heidelberg (2015)
13. Fox, M., Long, D., Magazzeni, D.: Automatic construction of efficient multiple battery usage policies. In: Walsh, T. (ed.) IJCAI, pp. 2620–2625. IJCAI/AAAI (2011)
14. Fränzle, M., Hahn, E.M., Hermanns, H., Wolovick, N., Zhang, L.: Measurability and safety verification for stochastic hybrid systems. In: HSCC, pp. 43–52. ACM Press, New York, NY, USA (2011)
15. Fränzle, M., Hermanns, H., Teige, T.: Stochastic satisfiability modulo theory: a novel technique for the analysis of probabilistic hybrid systems. In: Egerstedt, M., Mishra, B. (eds.) HSCC 2008. LNCS, vol. 4981, pp. 172–186. Springer, Heidelberg (2008)
16. Gilles, P.: Private communication (2014)
17. Gillespie, D.T.: A general method for numerically simulating the stochastic time evolution of coupled chemical reactions. J. Comput. Phys. **22**(4), 403–434 (1976)
18. GomSpace: Gomspace gomx-1, October 2014. http://gomspace.com/?p=gomx1
19. Henzinger, T.A.: The theory of hybrid automata. In: Kemal Inan, M., Kurshan, R.P. (eds.) Verification of Digital and Hybrid Systems. NATO ASI Series, vol. 170, pp. 265–292. Springer, Heidelberg (2000)
20. Henzinger, T.A., Sifakis, J.: The embedded systems design challenge. In: Misra, J., Nipkow, T., Sekerinski, E. (eds.) FM 2006. LNCS, vol. 4085, pp. 1–15. Springer, Heidelberg (2006)
21. Hermanns, H., Krcál, J., Nies, G.: Recharging probably keeps batteries alive. CoRR abs/1502.07120 (2015)
22. Jongerden, M., Haverkort, B., Bohnenkamp, H., Katoen, J.: Maximizing system lifetime by battery scheduling. In: DSN, pp. 63–72. IEEE (2009)

23. Jongerden, M.R., Haverkort, B.R.: Which battery model to use? IET Softw. **3**(6), 445–457 (2009)
24. Jongerden, M.R.: Model-based energy analysis of battery powered systems. Ph.d. thesis, Enschede, December 2010
25. Liaw, B.Y., Roth, E.P., Jungst, R.G., Nagasubramanian, G., Case, H.L., Doughty, D.H.: Correlation of arrhenius behaviors in power and capacity fades with cell impedance and heat generation in cylindrical lithium-ion cells. J. Power Sources **119**, 874–886 (2003)
26. Liu, J., Chou, P.H., Bagherzadeh, N., Kurdahi, F.: Power-aware scheduling under timing constraints for mission-critical embedded systems. In: DAC, pp. 840–845. ACM, New York, NY, USA (2001)
27. Manwell, J.F., McGowan, J.G.: Lead acid battery storage model for hybrid energy systems. Sol. Energy **50**(5), 399–405 (1993)
28. Rao, V., Singhal, G., Kumar, A., Navet, N.: Battery model for embedded systems. In: VLSI Design/ES Design, pp. 105–110. IEEE (2005)
29. SENSATION: Sensation, March 2015. http://www.sensation-project.eu/
30. Sproston, J.: Decidable model checking of probabilistic hybrid automata. In: Joseph, M. (ed.) FTRTFT 2000. LNCS, vol. 1926, p. 31. Springer, Heidelberg (2000)
31. Villén-Altamirano, M., Villén-Altamirano, J.: Restart: a straightforward method for fast simulation of rare events. In: WSC, pp. 282–289. IEEE (1994)
32. Wognsen, E.R., Hansen, R.R., Larsen, K.G.: Battery-aware scheduling of mixed criticality systems. In: Margaria, T., Steffen, B. (eds.) ISoLA 2014, Part II. LNCS, vol. 8803, pp. 208–222. Springer, Heidelberg (2014)
33. Zhang, L., She, Z., Ratschan, S., Hermanns, H., Hahn, E.M.: Safety verification for probabilistic hybrid systems. In: Touili, T., Cook, B., Jackson, P. (eds.) CAV 2010. LNCS, vol. 6174, pp. 196–211. Springer, Heidelberg (2010)

Fault Localization of Energy Consumption Behavior Using Maximum Satisfiability

Shin Nakajima[1,2]([⊠]) and Si-Mohamed Lamraoui[1,2]

[1] National Institute of Informatics, Tokyo, Japan
[2] SOKENDAI, Tokyo, Japan
nkjm@nii.ac.jp

Abstract. In model-based analysis of energy consumption behavior, detecting energy bugs is formulated as a model checking problem. Model checkers can check the energy consumption behavior automatically, but significant manual effort is required to study the generated counter-example trace for finding the root causes of the failure. This effort can be reduced by using a formula-based automatic fault localization method. The present paper proposes a new trace formula, encoding all potential transition sequences, with modest assumptions on the failure. The paper also discusses the precision of the identified root causes and limitations of the adapted failure model.

1 Introduction

Removing energy bugs is one of the primary concerns in constructing mobile systems, because the capacity of batteries is limited. Although hardware components are the direct consumers of battery power, programs must also be responsible for energy consumption because they control the usage of the hardware components. Such energy bugs (e-bugs) [22] are usually checked at runtime using energy profilers in, for example, Android-based mobile systems [1]. Some e-bugs are attributed to design faults, and model-based analysis methods (cf. [8,17]) are desirable for use in early stages of development.

Energy consumption behavior concerns both discrete and continuous dynamics [17], and linear hybrid automata (LHAs) [5] are appropriate as rigorous formal models. There are a number of early studies on the use of a subclass of LHAs, stopwatch automata [8] or n-rated timed systems [18]. Later, power consumption automaton (PCA) is introduced, which is a variant of weighted timed automata (WTAs) [3]. When we use linear temporal logic with freeze quantifiers to express properties to be checked, energy consumption analysis is reduced to a logical model checking problem [19,20]. Model checkers can check the energy consumption behavior automatically, but significant manual effort is required to study generated counter-example traces in order to find the root causes of e-bugs.

Automatic fault localization attempts to reduce the effort involved in finding root causes, and is successful for VLSI circuit designs [24] or imperative programs [11,12], which are formula-based approaches that adapt the model-based

© Springer International Publishing Switzerland 2015
C. Berger and M.R. Mousavi (Eds.): CyPhy 2015, LNCS 9361, pp. 99–115, 2015.
DOI: 10.1007/978-3-319-25141-7_8

diagnosis (MBD) framework [23] and use a Boolean satisfiability method or specifically a maximum satisfiability (MaxSAT) method (cf. [7]). In the MBD, a system and its property specification are encoded in a logic formula. The formula is unsatisfiable if the system violates the given property. The fault localization problem involves finding a subset of clauses in the formula so that removing the clauses in this subset makes the formula satisfiable. These clauses are obtained as a minimal correction subset (MCS) of the unsatisfiable formula [14].

The present paper proposes a formula-based fault localization method for PCAs [19] using MaxSAT. The main contributions are, (1) introducing a trace formula, encoding all potential transition sequences, with modest assumptions on a failure model, and (2) demonstrating the feasibility of the proposed method with experiments on a small example case using Yices-1, a partial MaxSAT solver [10]. We, then, discuss issues such as the limitation of the adapted failure model and the precision and efficiency of the fault localization method.

2   Energy Consumption Behavior

We first review an energy consumption model. The presentation is based on [17, 19] using an example of a Wi-Fi subsystem, referring to a diagrammatic representation of a PCA in Fig. 1. The example PCA consists of four power states and several transition edges between the states.

A Wi-Fi station (Wi-Fi STA or simply STA) of a smartphone operates in a passive scan mode [2]. An access point (AP) periodically sends beacon signals to notify the STA to start a data transfer. The STA is initially in the DeepSleep state and enters the HighPower state to send or receive data frames. The STA remains in the IdleListen state in order to determine whether additional frames will be received. When the STA recognizes a no-more-data flag in a transferred data frame, it enters the LightSleep state. The STA remains in this state to be ready for a quick re-start when a further data transfer is initiated. The STA

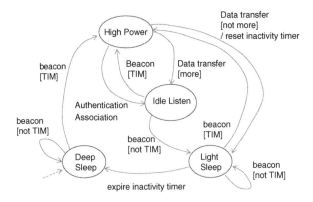

Fig. 1. PCA of a Wi-Fi Station

does not reenter the `DeepSleep` state immediately. An inactivity timer is used to generate a time-out event, which forces the STA into the `DeepSleep` state.

The amount of consumed energy is different in each power state. For example, the `HighPower` state consumes a lot of energy in order to decode the transferred frames. In the `DeepSleep` state, only power sufficient to activate a portion of the electric circuits is necessary, and thus the energy consumption rate is small. If we let $F^j(t)$ be a function of time that represents the rate of energy consumed at a state j, the total energy consumed in the time interval a to b is $E^j = \int_a^b F^j(t)dt$. Since the power states are visited many times as state transitions continue, the total energy consumption is calculated as a summation over E^js, $E = \sum_{j=0}^n E^j = \sum_{j=0}^n \int_{a^j}^{b^j} F^j(t)dt$. If we introduce a linear approximation such that $dE^j/dt = F^j(t) = M^j$ for a constant M^j in each power state, then $E = \sum_{j=0}^n M^j \times (b^j - a^j)$. Each constant M^ℓ is an average energy consumption rate for the power state ℓ, and is given as a specification of the hardware component.

The PCA falls within a subclass of LHAs [5] because the flow dynamics of the energy consumption variable E takes the form $dE/dt = M$, and the inactivity timer G is a clock variable such that $dG/dt = 1$ [17]. However, a PCA is more restricted than an LHA in that E is an observer and does not have any effect on the state-transition behavior, whereas G controls the timings of state-transitions. We regard a PCA as a WTA [3]. A WTA is a timed automaton (TA) in which a weight variable stores the accumulated consumed energy, $\sum_{j=0}^n E^j$, from the initial state to the current nth state. The weight variable E is initially zero. For example, if a PCA remains in the `DeepSleep` state for an amount of time t_1 and then remains in the `HighPower` state for t_2, E becomes $M^{DeepSleep} \times t_1 + M^{HighPower} \times t_2$. The weight E is increased as the PCA makes transitions between the power states.

From a naive viewpoint, a property on the energy consumption seems simple enough to state that a total amount of consumed energy must be less than a specified maximum value. However, because the amount of consumed energy is proportional to the duration in which the hardware components are used, this simple property is eventually violated. When we check a property on the energy consumption, we must specify a duration in which the property is checked. This can be captured by *duration-bounded cost constraint*, in which the cost refers to the amount of energy consumption [19].

3   Preliminaries

This section introduces basic concepts. The term *SAT method* here refers to both pure Boolean satisfiability and satisfiability modulo theories (SMT) methods.

Scope-Bounded Analysis. *SAT method* is a basis of various automatic analysis methods, such as bounded model checking (BMC) [6]. Given a system, we encode potential execution paths of the system in a trace formula (TF) φ_{TF}. If we let φ_{AS} be an assertion (AS), or a property to be checked, a BMC problem is to determine whether $\varphi_{TF} \wedge \neg\varphi_{AS}$ is satisfiable. If the whole formula is satisfied, then obtained assignments constitute a counter-example to demonstrate that the system (φ_{TF}) violates the property (φ_{AS}).

Fault Localization Problem. Let a formula φ_{FL} be $\varphi_{EI} \wedge \varphi_{TF} \wedge \varphi_{AS}$ for the above mentioned φ_{TF} and φ_{AS}, and φ_{EI} that encodes error-inducing input data values. We construct φ_{EI} by extracting from the counter-example a set of input data values that lead the system to such a failing execution. Thus, the φ_{FL} is unsatisfiable.

A fault localization problem is to find clauses in φ_{TF} that are responsible for this unsatisfiability. Clauses in the identified unsatisfiable core constitute a *conflict*, which is an erroneous situation containing root causes of the failure. Both φ_{EI} and φ_{AS} are supposed to be satisfiable because they encode the input data values and the property respectively. This is exactly a problem in which we search for root causes of the faulty system.

In what follows, C refers to a set of clauses that constitute a given formula φ in conjunctive normal form (CNF). We use C and φ interchangeably. For details about basic concepts, refer to the standard literature (cf. [7]).

Minimal Unsatisfied Subset. A set of clauses M, $M \subseteq C$, is a minimal unsatisfiable subset (MUS) *iff* M is unsatisfiable and $\forall c \in M : M \backslash \{c\}$ is satisfiable.

Maximal Satisfiable Subset. A set of clauses M, $M \subseteq C$, is a maximal satisfiable subset (MSS) *iff* M is satisfiable and $\forall c \in (C \backslash M) : M \cup \{c\}$ is unsatisfiable.

Minimal Correction Subset. A set of clauses M, $M \subseteq C$, is a minimal correction subset (MCS) *iff* $C \backslash M$ is satisfiable and $\forall c \in M : (C \backslash M) \cup \{c\}$ is unsatisfiable. By definition, an MCS is a complement of an MSS.

Hitting Set. Let Ω be a set of sets from some finite domain D. A hitting set of Ω, H, is a set of elements from D that covers every set in Ω by having at least one element in common with it. Formally, H is a hitting set of Ω *iff* $H \subseteq D$ and $\forall S \in \Omega : H \cap S \neq \emptyset$. A minimal hitting set is a hitting set from which no element can be removed without losing the hitting set property.

Partial Maximum Satisfiability. A maximum satisfiability (MaxSAT) problem for a CNF formula is finding an assignment that maximizes the number of satisfied clauses. Partial MaxSAT (pMaxSAT) is a variant of MaxSAT, in which some clauses are marked *soft* or relaxable, and the other clauses are marked *hard* or non-relaxable. A pMaxSAT problem is finding an assignment that satisfies all the hard clauses and maximizes the number of satisfied soft clauses.

Model-based Diagnosis Framework. In the MBD framework [23], fault localization involves finding a subset of clauses, called *diagnosis*, in the unsatisfiable formula φ_{FL} so that removing the clauses in this subset makes the formula satisfiable. A *conflict* is an erroneous situation and a *diagnosis* refers to the root causes. A faulty system usually contains multiple conflicts and diagnoses. Formally, diagnoses are a set of MCS elements (or MCSes), while conflicts are a set of MUS elements (or MUSes). MCSes and MUSes are related by a hitting set relationship [14]. The formula-based approach [11,12,24], adapted in the present paper, calculates an MSS to obtain an MCS by complementing the MSS and repeats this process to collect MCSes.

The fault localization problem requires means to represent the fact that φ_{EI} and φ_{AS} are satisfiable and that some clauses in φ_{TF} are suspicious. The pMaxSAT approach is well suited to satisfying this requirement [11,12]. The clauses in φ_{EI} and φ_{AS} are marked *hard*. Suspicious clauses in φ_{TF} are *soft*. The other clauses in φ_{TF} that are assumed to be bug-free are *hard*. This decision, in which clauses are marked *soft* in φ_{TF}, is dependent on a failure model.

An Example. Here is an example [13] to illustrate the basic concepts.

$$\begin{array}{cccc} C_1 & C_2 & C_3 & C_4 \end{array}$$
$$\varphi = (a) \wedge (\neg a) \wedge (\neg a \vee b) \wedge (\neg b)$$

Its MUSes, MCSes, and MSSes are the following.

$$\mathrm{MUSes}(\varphi) = \{\ \{C_1, C_2\},\ \{C_1, C_3, C_4\}\ \}$$
$$\mathrm{MCSes}(\varphi) = \{\ \{C_1\}, \qquad\quad \{C_2, C_3\}, \{C_2, C_4\}\ \}$$
$$\mathrm{MSSes}(\varphi) = \{\ \{C_2, C_3, C_4\}, \{C_1, C_4\}, \{C_1, C_3\}\ \}$$

$\mathrm{MUSes}(\varphi)$ and $\mathrm{MCSes}(\varphi)$ are related by a hitting set relationship.

Next, if we mark C_3 as *hard* and all the rest to be *soft*, a set consisting of two MCS elements, $\{\ \{C_1\}, \{C_2, C_4\}\ \}$, is obtained as MCSes. This illustrates that there are two possible diagnoses to make the formula φ satisfiable under the assumption that C_3 is correct. We may remove either a single clause (C_1) or two clauses (C_2 and C_4). We must decide which candidate we choose as a repair. This decision requires a piece of information beyond the fault localization method. Repairing is not the focus of the present paper.

4   A Method for Bounded Analysis

Bounded analysis methods rely on Boolean encoding of all possible transition sequences. The encoding of the trace formula is one of the primary concerns.

4.1   Power Consumption Automata

As mentioned above, PCAs are a variant of WTAs [3]. WTAs, an extension of TAs [4], are state-transition systems that have a finite numbers of non-negative real-valued clocks and weight variables. PCAs are different from WTAs in that PCA does not have weights on its edge. We first present a basic model of PCAs.

Basic Model. A PCA $\mathcal{A}$ is a tuple consisting of $\langle\ Loc, \ell_0, X, W, Edg, Flow, Inv\ \rangle$.

1. Loc is a non-empty finite set of locations.
2. ℓ_0 is the initial location, $\ell_0 \in Loc$.
3. X is a finite set of non-negative real ($\mathcal{R}_+$) clock variables. For a positive natural number $n(\in \mathcal{N})$ and an operator $\bowtie \in \{<, \leq, =, \geq, >\}$, constraints of the form $x \bowtie n$ and $x_1 - x_2 \bowtie n$ constitute a set of clock constraints $Z(X)$.
4. W is a finite set of weight variables that take non-negative real values.
5. Edg represents a set of transitions, and is a finite set $Loc \times Z(X) \times 2^X \times Loc$. An element of Edg, (l, g, r, l'), is written as $l \xrightarrow{g,r} l'$, where g is a guard condition in $Z(X)$, and r refers to a set of clock variables ($\in 2^X$) to reset.
6. $Flow$ represents the flow dynamics accounting for the change rate of weight variables, which is represented in terms of ordinary differential equations, $dw/dt = M_w^\ell$. $Flow : Loc \rightarrow (W \rightarrow \mathcal{R}_+)$
7. Inv is a mapping from Loc to clock constraints, $Inv : Loc \rightarrow Z(X)$. Each element in Inv defines a clock invariant defined at each location.

Parallel Composition. We represent a complex system as a parallel composition of PCAs, where two PCAs are synchronized for a same event. The PCAs are defined in terms of a finite set of events Σ and an empty symbol ϵ. A PCA $\mathcal{A}$ is $\langle Loc, \ell_0, X, W, \Sigma \cup \{\epsilon\}, Edg, Flow, Inv \rangle$.

Edg is $Loc \times (\Sigma \cup \{\epsilon\}) \times Z(X) \times 2^X \times Loc$, and its element (l, a, g, r, l') is written as $l \xrightarrow{a,g,r} l'$. Parallel composition is defined for two given PCAs $\mathcal{A}^{(1)}$ and $\mathcal{A}^{(2)}$, where $\Sigma^{(1)} \cap \Sigma^{(2)} \neq \emptyset$ and $W^{(1)} \cap W^{(2)} = \emptyset$. Locations of the composed automaton are pairs of locations, $\langle l^{(1)}, l^{(2)} \rangle \in Loc^{(1)} \times Loc^{(2)}$. An invariant at each location is a conjunction, $Inv^{(1)}(l^{(1)}) \wedge Inv^{(2)}(l^{(2)})$. Symbols common to both alphabets ($a \in \Sigma^{(1)} \cap \Sigma^{(2)}$) synchronize two automata. For such a common alphabet, $\mathcal{A}^{(1)}$ and $\mathcal{A}^{(2)}$ take transitions simultaneously.

Power Consumption Automata. PCAs add internal state variables to the basic model and discriminate input-output actions. We introduce a finite set of variables V, whose values are Booleans, naturals or elements in some finite discrete domains. Such variables are updated along with a transition, $Update$. Here, Edg is $Loc \times (\Sigma \cup \{\epsilon\}) \times Z(X) \times 2^X \times Update \times Loc$, and its element (l, a, g, r, u, l') is written as $l \xrightarrow{a,g,r,u} l'$. Furthermore, parallel composition is communication between two PCAs. The participants in such a parallel composition use unidirectional communication. The alphabet involved in the synchronous transitions consists of two disjoint sets, Σ and $\overline{\Sigma}$. Here, $a \in \Sigma$ indicates that $\overline{\Sigma}$ contains its counterpart $\overline{a}$, where Σ denotes *receive*, and $\overline{\Sigma}$ denotes *send*. Two transitions with a and $\overline{a}$ are taken simultaneously. Formal model of PCAs is now $\langle Loc, \ell_0, X, W, V, (\Sigma \cup \overline{\Sigma}) \cup \{\epsilon\}, Edg, Flow, Update, Inv \rangle$.

4.2 Boolean Encoding

Fault localization, as well as bounded model checking, requires Boolean encoding of a trace formula φ_{TF}. We follow the encoding method of TAs in [25] and extend this method to PCAs. In the following, we use an abbreviation $\hat{x}$ to refer to a vector of variables $(x_1, \dots, x_n) \in X^n$.

Trace Formula. A state of a single PCA $\mathcal{A}$ is characterized by a location variable (at), clock variables ($\hat{x}$), weight variables ($\hat{w}$), and discrete variables ($\hat{v}$). We introduce a set $S=\{at,\ \hat{x},\ \hat{w},\ \hat{v}\}$, where $\hat{x}$, $\hat{w}$, and $\hat{v}$ are vectors of a suitable number of variables, $\hat{x} \in X^n$, $\hat{w} \in W^m$, and $\hat{v} \in V^l$. Here, a PCA $\mathcal{A}$ is defined as $\langle I, T \rangle$ over S.

1. Initial State: Variables in $\hat{v}$ are appropriately initialized.

   $$I=(at = \ell_0 \wedge \hat{x} = 0 \wedge \hat{w} = 0 \wedge \hat{v} = init)$$

2. Discrete Transition Step:

   $T(e)$ is a relation on S and S', where $e = l \xrightarrow{g,r,u} l'$, and $z_i = 0$ if $x_i \in r$, $z_i = x_i$ otherwise. The internal variable v_i is modified using an updating function $f_i \in u_i$.
   $$T(e)=(at = l \wedge at' = l' \wedge g \wedge \hat{x}' = \hat{z} \wedge \hat{w}' = \hat{w} \wedge \hat{v}' = \hat{f}(\hat{v}) \wedge Inv(l')(\hat{x}'))$$

3. Delay Transition Step:

   $D(\delta, \ell)$ is a relation on S and S' at a location $\ell \in Loc$, where δ is a positive real value of delay, and M^ℓ is a non-negative real-valued constant given at each location. In particular, weight variables are updated in accordance with the flow dynamics (cf. *Flow*).

   $$D(\delta, \ell)= (Inv(\ell)(\hat{x}') \wedge at' = at \wedge \hat{x}' = \hat{x} + \delta \wedge \hat{w}' = \hat{w} + M^\ell \times \delta \wedge \hat{v}' = \hat{v})$$

4. Transition Relation:

   T is a relation on S and S'.
   $$T= (\bigvee_{e \in Edg} T(e)) \vee (\exists\ \delta \geq 0 . \bigvee_{\ell \in Loc} D(\delta, \ell))$$

5. K-step Unfolding of PCA:

   φ_{TF}^K is a trace formula encoding potential K-step transition sequences. Let S_j be a set of j-indexed variables $\{at^j, \hat{x}^j,\ \hat{w}^j,\ \hat{v}^j\}$. Here, S in I is S_0. S and S' in T_j are S_{j-1} and S_j, respectively.
   $$\varphi_{TF}^K = I \wedge (\bigwedge_{j=1..K} T_j)$$

Next, we consider parallel composition cases. In order to define delay transition steps, we introduce a special symbol *delay* to represent that the automaton takes a delay transition. In the definition of a PCA, synchronization symbols are either receive (Σ) or send ($\overline{\Sigma}$). The Boolean encoding here does not discriminate the annotation because the symbols are just meant for synchronizing transitions. Therefore, the input alphabet is $\Sigma \cup \{\epsilon,\ delay\}$. The set S is extended to include a variable act referring to an input symbol ($S \cup \{\ act\ \}$).

1. Inactivity Transition:

   $$F=(at' = at \wedge \hat{x}' = \hat{x} \wedge \hat{w}' = \hat{w} \wedge \hat{v}' = \hat{v} \wedge (\bigwedge_{\alpha \in (\Sigma \cup \{delay\})} act \neq \alpha))$$

2. Discrete Transition Step for $e = l \xrightarrow{a,g,r,u} l'$.

$$T(e) = (at = l \wedge at' = l' \wedge act = a \wedge g \wedge \hat{x}' = \hat{z} \wedge \hat{w}' = \hat{w} \wedge \hat{v}' = \hat{f}(\hat{v})$$
$$\wedge \, Inv(\ell')(\hat{x}'))$$

3. Delay Transition Step:

$$D(\delta, \ell) = (Inv(\ell)(\hat{x}') \wedge at' = at \wedge act = delay \wedge \hat{x}' = \hat{x} + \delta \wedge \hat{w}' = \hat{w} + M^{\ell} \times \delta$$
$$\wedge \, \hat{v}' = \hat{v})$$

4. Transition Relation:

$$T = (\bigvee_{e \in Edg} T(e)) \vee (\exists \, \delta \geq 0 . \bigvee_{\ell \in Loc} D(\delta, \ell)) \vee F$$

5. K-step Unfolding of N numbers of PCAs: A total of N PCAs $A^{(1)} \ldots A^{(N)}$ are composed, where $A^{(i)}$ is $\langle I^{(i)}, T^{(i)} \rangle$. Here, $I^{(i)}$ and $T^{(i)}$ define the initial state and transition relation of an i-th automaton.

$$\varphi_{TF}^{K} = \bigwedge_{i=1..N}(I^{(i)} \wedge (\bigwedge_{j=1..K} T_j^{(i)})), \text{ which is rewritten as } I \wedge (\bigwedge_{j=1..K} T_j)$$
where $I = \bigwedge_{i=1..N} I^{(i)}$ and $T_j = \bigwedge_{i=1..N} T_j^{(i)}$.

An Example. We show a Boolean encoding of a client that will appear later in Fig. 3. This automaton does not have weight variables and thus is a TA.

1. Initial State:

$$I = (at = \ell_0 \wedge X_c = 0)$$

2. Discrete Transition Steps:

$$T(e_1) = (at = \ell_0 \wedge at' = \ell_1 \wedge X'_c = 0 \wedge act = \overline{lock})$$
$$T(e_2) = (at = \ell_1 \wedge at' = \ell_0 \wedge X_c \geq C'_1 \wedge act = \overline{unlock})$$

3. Delay Transition Steps:

$$D(\delta, \ell_0) = (at' = at \wedge at = \ell_0 \wedge act = delay \wedge X'_c = X_c + \delta)$$
$$D(\delta, \ell_1) = ((X'_c \leq C_1) \wedge at' = at \wedge at = \ell_1 \wedge act = delay \wedge X'_c = X_c + \delta)$$

4. Inactivity Transition:

$$F = (at' = at \wedge X'_c = X_c \wedge act \neq \overline{lock} \wedge act \neq \overline{unlock} \wedge act \neq delay)$$

5. Transition Relation: $T = (T(e_1) \vee T(e_2) \vee D(\delta, \ell_0) \vee D(\delta, \ell_1) \vee F)$

4.3   Scope-Bounded Analysis

Bounded Model Checking. We introduce a labeling function Lab from each location to a set of atomic propositions, $Lab : Loc \rightarrow 2^{Prop}$. Here, $Prop$ is defined over state variables U such that $U = S \backslash \{at\} = \{\hat{x}, \hat{w}, \hat{v}\}$. Specifically, a proposition p $(p \in Prop)$ takes the form of clock constraints $Z(X)$ for clock variables (x_j), and of weight constraints $Z(W)$ for weight variables. These constraints are represented in linear real arithmetic (LRA) theory.

Although a BMC problem is usually defined for arbitrary formulas of linear temporal logic (LTL) [6,25], we restrict to consider safety properties only. We let $\psi(\hat{u})$ be a propositional formula constructed from $Prop$, and $\hat{u}_j$ be state variables in U^j. A safety property is expressed in LTL as $\Box\psi$. Recall a BMC problem is checking the satisfiability of $\varphi_{TF} \wedge \neg\varphi_{AS}$. Because $\neg(\Box\psi) = \Diamond\neg\psi$, the entire formula for the K-unfolded case is

$$\varphi_{safety} \;=\; I(\hat{u}_0) \wedge (\bigwedge_{j=1..K} T_j(\hat{u}_{j-1}, \hat{u}_j)) \wedge (\bigvee_{j=1..K} \neg\psi(\hat{u}_j)).$$

This BMC problem is searching for an erroneous state, that satisfies $\neg\psi(\hat{u}_j)$, within K transition steps from an initial state.

Guide Constraints. The energy consumption analysis is a duration-bounded cost constraint problem (see Sect. 2). We need means to specify a duration in which numerical constrains on weight variables are checked. Such a duration is defined by an LTL formula φ_G, a *guide constraint*. Then, the entire formula for a BMC problem is $\varphi_{TF} \wedge \neg(\varphi_G \Rightarrow \varphi_{AS})$, which is $(\varphi_{TF} \wedge \varphi_G) \wedge \neg\varphi_{AS}$.

δ-Stuttering. A PCA has delay transitions in addition to discrete transitions. When a discrete transition at a location ℓ is not enabled, there is a chance to fire a delay transition so long as the invariant at the location ℓ is satisfied. The amount of such a delay, δ in the definition, can be arbitrary, which implies, in principle, that a countable number of delay transitions are able to fire on the same location ℓ. The number of such transitions may increase to reach the bound K with no meaningful discrete transition at all. Such δ-*stuttering* is effectively the same as the scope being chosen to be smaller than K.

We remove the δ-stuttering from the transition sequences. A transition sequence containing δ-stuttering has a sub-sequence that consists of consecutive delay transitions and either is ended with a discrete transition or reaches the scope limit. Here, we write such a sub-sequence ended with a discrete transition e^n, where $e^n = \ell_s \rightarrow \ell_t$, to be $\langle D(\delta_1, \ell_s), \cdots, D(\delta_{n-1}, \ell_s), T(e^n) \rangle$. We compress the delay transition fragment to be $D(\delta_T, \ell_s)$ where $\delta_T = \Sigma_{i=1}^{n-1} \delta_i$. Then, the sub-sequence becomes $\langle D(\delta_T, \ell_s), T(e^n) \rangle$. For the case of reaching the scope limit, we simply truncate the sequence by removing the delay transitions.

Practically, we can remove δ-stuttering by choosing a scope bound of a BMC carefully. Imagine that we notice δ-stuttering in a counter-example trace of a K-bounded BMC. If the δ-stuttering has N consecutive delay transitions, we re-run the BMC in which its scope is chosen to be smaller than K, for example

$(K - N + 1)$. We ensure that δ-stuttering does not appear anymore in a newly generated counter-example.

5   Automatic Fault Localization

5.1   Fault Localization Method

Fault Localization Problem for PCA. Parallel compositions of PCAs are *closed* in that there is no *free* event symbol; any symbol a $(\in \Sigma)$ has a matching $\bar{a}$ $(\in \overline{\Sigma})$. Although the original fault localization problem in Sect. 3 refers to the error-inducing input φ_{EI}, the problem here does not need to consider this condition. Because a set of PCAs are closed, there is no input data that is given externally. However, as discussed above, we must take into account of the guide constraint φ_G. Therefore, the formula φ_{FL} used in the fault localization problem for PCAs takes the form such that $\varphi_{FL} = \varphi_{TF} \wedge \varphi_G \wedge \varphi_{AS}$. The problem is searching for MCS elements in φ_{TF} of the unsatisfiable φ_{FL}.

Failure Model. PCAs are state transition systems that control the enabling of transitions by non-negative real-valued clocks. Weight variables are *observers* and does not affect the enabling of transitions. When multiple PCAs are composed, synchronization can be considered to result in introducing further constraints on transition sequences of the constituent PCAs, which indirectly affects possible transition sequences controlled by the clock variables.

We assume that faulty behavior in PCAs is originated from some faults in using clock variables. PCAs refer to clocks in invariants, or transition guards and resets, $Inv(l)$, or g and r on an edge of $l \xrightarrow{a,g,r,u} l$. We consider possibilities that the elements referring to clocks may contain root causes, These are suspicious elements in faulty systems. We do not consider *structural* bugs such as missing edges or redundant edges. Now, the fault localization problem involves checking a set of clock constraints collected from a failing trace with respect to a given property φ_{AS}.

In a fault localization problem using the pMaxSAT approach, these suspicious elements are marked *soft*. Since the initial state is usually definite, all of the elements in the initial state formula (I) are *hard*. The inactivity transition F, in parallel compositions of automata, is also definite because it encodes situations in which a constituent automaton does not take any transition.

Next, we consider the discrete transition step $T(e)$ and the delay transition step $D(\delta, \ell)$. Elements, which are related to invariants in the transition step, guards and resets, are marked *soft*. Below the notation p^H (or, p^S) indicates that p is *hard* (or, *soft*).

1. Discrete Transition Step:

$$T(e) = (\ (at = l)^H \wedge (at' = l')^H \wedge (act = a)^H \wedge (g)^S$$
$$\wedge (\hat{x}' = \hat{z})^S \wedge (\hat{w}' = \hat{w})^H \wedge (\hat{v}' = \hat{f}(\hat{v}))^H \wedge (Inv(\ell')(\hat{x}'))^S\ )$$

2. Delay Transition Step:

$$D(\delta, \ell) = ((Inv(\ell)(\hat{x}'))^S \wedge (at' = at)^H \wedge (act = delay)^H$$
$$\wedge (\hat{x}' = \hat{x} + \delta)^H \wedge (\hat{w}' = \hat{w} + M^\ell \times \delta)^H \wedge (\hat{v}' = \hat{v})^H)$$

Non-deterministic Transitions. PCAs have non-deterministic transitions, i.e. more than one transition can be enabled simultaneously. A PCA may have multiple edges e_i such that $e_i = l_s \xrightarrow{a_s, g_i, r_i, u_i} l_i$. The edges share a common source location l_s and enabling conditions, but have a different reset r_i, an update u_i, and a destination location l_i, where the enabling conditions are described in terms of a common input symbol a_s and overlapped guard conditions g_i. Furthermore, a PCA has a delay transition $D(\delta, l_s)$ at the same source location l_s, which is competing with discrete transitions. We have a set of transitions that are enabled non-deterministically, $\{D(\delta, l_s), T(e_1), \ldots, T(e_N)\}$.

Non-deterministic transitions complicate fault localization. The formula-based fault localization method relies on the fact that MCSes are calculated from the unsatisfiability of the φ_{FL}. However, if the system has non-deterministic transitions, it can take transitions other than that in the failing execution and some of the paths may be successful. Consequently, φ_{FL} may be satisfiable and have an empty MCSes.

The above observation implies that we cannot use the full flow-sensitive trace formula, which is successful for the case of imperative programs [12]. The trace formula used in the BMC is full flow-sensitive because the formula encodes all potential execution paths and thus contains non-deterministic transitions when we consider PCAs. Note that imperative programs are deterministic, and that this issue does not come up.

Trace Formula for Fault Localization. Since φ_{FL} is $\varphi_{TF} \wedge \varphi_G \wedge \varphi_{AS}$, the φ_{TF} in the unsatisfiable formula φ_{FL} can be restricted to capture conflict situations only. These are in a subset of all potential transition sequences, and the φ_{TF} does not need to encode all the sequences. Furthermore, a conflict situation is related to a counter-example trace that a K-scoped BMC procedure returns[1]. The trace contains a transition sequence leading to the violation of φ_{AS} and other information. The sequence is actually a mixture of discrete step $(T(e_j^i))$ and delay transition step $(D(\delta^i, \ell^i))$. Here, $T(e_j^i)$ is a discrete transition $T(e_j)$ taken as the i-th step. If the length is K, the sequence is encoded to be $\bigwedge_{i=1..K}(T(e_j^i) \text{ or } D(\delta^i, \ell^i))$.

Recall that the formula φ_{AS} is a safety property ($\Box \psi$). If it is violated, then there is an index L ($L \leq K$) such that L is the state at which φ_{AS} violates at the first time, a minimum of such indices. Since the transition sequence up to L contains enough information leading to the violation, the sequence is encoded in a formula $\bigwedge_{i=1..L}(T(e_j^i) \text{ or } D(\delta^i, \ell^i))$. We can ensure that $I(\hat{u}_0) \wedge (\bigwedge_{i=1..L}(T(e_j^i) \text{ or } D(\delta^i, \ell^i))) \wedge \neg\psi(\hat{u}_L)$ is satisfiable.

---

[1] We can assume here the counter-example trace is free from the δ-stuttering issue.

A Sliced Transition Sequence. We use a *sliced transition sequence* as the trace formula (φ_{TF}^{sliced}) for the fault localization. It is a conjunction of transition steps in a L-scoped counter-example trace. $\varphi_{TF}^{sliced} = I \wedge (\bigwedge_{i=1..L}(T(e_j^i) \text{ or } D(\delta^i, \ell^i)))$. The formula involves *soft* clauses referring to clock variables. Since *soft* clauses are relaxable, we can find MCS elements that make the formula $\varphi_{TF}^{sliced} \wedge \varphi_{AS}$ satisfiable. Note that the formula φ_G does not appear because φ_{TF}^{sliced}, by construction, satisfies the guide constraint.

Fault Localization Steps. The fault localization steps are described below.

1. Execute K-scope BMC of $\varphi_{TF} \wedge \varphi_G \wedge \neg\varphi_{AS}$.
2. Remove δ-stuttering if present by executing BMC with a chosen small scope.
3. Construct φ_{TF}^{sliced} (a sliced transition) from the counter-example trace.
4. Use pMaxSAT for $\varphi_{TF}^{sliced} \wedge \varphi_{AS}$ to enumerate MCSes.

6   An Example Case

In the following, we present a simple example case conducted as an initial study under MacO/S 10.9.5 on a 1.3 GHz Intel Core i5, using Yices-1, a pMaxSAT solver supporting LRA theory [10].

Scenario. Figures 2 and 3 illustrate a diagrammatic representation of automata used in the example. This is a simplified scenario reported in [21].

The client locks or unlocks the Lock controlling the Wi-Fi STA, which communicates with the Wi-Fi AP. The Wi-Fi STA (Fig. 2) is a PCA that has three power states; ℓ_0 is a deep-sleep state whose battery consumption rate (M^0) is small, ℓ_1 is a light-sleep state whose battery consumption rate (M_1) is larger than M^0 so as to be ready for a quick re-start in the near future, and ℓ_2 is an active state in which the battery consumption rate (M_2) is the largest because incoming data frames are decoded. If the Lock is disabled, the Wi-Fi STA takes a transition from ℓ_2 to ℓ_1 when a data transfer is finished. An expiration timer

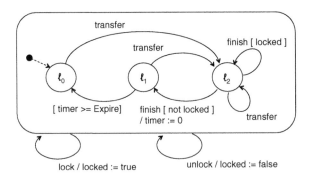

Fig. 2. A simplified Wi-Fi STA with a Lock

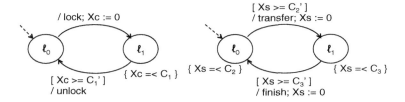

Fig. 3. A client (left) and a simplified Wi-Fi AP (right)

enables a transition from ℓ_1 to ℓ_0. Alternatively, if the Lock is enabled, the system stays in the ℓ_2 state even if the transfer is finished. The Client and Wi-Fi AP in Fig. 3 are TAs since they have clock variables, but no weight variable.

BMC Problem. We introduce a simple safety property to specify that a total energy consumption E is less than a given threshold C_0. This relationship is expressed in an LTL formula such that $\varphi_{AS} = \Box(E \leq C_0)$. We also specify a duration for the analysis such that the interval starts with a `lock` message and eventually involves a `finish` followed by a `transfer`, which is encoded in a guide constraint φ_G such that $\varphi_G = \text{lock} \wedge \Diamond(\text{finish} \wedge \Diamond\text{transfer})$. Because $\neg\varphi_{AS} = \Diamond(E > C_0)$, the formula for our BMC problem is $\varphi_{TF} \wedge \varphi_G \wedge \Diamond(E > C_0)$, where the formula φ_{TF} encodes all possible interleaving execution paths generated by the parallel composition of three automata.

In the experiments, we set concrete values to the parameters, those appeared in the clock invariants (C_1, C_2, and C_3), in the guard conditions on the clocks (C'_1, C'_2, and C'_3), and in the property to check (C_0). In particular, we choose a large value for C_2 and C'_2, which is a source of potential e-bugs injected so that Wi-Fi STA (Fig. 2), if locked, remains at the location ℓ_2 for a long time.

Failing Execution. We conducted BMC with a scope bound of nine, which is just an initial guess. The BMC procedure returns a counter-example that contains a sub-sequence involving δ-stuttering of a length two. We re-run the BMC with a new scope bound of seven. The resultant transition sequence is $(\text{lock}, \delta_2, \text{transfer}, \delta_4, \text{finish}, \delta_6, \text{transfer})$. Figure 4 illustrates the obtained

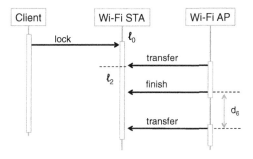

Fig. 4. A Failing Execution

failing execution trace in a message sequent chart. Three PCAs execute in parallel, and the trace is an instance of possible interleaving that results in violating the property. The Wi-Fi STA, first in the ℓ_0 state, enters the ℓ_2 in response to receiving a `transfer`. Although it receives a `finish`, the Wi-Fi STA stays at the same state. After an amount of time d_6 is passed, another `transfer` event occurs where $d_6 \geq C'_2$ is satisfied. Because C'_2 is large, the total energy E consumed up to this point violates the given condition. E is equal to $M_0 \times d_2 + M_2 \times d_4 + M_2 \times d_6$. From this we constructed a sliced trace formula φ_{TF}^{sliced} that encodes the obtained counter-example transition sequence.

Localizing Faults. We constructed a formula φ_{FL} to be $\varphi_{TF}^{sliced} \wedge \Box(E \leq C_0)$ whose scope is seven, and iteratively invoked Yices-1 pMaxSAT procedure to enumerate all MCS elements. The result is MCSes to have two MCS elements, $\{\{[X_s \geq C'_2]\ on\ \ell_0 \rightarrow \ell_1\}, \{(X_s := 0)\ on\ \ell_1 \rightarrow \ell_0\}\}$, which concern with clocks in Wi-Fi AP (Fig. 3 - right).

The first MCS element, $\{[X_s \geq C'_2]\ on\ \ell_0 \rightarrow \ell_1\}$, shows that the time between the last `finish` and a coming `transfer` is large because C'_2 is large. The Wi-Fi STA waits for another `transfer` at the state ℓ_2 and consumes a lot of energy. The second MCS element, $\{(X_s := 0)\ on\ \ell_1 \rightarrow \ell_0\}$, may suggest a repair in which the clock X_s is initialized to be larger than zero so that the guard condition on the edge from ℓ_0 to ℓ_1 is enabled sooner. PCA, however, allows only a reset, assigning zero to a clock. This second MCS element is not a real root cause.

7   Discussion and Conclusion

Precision of Identified Root Causes. Because diagnoses of a fault in the formula-based fault localization method are MCS elements, we have two aspects to discuss in regard to the precision of identified root causes. First, MCS is not minimum and may have extra clauses, which implies that a diagnosis may not be accurate enough to pinpoint a specific fault location. However, in our experience of either PCA or imperative programs [12] and in existing work on imperative programs [11,26], an MCS element consists of a single clause or at most a few. Thus, being minimal is not an issue in practice.

Second, the number of MCS elements is sometimes large, which means that there are many root cause candidates. It requires human insight to determine which candidate MCS is a real root cause to repair. The fault localization method is not concerned with such differences. In our experiment in Sect. 6, the obtained MCSes contains a real root cause ($\{[X_s \geq C'_2]\ on\ \ell_0 \rightarrow \ell_1\}$) and a spurious one ($\{(X_s := 0)\ on\ \ell_1 \rightarrow \ell_0\}$).

Trace Formula for Fault Localization. The trace formula, playing a primary role in the fault localization method, depends on computational models, the operational semantics of PCAs in our case. Because of the issue on non-deterministic transitions in PCA, we used a sliced trace formula φ_{TF}^{sliced} for the fault localization. The formula is essentially encoding a counter-example transition sequence obtained by a BMC method. The sliced trace formula is similar to a flow-insensitive trace formula for imperative programs in BugAssist [11]. The flow-insensitive trace formula is introduced in order to counter a less efficient MCS algorithm that the tool uses. However, it cannot deal with failures due to bugs in control flows of programs [9]. SNIPER [12] showed that the full flow-sensitive trace formula was able to identify such control flow bugs and the adapted algorithm was as efficient as that of BugAssist. The sliced trace formula φ_{TF}^{sliced} in this paper is introduced not for an efficiency reason, but is essential because of the issues relating to non-deterministic transitions.

Limitation of Failure Model. The failure model in this paper is based on an assumption that PCA elements referring to clock variables are suspicious (Sect. 5.1). Here, φ_{TF}^{sliced} is considered as a sequence of transition steps and each transition step has a conjunct of conditions on clock variables as its sub-formula (Sect. 4.2). The sliced trace formula is essentially a set of conditions on clock variables that are collected along the counter-example transition sequence. We denote ϕ_{clk} a formula encoding such constraints here. Imagine that a given property ϕ_{AS} uses clock variables and weight variables. Since values of the weight variables are dependent on time, the formula ϕ_{AS} can be considered as clock constraints. A violation of a given LTL property is indeed an unsatisfiability of clock constraints, $\phi_{clk} \wedge \phi_{AS}$. The example case in Sect. 6 was exactly an instance of this constraint problem.

The failure model currently does not consider possible structural bugs. We can, however, extend our method to consider such a bug, but in a restricted case only. Recall that the method relies on finding MCS elements, which is indeed finding clauses that must be removed. If a new failure model considers a case in which a certain transition step, or an edge in PCA, is suspicious, then an edge, actually a clause corresponding to the edge, can be a candidate to be relaxed. Contrarily, if a bug appears because of a missing edge, we cannot find any root cause. There is no MCS element to account for the missing edge. This limitation is unavoidable in the MBD approaches.

Efficiency of MCS Enumeration. Enumerating all MCSes is time-consuming and a scalability problem remains. We may use an efficient method in [12] implemented using Yices-1, which adapts a technique for blocking MCS [16], or may use recent new algorithms such as the one in [15].

Last, as far as we know, the present paper is the first report on formula-based fault localization of energy consumption behavior, or a variant of WTA. The work is still preliminary, but we believe it can be a start of further research.

Acknowledgements. This work is partially supported by JSPS KAKENHI Grant Numbers 24300010 and 26330095, and the Kayamori Foundation of Informational Science Advancement.

References

1. Android. http://developer.android.com
2. IEEE Standard 802.11, Wireless LAN Medium Access Control (MAC) and Physical Layer (PHY) Specifications (1999)
3. Alur, R., Courcoubetis, C., Henzinger, T.A.: Computing accumulated delays in real-time systems. CAV 1993. LNCS, vol. 697, pp. 181–193. Springer, Heidelberg (1993)
4. Alur, R., Dill, D.L.: A theory of timed automata. TCS **126**, 183–235 (1994)
5. Alur, R., Courcoubetis, C., Halbwachs, N., Henzinger, T.A., Ho, P.-H., Nicollin, X., Olivero, A., Sifakis, J., Yovine, S.: The algorithmic analysis of hybrid systems. Theoret. Comput. Sci **138**, 3–24 (1995)
6. Biere, A., Cimatti, A., Clarke, E., Zhu, Y.: Symbolic model checking without BDDs. In: Cleaveland, W.R. (ed.) TACAS 1999. LNCS, vol. 1579, pp. 193–207. Springer, Heidelberg (1999)
7. Biere, A., Heule, M., Van Maaren, H., Walsh, T. (eds.): Handbook of Satisfiability. IOS Press, Amsterdam (2009)
8. Brekling, A., Hansen, M.R., Madsen, J.: MoVES - a framework for modeling and verifying embedded systems. In: Proceedings of the ICM2009, pp. 149–152 (2009)
9. Christ, J., Ermis, E., Schäf, M., Wies, T.: Flow-sensitive fault localization. In: Giacobazzi, R., Berdine, J., Mastroeni, I. (eds.) VMCAI 2013. LNCS, vol. 7737, pp. 189–208. Springer, Heidelberg (2013)
10. Dutertre, B., de Moura, L.: The Yices SMT Solver (2006). http://yices.csl.sri.com
11. Jose, M., Majumdar, R.: Cause clue clauses: error localization using maximum satisfiability. In: Proceedings of the PLDI 2011, pp. 437–446 (2011)
12. Lamraoui, S.-M., Nakajima, S.: A formula-based approach for automatic fault localization of imperative programs. In: Merz, S., Pang, J. (eds.) ICFEM 2014. LNCS, vol. 8829, pp. 251–266. Springer, Heidelberg (2014)
13. Liffiton, M.H., Sakallah, K.A.: On finding all minimally unsatisfiable subformulas. In: Bacchus, F., Walsh, T. (eds.) SAT 2005. LNCS, vol. 3569, pp. 173–186. Springer, Heidelberg (2005)
14. Liffiton, M.H., Sakallah, K.A.: Algorithms for computing minimal unsatisfiable subsets of constraints. J. Autom. Reasoning **40**(1), 1–33 (2008)
15. Liffiton, M.H., Malik, A.: Enumerating infeasibility: finding multiple MUSes quickly. In: Gomes, C., Sellmann, M. (eds.) CPAIOR 2013. LNCS, vol. 7874, pp. 160–175. Springer, Heidelberg (2013)
16. Morgado, A., Liffiton, M., Marques-Silva, J.: MaxSAT-based MCS enumeration. In: Biere, A., Nahir, A., Vos, T. (eds.) HVC. LNCS, vol. 7857, pp. 86–101. Springer, Heidelberg (2013)
17. Nakajima, S.: Model-based power consumption analysis of smartphone applications. In: Proceedings of the ACES-MB 2013, pp. 5:1–5:10 (2013)
18. Nakajima, S.: Everlasting challenges with the OBJ language family. In: Iida, S., Meseguer, J., Ogata, K. (eds.) Specification, Algebra, and Software. LNCS, vol. 8373, pp. 478–493. Springer, Heidelberg (2014)
19. Nakajima, S.: Model checking of energy consumption behavior. In: Cardin, M.-A., Krob, D., Lui, P.C., Tan, Y.H., Wood, K. (eds.) Proceedings of the 1st CSDM Asia, pp. 3–14. Springer, Switzerland (2014)
20. Nakajima, S.: Using real-time maude to model check energy consumption behavior. In: Bjørner, N., de Boer, F. (eds.) FM 2015. LNCS, vol. 9109, pp. 378–394. Springer, Heidelberg (2015)

21. Nakajima, S.: Formal analysis of android application behavior with real-time maude. In: Proceedings of the CPSNA 2015, pp. 7–12 (2015)
22. Pathak, A., Hu, Y.C., Zhang, M.: Bootstrapping energy debugging on smartphones: a first look at energy bugs in mobile devices. In: Proceedings of the Hotnets 2011, pp. 5:1–5:6 (2011)
23. Reiter, R.: A theory of diagnosis from first principles. Artif. Intell. **32**(1), 57–95 (1987)
24. Safarpour, S., Mangassarian, H., Veneris, A., Liffiton, M.H., Sakallah, K.A.: Improved design debugging using maximum satisfiability. In: Proceedings of the FMCAD 2007, pp. 13–19 (2007)
25. Sorea, M.: Bounded model checking for timed automata. ENTCS **68**(5), 116–134 (2002)
26. Wotawa, F., Nica, M., Moraru, I.: Automated debugging based on a constraint model of the program and a test case. J. Logic Algebraic Program. **81**(4), 390–407 (2012)

Hybrid Secure Data Aggregation in Wireless Sensor Networks

Keyur Parmar$^{(\boxtimes)}$ and Devesh C. Jinwala

S.V. National Institute of Technology, Surat, India
{keyur.mtech,dcjinwala}@gmail.com

Abstract. Secure data aggregation aims at combining security and data aggregation together to meet the requirements of data-centric networks such as wireless sensor network. Secure data aggregation protocols provide either hop-by-hop security or end-to-end security. However, hop-by-hop secure data aggregation is vulnerable to attackers at intermediate nodes while end-to-end secure data aggregation increases the communication overhead. In this paper, we propose a hybrid secure data aggregation protocol to balance the trade-off between privacy and communication overhead. The proposed protocol uses the symmetric-key based privacy homomorphism to ensure the privacy of sensor readings at intermediate nodes. In addition, the proposed protocol efficiently deals with the key management issues that exist in the state-of-the-art symmetric-key based protocols. The proposed protocol also reduces the communication overhead as compared to the existing end-to-end secure data aggregation protocols. Comprehensive analysis and comparisons validate the viability of the proposed protocol in resource-constrained wireless sensor networks.

Keywords: Wireless sensor networks · Security · Secure data aggregation · Privacy homomorphism · Communication overhead

1 Introduction

Wireless sensor network (WSN), a collection of tiny and cost-effective sensor devices, has envisioned many applications such as battlefield surveillance, target tracking, environmental & health care monitoring and traffic regulation. [1]. These tiny sensor devices have very limited resources such as memory, processor, energy and bandwidth [1]. Amongst these resources, energy is the most limiting factor that has a profound impact on the WSNs' lifetime [6]. Therefore, the major objective of WSNs' protocols is to reduce the energy consumption. In addition, as communication operations in WSNs consume significantly more energy than computation operations [11], WSNs' protocols aim at reducing communication overhead. One of the techniques used for reducing the communication overhead is "In-network data aggregation" [6]. In-network data aggregation processes the raw sensor readings at intermediate nodes, and forwards the aggregated result towards the base station. Along with data aggregation, data security becomes

© Springer International Publishing Switzerland 2015
C. Berger and M.R. Mousavi (Eds.): CyPhy 2015, LNCS 9361, pp. 116–131, 2015.
DOI: 10.1007/978-3-319-25141-7_9

an important design parameter due to hostile and unattended deployments and unreliable communication channel [4,25].

The requirement to bind the security and data aggregation together leads the development of secure data aggregation protocols. Secure data aggregation protocols have been classified as either hop-by-hop secure data aggregation protocols or end-to-end secure data aggregation protocols. Hop-by-hop secure data aggregation protocols [12,18] assume that intermediate nodes are trustworthy. Hence, data forwarded by leaf nodes can be decrypted at intermediate nodes. Intermediate nodes perform the aggregation operations over raw sensor readings and encrypt the aggregated data before forwarding the result towards the next hop. Though viable, such hop-by-hop aggregation becomes problematic when intermediate nodes are not trustworthy. Malicious intermediate nodes can read and modify the sensor readings that eventually violate the privacy and confidentiality of sensor readings. In addition, hop-by-hop secure data aggregation also incurs extra computation overhead at intermediate nodes. Intermediate nodes have to decrypt the sensor readings, perform the aggregation, and re-encrypt the aggregated data before forwarding it to the parent nodes. Hence, with the aim to protect the privacy of sensor readings, and to reduce the computation overhead at intermediate nodes, Girao et al. [8] proposed the end-to-end secure data aggregation (also known as concealed data aggregation).

End-to-end secure data aggregation protocols [8,17,18,20] process the encrypted data at intermediate nodes. End-to-end secure data aggregation uses privacy homomorphism [23] to support encrypted data processing. End-to-end secure data aggregation can be classified in three categories: (1) Symmetric-key based end-to-end secure data aggregation [3,8] (2) Asymmetric-key based end-to-end secure data aggregation [17], and (3) Elliptic curve cryptography (ECC) based end-to-end secure data aggregation [7,19]. Amongst these protocols, asymmetric-key/ECC based protocols are not viable for resource-constrained sensor devices due to their high computation and communication overhead [12]. In addition, symmetric-key cryptosystems, such as SKIPJACK, with 80-bit key size can provide the same level of security as compared to the asymmetric-key based cryptosystems such as the RSA [24] with 1024-bit key size [10]. However, there exist numerous research articles [17,18,22] that use asymmetric-key/ECC based cryptosystems in WSNs. The only reason to pursue the costly asymmetric-key/ECC based cryptosystems is the key management issues related to the symmetric-key based cryptosystems.

Symmetric-key based cryptosystems use a shared secret key at both ends of the communication channel. Moreover, if data are encrypted with different pairwise keys in symmetric-key based protocols, such as Domingo-Ferrer's cryptosystem [5], aggregator nodes cannot perform the in-network processing. Hence in order to perform the in-network processing of encrypted data, the global shared secret key needs to be distributed throughout the network. In WSNs where the deployment of nodes is in hostile environments, such a global shared secret key mechanism has a devastating effect on the overall aggregated result. The only symmetric-key based cryptosystem that does not require the global shared secret key across all nodes is Castelluccia et al.'s cryptosystem (The CMT cryptosystem) [2,3]. Although the CMT cryptosystem [2,3] mitigates the key management issues typically found in other symmetric-key based cryptosystems [8,21,26], it has an identity management issue. Each node in the CMT cryptosystem shares a unique secret key with the base station. Hence, if there exist non-responding nodes in the network, then the identities of non-responding nodes need to be forwarded towards the base station. The identity of a node is used to uniquely identify the node and to find the secret key it shares with the base station. As the identity-related information cannot be aggregated in the same way as the sensor readings, transmission of the identities of nodes increases the significant communication overhead.

In this paper, we propose a hybrid secure data aggregation protocol to deal with the challenges typically found in existing hop-by-hop as well as end-to-end secure data aggregation protocols. The proposed protocol uses the symmetric-key based privacy homomorphism to ensure the privacy of sensor readings nearer to the base station. In addition, the proposed protocol attempts to balance the trade-off between privacy and communication overhead. Finally, we compare the proposed protocol with existing hop-by-hop and end-to-end secure data aggregation protocols and validate the viability of the proposed protocol in resource-constrained WSNs.

The rest of the paper is organized as follows. In Sect. 2, we discuss the relevant literature. In Sect. 3, we provide a brief overview of the symmetric-key based CMT cryptosystem. Section 4 presents the proposed protocol for hybrid secure data aggregation. We analyze the resource overhead of the proposed protocol in Sect. 5. In Sect. 6, we analyze the security strength of the proposed protocol. Section 7 concludes the paper by emphasizing our contributions.

2   Related Work

Although security and data aggregation are vital design parameters for WSNs' protocols, their objectives are contradictory. Data aggregation protocols aim at reducing the communication traffic while security protocols increase the communication traffic. The need to provide security and data aggregation together has initiated secure data aggregation. Initial secure data aggregation protocols [12,18] aim at providing security in a hop-by-hop manner. Hu et al. [12] proposed a secure data aggregation protocol that ensures hop-by-hop security and en route data aggregation. Although, there have been numerous solutions [12,18] that provides hop-by-hop security, all of them consider the trustworthy intermediate nodes. Hence, intermediate aggregator nodes that contain a large volume of information gathered from their child nodes become the prime target for attackers.

Girao et al. [8] proposed a concealed data aggregation to protect the sensor readings at intermediate nodes. Authors used the privacy homomorphism introduced by Rivest et al. [23] to perform the encrypted data processing. Privacy homomorphism can be classified as either symmetric-key based [3,21], asymmetric based key [5,24] or ECC based [13] privacy homomorphism. Asymmetric-key based and ECC based privacy homomorphism have much higher resource consumption than the symmetric-key based privacy homomorphism [9,15]. Although, Gura et al. [9] and Malan et al. [15] argue in favor of asymmetric-key based and ECC based cryptosystems, their results clearly show that the resource overhead of their protocols are significantly higher than the protocols based on symmetric-key based cryptosystems [3,8].

The reason to pursue asymmetric-key based or ECC based privacy homomorphism in sensor networks is due to the key management issue of symmetric-key based techniques, such as [8,21,26], or the identity management issue of symmetric-key based techniques such as [2,3,21]. Mlaih et al. [16] proposed the protocol to combine the hop-by-hop and end-to-end secure data aggregation to provide the flexibility during aggregation and optimal data privacy at intermediate nodes. However, their proposed protocol requires the identity transfer similar to the one required by the CMT cryptosystem. Hence, the communication cost incurred by identity transfer remains as high as the CMT cryptosystem.

3   Preliminaries

In this section, we briefly discuss Castelluccia et al.'s [2,3] stream cipher based additively homomorphic cryptosystem (The CMT cryptosystem). As the CMT cryptosystem supports additive homomorphism, it can be used to compute the mean, variance and standard deviation over encrypted data without performing any decryption. The majority of sensor network's applications require computing an optimum value, such as the sum, minimum, maximum, variance, movement detection, etc., over data [2,26]. Such operations can be easily computed with the help of the additively homomorphic CMT cryptosystem.

The CMT Cryptosystem

Encryption $\mathcal{E}$:
  1. Represent a plaintext m as an integer $m \in [0, M-1]$, where M is the modulus.
  2. Let k be a pseudo random number such that $k \in [0, M-1]$.
  3. Compute the ciphertext, $c = \mathcal{E}_k(m) = m + k \bmod M$.
Decryption $\mathcal{D}$:
  1. Decrypt the ciphertext, $\mathcal{D}_\mathcal{K}(c) = c - k \bmod M = m$.
Ciphertexts Aggregation $\mathcal{A}$:
  1. Given $c_1 = \mathcal{E}_{k_1}(m_1)$ and $c_2 = \mathcal{E}_{k_2}(m_2)$.
  2. Compute an aggregated ciphertext, $C = c_1 + c_2 \bmod M = \mathcal{E}_K(m_1 + m_2)$ where $K = k_1 + k_2 \bmod M$.

To ensure the correctness, modulus M should be sufficiently larger than the sum of individual messages such as $M > \sum_{i=1}^{n}(m_i)$. If modulus M is smaller than the sum of aggregated messages, the correctness does not hold.

4   The Proposed Hybrid Secure Data Aggregation

The major advantage of using end-to-end secure data aggregation over hop-by-hop secure data aggregation is due to the privacy protection of sensor readings at intermediate aggregator nodes. However, end-to-end secure data aggregation protocols, such as the CMT cryptosystem, increase the communication overhead. As shown by Castelluccia et al. [2,3], the requirement of transmitting node identities (responding or non-responding, whichever is less) to the base station increases the communication overhead that in turn depletes the energy of sensor nodes. Due to the identity transfer of non-responding nodes, the communication overhead of the CMT cryptosystem remains nearly same as any non-aggregation based protocols when there exist a high number of non-responding nodes. In no-aggregation based approaches, data are not aggregated at intermediate nodes while in the CMT cryptosystem, the identities of nodes are not aggregated.

In this section, we present the proposed hybrid secure data aggregation protocol. The proposed protocol reduces the communication overhead and protects the privacy of sensor readings at aggregator nodes nearer to the base station. In Table 1, we describe the notations used in the proposed protocol.

Table 1. Notations used in the proposed protocol

Symbol	Description
i	A sensor node (leaf node) ID
j	An intermediate node (Aggregator)
$k_{i,j}$	A pair-wise secret key between a node i and its parent node j
m	The distance between a node i and a node j (in hops)
$k_{m'}$	A shared secret key between an intermediate node at m^{th} hop and the base station
S_i	A plaintext value sensed by a sensor node i
c_i	A ciphertext generated by a node i
S_j	An aggregated plaintext value generated by an aggregator node j
c_j	A ciphertext generated by an aggregator node j
$S_{m'}$	An aggregated plaintext value generated by an aggregator node at m^{th}-hop
$c_{m'}$	A ciphertext generated by an aggregator node at m^{th}-hop
$c_{m''}$	An aggregated ciphertext
h	A height of the data aggregation tree for a node at level m
p_m	An identity of a non-responding node, stored at its parent node at $(m + h)^{\text{th}}$-hop
$p_{m''}$	A product of non-responding nodes' identities
C	An aggregated ciphertext received at the base station
S	An aggregated plaintext retrieved at the base station

The Proposed Protocol for Hybrid Secure Data Aggregation

Upto m^{th} - hop

Encryption:

1. Each leaf node i, encrypts a sensor reading S_i using a shared secret key $k_{i,j}$ of a node i and its parent node j.
2. Compute $c_i = Enc_{k_{i,j}}(S_i)$.

Decryption:

1. Each parent node j, decrypts a ciphertext c_i using a shared secret key $k_{i,j}$ of a node j and its child node i.
2. Compute $S_i = Dec_{k_{i,j}}(c_i)$.

Plaintext Aggregation:

1. Each parent node j, aggregates the decrypted data S_i for all $i \in [1..n]$
2. Compute $S_j = \sum_{i=1}^{n} S_i$.
3. Node j re-encrypts the aggregated sensor readings S_j, using a shared secret key $k_{j,m'}$ of a node j and its parent node m'.
4. Compute $c_j = Enc_{k_{j,m'}}(S_j)$.

At m^{th} hop

Decryption:

1. Each node m' at m^{th} hop decrypts the ciphertext c_j using a shared secret key $k_{j,m'}$ of a node m' and its child node j.
2. Compute $S_j = Dec_{k_{j,m'}}(c_j)$.

Plaintext Aggregation:

1. Each node m' aggregates the decrypted data.
2. Compute $S_{m'} = \sum_{j=1}^{n} S_j$.

Encryption:

1. Each node m', encrypts an aggregated data $S_{m'}$ using a shared secret key $k_{m'}$.
2. $c_{m'} = Enc_{k_{m'}}(S_{m'})$.

m^{th} - hop onwards

Ciphertext Aggregation:

1. Each node m'' at $(m + h)$th hop, where $h \in [1...x]$, aggregates the encrypted data $c_{m'}$. Here, x is a height of a data aggregation tree.
2. $c_{m''} = \sum_{m'=1}^{n}(c_{m'})$.

Key Management:

1. Each node m'' at $(m + h)$th hop, where $h \in [1...x]$, computes the product of its child nodes' identities p_m that do not responded during the aggregation process.
2. $p_{m''} = \prod_{m=1}^{n}(p_m)$.

At the Base Station

Key Management:

1. The base station uniquely identifies the non-responding/responding nodes using the received product of primes $p_{m''}$.
2. $p_{m''} = \prod_{m=1}^{n}(p_m)$.
3. The base station uses these primes to uniquely identify the nodes at m^{th} hop and their respective keys $k_{m'}$.

Decryption:

1. The base station removes the shared secret keys $k_{m'}$ where $m' \in [1..n]$, of nodes at m^{th} hops, who responded during the aggregation process.
2. Compute $Dec(C) = c_{m''} - \sum_{m'=1}^{n} k_{m'} = \sum_{i=1}^{n} S_i$. Here, $n \in [1....x]$ represents the sensor nodes at m^{th} hops, that provided the sensor readings S_i.

5   Overhead Analysis

In this section, we comparatively evaluate the performance of the proposed protocol with hop-by-hop secure data aggregation and end-to-end secure data aggregation (The CMT cryptosystem) scenarios. For ease of calculation, we assume a ternary tree-based data aggregation topology in which the packets are forwarded from leaf nodes towards the base station. However, the proposed protocol can be seamlessly adopted for other network topologies such as, a cluster-based network topology or a hybrid network topology. In addition, we consider a network model similar to the one found in Castelluccia et al. [2] to calculate the bandwidth consumption.

5.1   Network Model

Let us assume a balanced k-ary tree with a sink node and multitude of sensor nodes. In Fig. 1, we present a ternary tree where $k = 3$. In addition, for the ease of calculation, we assume that leaf nodes are sensor nodes and remaining intermediate nodes are forwarders. We also assume that the sensor reading, S_i, of node i, (e.g. Temperature ranges between 0 and 127 Fahrenheit) is 7-bit long.

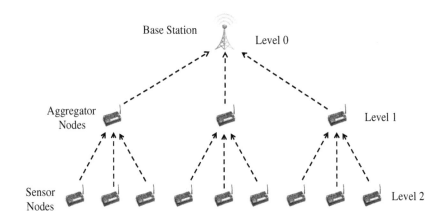

Fig. 1. Ternary tree-based data aggregation topology

We analyze the bandwidth consumption of nodes at various levels in the hierarchy by computing number of bits transmitted by the nodes. We consider a packet format used in TinyOS [14], an operating system for embedded devices, where the packet header (HDR) is of 56-bit and the maximum supported payload is 232 bits. We compare the proposed protocol with hop-by-hop secure data aggregation and end-to-end secure data aggregation scenarios. In addition, three scenarios considered for evaluation are as follows: (1) All nodes reply to their parent nodes (2) 10 % nodes are exhausted/compromised and do not reply (3) 30 % nodes are exhausted/compromised and do not reply. Here, we assume that non-responding nodes are distributed uniformly across the network.

5.2   Communication Overhead

In hop-by-hop secure data aggregation (SDA), a total number of bits transmitted by a node vary depending on the node's position in the hierarchy. As symmetric-key cryptosystems have negligible message expansion compared to asymmetric-key cryptosystems, a total number of bits transmitted by leaf nodes, remains the same as raw sensor readings, $log_2(t)$. Here, the total number of bits transmitted by leaf nodes in no aggregation based scenarios and hop-by-hop secure data aggregation scenarios remains nearly same. However, aggregator nodes in hop-by-hop secure data aggregation require to transmit a few more bits compared to the leaf nodes as they receive more data compared to the leaf nodes.

As shown in Fig. 2, the total number of bits transmitted by a leaf node in hop-by-hop encryption is HDR + $log_2(t)$, where t is the range of all possible sensor measurements. As shown above, temperature sensor requires 7-bit, $log_2(127)$, to represent 127 different temperature values. Hence, $56 + 7 = 63$-bit data are transmitted by each leaf node. Moreover, each intermediate node has to transmit $log_2(n' \cdot t)$ bits, where n' represents the aggregation of child nodes' sensor readings. Hop-by-hop encryption does not incur any additional communication overhead when there exist 10 % or 30 % non-responding nodes (NRN) in the network. In addition, the communication overhead reduces in these scenarios due to the less number of packets coming for aggregation.

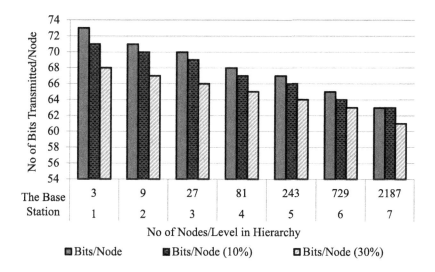

Fig. 2. Communication overhead of hop-by-hop SDA

If there aren't any non-responding nodes, the CMT cryptosystem (end-to-end secure data aggregation) performs nearly as good as hop-by-hop secure data aggregation protocols. In the CMT cryptosystem, a total number of bits transmitted by a node (leaf/intermediate node) remains constant due to en route aggregation. The ciphertext size in the CMT cryptosystem depends on the modulus M. The total number of bits transmitted by the CMT cryptosystem is calculated as HDR $+log_2(n)+log_2(t)$, where n represents the total number of nodes in the network and t represents the range of sensor readings. Here, each sensor node has to transmit $56 + 12 + 7 = 75$-bit. However, due to non-responding nodes' identity transfer, communication overhead increases drastically.

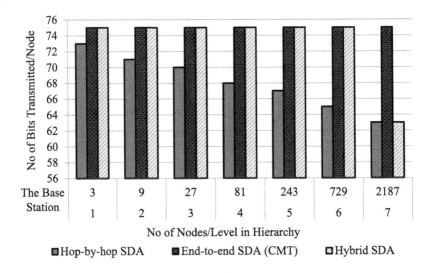

Fig. 3. Communication overhead of hybrid SDA ($m = 1$ and 0% NRN)

As shown in Fig. 3, the proposed hybrid secure data aggregation protocol has the same communication overhead as a hop-by-hop secure data aggregation protocol between leaf nodes to m^{th} hop intermediate nodes. In addition, from m^{th} hop onwards, the communication overhead of the proposed protocol remains same as the CMT cryptosystem. Figure 4 comparatively evaluates the performance of the proposed protocol and presents the communication overhead when data are aggregated after 2nd hop intermediate node, $m = 2$. In addition, when we compared the proposed hybrid secure data aggregation protocol with hop-by-hop secure data aggregation, it has negligible additional communication overhead. The proposed protocol does not require the extra computation overhead at each intermediate nodes as required by the hop-by-hop secure data aggregation protocols. In addition, unlike hop-by-hop secure data aggregation protocols, the proposed protocol ensures the privacy of sensor readings at intermediate nodes.

As shown in Fig. 5, when we choose $m = 1$ and if 10% nodes are not responding to the aggregator nodes, the communication overhead of the proposed protocol is 2.2 times less compared to the end-to-end secure data aggregation protocol. In addition, the proposed protocol has 1.9 times more communication overhead compared to the hop-by-hop secure data aggregation protocol. However, the

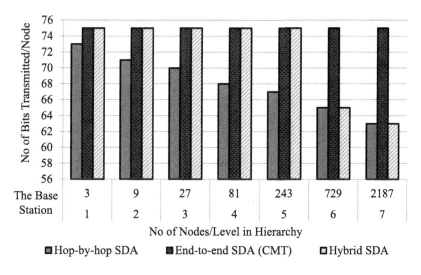

Fig. 4. Communication overhead of hybrid SDA ($m = 2$ and 0% NRN)

increase in communication overhead is due to the much higher level of security at intermediate nodes in the network. The communication overhead of the proposed protocol remains same as the hop-by-hop secure data aggregation for the 1st hop ($m = 1$), it reduces significantly compared to the CMT cryptosystem after 1st hop onwards ($m = 1$). The communication overhead of the proposed protocol after m^{th} hop is HDR $+log_2(n) + log_2(t) + log_2(n'')$. Here, n'' represents the number of bits used to uniquely identify the child nodes of an intermediate node at ($m + 1$)th hop. Moreover, the proposed protocol ensures the privacy of sensor readings at intermediate nodes higher than 1st hop intermediate nodes. In addition, for 30% non-responding nodes (Fig. 6), the proposed protocol has nearly 2.9 times less communication overhead compared to the end-to-end secure data aggregation protocol.

As shown in Fig. 7, if we choose $m = 2$, the proposed protocol has 3.5 times less communication overhead compared to the end-to-end secure data aggregation protocol. In addition, the communication overhead of the proposed protocol is only 1.2 times more compared to the hop-by-hop secure data aggregation. For 30% non-responding nodes at level $m = 2$ (Fig. 8), the proposed protocol has nearly 7 times less communication overhead compared to the CMT cryptosystem. In addition, the communication overhead of the proposed protocol is only 1.6 times more compared to the hop-by-hop secure data aggregation. The comparison of the proposed protocol with hop-by-hop secure data aggregation and end-to-end secure data aggregation protocol proves that the proposed hybrid secure data aggregation protocol reduces the significant communication overhead without affecting the privacy of a major part of the network.

The reason to pursue the hybrid secure data aggregation protocol is to reduce the communication overhead of symmetric-key based cryptosystem [3], or

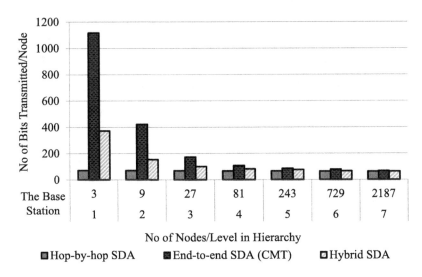

Fig. 5. Communication overhead of hybrid SDA ($m = 1$ and 10% NRN)

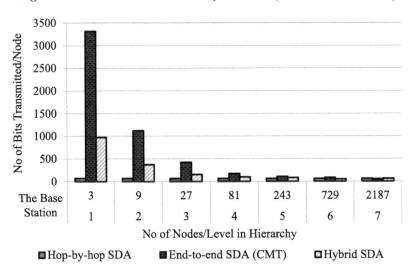

Fig. 6. Communication overhead of hybrid SDA ($m = 1$ and 30% NRN)

asymmetric-key based or ECC based cryptosystems. In addition, without affecting the privacy of a network at a large, we can achieve a significant reduction in communication traffic. Hence, instead of having hop-by-hop or end-to-end secure data aggregation protocols, if we choose the hybrid secure data aggregation protocol, we can trade-off between communication overhead and privacy requirements for different applications, depending on the needs of applications.

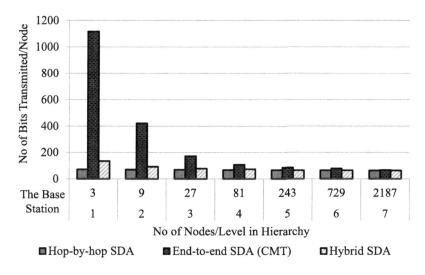

Fig. 7. Communication overhead of hybrid SDA ($m = 2$ and 10% NRN)

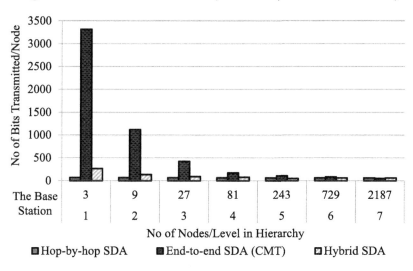

Fig. 8. Communication overhead of hybrid SDA ($m = 2$ and 30% NRN)

Computation operations also consume sensor nodes' limited resources. However, energy consumption due to the CPU processing is negligible compared to the radio frequency operations. As shown by Hill et al. [11], transmitting a single bit over a meter range requires the same amount of energy as required by the 1000 CPU instructions. Hence, in this paper, we focus on the communication overhead only, and we neglect the computation overhead that is negligible [11] compared to the communication overhead.

6   Security Analysis

In this section, we discuss the resilience of the proposed protocol against well-known cryptographic attacks [22]. In addition, we analyze the security of the proposed protocol against active and passive adversaries.

Ciphertext Analysis. In the ciphertext analysis, an adversary eavesdrops the ciphertexts and analyzes them to infer knowledge about the corresponding plaintexts or the key(s). In the proposed protocol, two different symmetric-key based cryptosystems have been used to secure the communication. Symmetric-key based cryptosystems remain secure against ciphertext analysis as long as the key being shared remains secret. Here, the shared secret key needs to be updated periodically to thwart the ciphertext analysis attacks.

Known-Plaintext Attack. In a known-plaintext attack, an adversary has plaintext-ciphertext pairs and the objective is to recover the complete or partial information related to the secret key or the plaintext(s). As WSNs are deployed in hostile and unattended environments, for an adversary to capture the plaintext-ciphertext pairs becomes relatively easy. In the proposed protocol, we use two different symmetric-key based cryptosystems. The proposed protocol can use symmetric-key based cryptosystem, such as AES, DES, or Triple DES, for communication between the leaf nodes to the mth hop nodes. Any node before m^{th} hop shares a unique secret key with its parent node. Hence, if an adversary gets the hold of the node's secret key, it cannot decrypt the ciphertexts produced by other sensor nodes. From m^{th} hop onwards, we use additively homomorphic symmetric-key based CMT cryptosystem. In the CMT cryptosystem, each node shares a unique pairwise key with the base station. As the CMT cryptosystem does not have a limitation to share a global shared secret key in order to perform en route aggregation, the proposed protocol remains secure against known-plaintext attacks.

Forge Packets. If an adversary can generate a valid ciphertext with a specific content, then it does not have to modify the existing ciphertexts. An attacker can easily insert the ciphertext into the network without being detected. Any asymmetric-key based cryptosystem, where the public key is used to generate the ciphertext, is vulnerable to this attack. However, in the proposed cryptosystem, we use symmetric-key based cryptosystems. Hence, an adversary must have to compromise a sensor node and extracts the shared secret key in order to generate a valid ciphertext.

Denial of Service Attacks. Amongst the various types of denial of service attacks, sensor networks are more prone to the attacks where the scarce energy is a target. In this attack, an adversary's goal is to keep sensor nodes busy doing activities that deplete sensor nodes' precious energy. In addition, there cannot be any cryptographic solution for such attacks as the cryptographic solution also consumes the energy. In the proposed protocol, the communication overhead is significantly less compared to the end-to-end secure data aggregation. In addition, although it requires a little bit more communication overhead compared to the hop-by-hop secure data aggregation, the privacy preservation at intermediate nodes compensates that extra communication overhead. As the radio frequency operations has the highest impact on the energy consumption [11], the reduced communication overhead can significantly improve the performance against denial of service attacks.

7 Conclusions

Although data aggregation and security remain essential design parameters for secure data aggregation protocols, both of them have conflicting requirements. Data aggregation protocols lessen the communication overhead in order to reduce the energy consumption while the security protocols add extra communication overhead in order to ensure the security of sensor readings. Amongst secure data aggregation protocols, hop-by-hop secure data aggregation protocols ensure lesser communication overhead while end-to-end secure data aggregation protocols ensure the privacy of sensor readings at intermediate nodes. Hence, with the intent to reduce the communication overhead and to ensure the privacy of sensor readings at intermediate nodes, we proposed a hybrid secure data aggregation protocol. The proposed protocol balances the trade-off between privacy and communication overhead. It protects the privacy of sensor readings nearer to the base station where it is required the most. In addition, the proposed protocol ensures lesser communication overhead that eventually increases the lifespan of WSNs. As per our knowledge, the proposed protocol is the first that achieves advantages of both hop-by-hop secure data aggregation and end-to-end secure data aggregation. As future work, we intend to formalize the security analysis. In addition, we plan to implement the proposed protocol for measuring the impact of computation and communication operations on the energy of sensor devices.

Acknowledgments. This research was a part of the project "A Secure Data Aggregation System and An Intrusion Detection System for Wireless Sensor Networks". It was supported by the Department of Electronics and Information Technology, Ministry of Communications and Information Technology, Government of India.

References

1. Akyildiz, I.F., Su, W., Sankarasubramaniam, Y., Cayirci, E.: Wireless sensor networks: a survey. Comput. Netw. Int. J. Comput. Telecommun. Netw. **38**(4), 393–422 (2002)
2. Castelluccia, C., Chan, A.C.F., Mykletun, E., Tsudik, G.: Efficient and provably secure aggregation of encrypted data in wireless sensor networks. ACM Trans. Sens. Netw. (TOSN) **5**(3), 20:1–20:36 (2009)

3. Castelluccia, C., Mykletun, E., Tsudik, G.: Efficient aggregation of encrypted data in wireless sensor networks. In: Proceedings of the 2nd Annual International Conference on Mobile and Ubiquitous Systems: Networking and Services, MOBIQUI-TOUS 2005, pp. 109–117. IEEE, Washington, D.C., July 2005
4. Chan, H., Perrig, A.: Security and privacy in sensor networks. Computer **36**(10), 103–105 (2003)
5. Domingo-Ferrer, J.: A provably secure additive and multiplicative privacy homomorphism. In: Chan, A.H., Gligor, V.D. (eds.) ISC 2002. LNCS, vol. 2433, pp. 471–483. Springer, Heidelberg (2002)
6. Fasolo, E., Rossi, M., Widmer, J., Zorzi, M.: In-network aggregation techniques for wireless sensor networks: a survey. Wirel. Commun. **14**(2), 70–87 (2007)
7. Girao, J., Westhoff, D., Mykletun, E., Araki, T.: TinyPEDS: tiny persistent encrypted data storage in asynchronous wireless sensor networks. Ad Hoc Netw. **5**(7), 1073–1089 (2007)
8. Girao, J., Westhoff, D., Schneider, M.: CDA: concealed data aggregation for reverse multicast traffic in wireless sensor networks. In: Proceedings of the 40th International Conference on Communications, ICC 2005, pp. 3044–3049. IEEE, Seoul, May 2005
9. Gura, N., Patel, A., Wander, A., Eberle, H., Shantz, S.C.: Comparing elliptic curve cryptography and RSA on 8-bit CPUs. In: Joye, M., Quisquater, J.-J. (eds.) CHES 2004. LNCS, vol. 3156, pp. 119–132. Springer, Heidelberg (2004)
10. Hankerson, D., Menezes, A.J., Vanstone, S.: Guide to Elliptic Curve Cryptography, 1st edn. Springer, Secaucus (2003)
11. Hill, J., Szewczyk, R., Woo, A., Hollar, S., Culler, D., Pister, K.: System architecture directions for networked sensors. ACM SIGPLAN Not. **35**(11), 93–104 (2000)
12. Hu, L., Evans, D.: Secure aggregation for wireless networks. In: Proceedings of the Symposium on Applications and the Internet Workshops, SAINT 2003, pp. 384–391. IEEE, Washington, D.C., January 2003
13. Koblitz, N.: Elliptic curve cryptosystems. Math. Comput. **48**(177), 203–209 (1987)
14. Levis, P., Madden, S., Polastre, J., Szewczyk, R., Whitehouse, K., Woo, A., Gay, D., Hill, J., Welsh, M., Brewer, E., Culler, D.: TinyOS: an operating system for sensor networks. In: Weber, W., Rabaey, J.M., Aarts, E. (eds.) Ambient Intelligence, pp. 115–148. Springer, Heidelberg (2005)
15. Malan, D.J., Welsh, M., Smith, M.D.: A public-key infrastructure for key distribution in TinyOS based on elliptic curve cryptography. In: Proceedings of the 1st Annual IEEE Communications Society Conference on Sensor and Ad Hoc Communications and Networks, SECON 2004, pp. 71–80. IEEE, Santa Clara, October 2004
16. Mlaih, E., Aly, S.A.: Secure hop-by-hop aggregation of end-to-end concealed data in wireless sensor networks. In: Proceedings of the 2nd IEEE Workshop on Mission Critical Networking in Conjunction with Infocom 2008, MCN 2008, pp. 1–6. IEEE, Phoenix, April 2008
17. Mykletun, E., Girao, J., Westhoff, D.: Public key based cryptoschemes for data concealment in wireless sensor networks. In: Proceedings of the IEEE International Conference on Communications, ICC 2006, pp. 2288–2295. IEEE, Istanbul, June 2006
18. Ozdemir, S., Xiao, Y.: Secure data aggregation in wireless sensor networks: a comprehensive overview. Comput. Netw. Int. J. Comput. Telecommun. Netw. **53**(12), 2022–2037 (2009)

19. Parmar, K., Jinwala, D.C.: Malleability resilient concealed data aggregation. In: Kermarrec, Y. (ed.) EUNICE 2014. LNCS, vol. 8846, pp. 160–172. Springer, Heidelberg (2014)
20. Parmar, K., Jinwala, D.C.: Symmetric-key based homomorphic primitives for end-to-end secure data aggregation in wireless sensor networks. J. Inf. Secur. **6**(1), 38–50 (2015)
21. Peter, S., Piotrowski, K., Langendoerfer, P.: On concealed data aggregation for WSNs. In: Proceedings of the 4th IEEE Consumer Communications Networking Conference, CCNC 2007, pp. 192–196. IEEE, Las Vegas, January 2007
22. Peter, S., Westhoff, D., Castelluccia, C.: A survey on the encryption of convergecast traffic with in-network processing. IEEE Trans. Dependable Secure Comput. **7**(1), 20–34 (2010)
23. Rivest, R.L., Adleman, L., Dertouzos, M.L.: On data banks and privacy homomorphisms. Found. Secure Comput. **4**(11), 169–180 (1978)
24. Rivest, R.L., Shamir, A., Adleman, L.: A method for obtaining digital signatures and public-key cryptosystems. Commun. ACM **21**(2), 120–126 (1978)
25. Wang, Y., Attebury, G., Ramamurthy, B.: A survey of security issues in wireless sensor networks. IEEE Commun. Surv. Tutor. **8**(2), 2–23 (2006)
26. Westhoff, D., Girao, J., Acharya, M.: Concealed data aggregation for reverse multicast traffic in sensor networks: encryption, key distribution, and routing adaptation. IEEE Trans. Mob. Comput. **5**(10), 1417–1431 (2006)

Formally Analyzing Continuous Aspects of Cyber-Physical Systems Modeled by Homogeneous Linear Differential Equations

Muhammad Usman Sanwal[1] and Osman Hasan[2]($^{\boxtimes}$)

[1] Computational Biomodeling Laboratory,
Turku Centre for Computer Science and Department of Computer Science,
Abo Akademi University, Turku, Finland
muhammad.sanwal@abo.fi
[2] School of Electrical Engineering and Computer Science,
National University of Sciences and Technology (NUST), Islamabad, Pakistan
osman.hasan@seecs.nust.edu.pk

Abstract. Traditionally, the continuous aspects of cyber-physical systems (CPS), usually modeled by differential equations, are analyzed using paper-and-pencil proof methods, computer based numerical methods or computer algebra systems. All these methods are error-prone and thus the analysis cannot be termed as accurate, which poses a serious threat to the accuracy of the cyber-physical systems. To guarantee the correctness of analysis, we propose to use higher-order-logic theorem proving to reason about the correctness of solutions of differential equations. This paper presents a formalization framework to express homogeneous linear differential equation of arbitrary order and formally verify their solutions within the sound core of the higher-order-logic theorem prover HOL4. In order to illustrate the usefulness of the proposed formalization, we utilize it to formally verify a couple of CPS used in the domain of bio-medicine, namely, a heart pacemaker and a fluid-filled catheter.

1 Introduction

Cyber-physical systems (CPS) [26] are characterized as computational systems, with software and digital and/or analog hardware components, that closely interact with their continuously changing physical surroundings. These days, CPS are widely being used and advocated to be used in a variety of applications ranging from ubiquitous consumer electronic devices, such as tele-operated health-care units and autonomous vehicles, to not so commonly used but safety-critical domains, such as tele-surgical robotics, space-travel and smart disaster response and evacuation. Due to the tight market windows or safety-critical nature of their applications, it has become a dire need to design error-free CPS and thus a significant amount of time is spent on ensuring the correctness of CPS designs.

Traditionally, physical and continuous aspects of a CPS are analyzed by capturing their behaviors by appropriate differential equations [33] and then solving

© Springer International Publishing Switzerland 2015
C. Berger and M.R. Mousavi (Eds.): CyPhy 2015, LNCS 9361, pp. 132–146, 2015.
DOI: 10.1007/978-3-319-25141-7_10

these differential equations to obtain the required design constraints. This kind of analysis can be done using paper-and-pencil proof methods or computer based numerical techniques. Whereas, the software and digital hardware components of a CPS are usually analyzed using computer based testing or simulation methods, where the main idea is to deduce the validity of a property by observing its behavior for some test cases. However, all the above mentioned analysis techniques, i.e., paper-and-pencil proof methods, numerical methods and simulation, cannot ascertain the absence of design flaws in a design. For example, paper-and-pencil proof methods are error prone due to the human error factor. Moreover, it is quite often the case that many key assumptions of the results obtained using paper-and-pencil proof methods are in the mind of the mathematician and are not documented. Such missing assumptions may also lead to erroneous CPS designs. Similarly, computer based numerical methods cannot attain 100 % accuracy as well due to the memory and computation limitations and round-off errors introduced by the usage of computer arithmetics. Thus, given the above mentioned inaccuracies, these traditional techniques should not be relied upon for the analysis of CPS, especially when they are used in safety-critical areas, such as medicine and transportation, where inaccuracies in the analysis could result in design bugs that in turn may even lead to the loss of human life.

In the past couple of decades, formal methods [5] have been successfully used for the precise analysis of a variety of software, hardware and physical systems. The main principle behind formal analysis of a system is to construct a computer based mathematical model of the given system and formally verify, within a computer, that this model meets rigorous specifications of intended behavior. Two of the most commonly used formal verification methods are model checking [4] and higher-order-logic theorem proving [16]. Model checking is an automatic verification approach for systems that can be expressed as a finite-state machine. Higher-order-logic theorem proving, on the other hand, is an interactive approach but is more flexible in terms of tackling a variety of systems. The rigorous exercise of developing a mathematical model for the given system and analyzing this model using mathematical reasoning usually increases the chances for catching subtle but critical design errors that are often ignored by traditional techniques like paper-and-pencil based proofs or simulation.

Given the extensive usage of CPS in safety-critical applications, there is a dire need of using formal methods for their analysis. However, the frequent involvement of ordinary differential equations (ODEs) in their analysis is a main limiting factor in this direction. For example, ODEs are essential for modeling the motion of mechanical parts, analog circuits and control systems, which are some of the most common elements of any CPS. Thus, automatic state-based formal methods, like model checking, and automatic theorem provers cannot be used to model and analyze the true CPS models due to their inability to model continuous systems. This is the main reason why most of the formal verification work about CPS utilizes their abstracted discrete models (e.g., [30]). Hybrid model-checking and theorem proving based approaches, e.g., [1], have been generally used for analyzing systems that can be modeled as differential equations. Moreover, safety properties of such systems have also been formally verified using differential invariants [3, 24] based on fixed point algorithms. Similarly, the Coq theorem prover has been used to formally verify the convergence of numerical solutions for a widely used partial differential wave equation [6]. Other notable higher-order-logic formalizations related to differential equations include verification of the convergence of numerical solutions for differential equations [6] and the approximate numerical solution of ordinary differential equations using the one-step method [19]. However, to the best of our knowledge, none of these formal approaches allow us to verify the solutions of differential equations.

These limitations can be overcome by using higher-order-logic theorem proving [13] for conducting the formal analysis of CPS since the high expressiveness of higher-order logic can be leveraged upon to model elements of continuous nature. However, the main challenge in this direction is the enormous human guidance required in the formal verification of CPS due to the non-decidable nature of higher-order logic. As a first step towards using a higher-order-logic theorem prover for formally verifying solutions of differential equations, we presented the formal reasoning support for the solutions of second-order homogeneous linear differential equations [23], i.e., a simple yet the most widely used class of differential equations, in [27]. In the current paper, we extend this work by presenting a formal definition that can be used to specify arbitrary order homogeneous linear differential equations. Moreover, we provide the formal verification of some mathematical facts, like a couple of general solutions of arbitrary order homogeneous linear differential equations and the quadratic formula, that allow us to reason about the correctness of the solutions of arbitrary order homogeneous linear differential equations in a very straightforward way. The prime advantage of these results is that they greatly minimize the user intervention for formal reasoning about differential equations and thus facilitate the usage of higher-order-logic theorem proving for verifying the solutions of differential equations for real-world industrial problems. In order to demonstrate the practical effectiveness and utilization of our formalization, we utilize it to analyze two CPS used in biomedical applications, i.e., a heart pacemaker and fluid-filled catheter.

Our formalization primarily builds upon the higher-order-logic formalization of the derivative function and its associated properties. This formalization is available in a number of theorem provers like HOL4 [14], PVS [8] and Coq [10]. Our work is based on Harrison's formalization [14] that is available in the HOL4 theorem prover [29]. The main motivations behind this choice is include the availability of formalized transcendental functions, which play a key role in the reported work, and the general richness of Harrison's real analysis related theories. Though, it is important to note here that the ideas presented in this paper are not specific to the HOL4 theorem prover and can be adapted to any other LCF style higher-order-logic theorem prover as well.

2   Related Work

Formal methods have been extensively used these days for analyzing CPS due to their ever increasing usage in various safety and financial-critical domains.

Zhang et al. [21] proposed to use formal specification for CPS in order to reduce the infinite set of test parameters in a finite set. Similarly, the aspect-oriented programming based on the UML and formal methods is utilized for QoS modeling of CPS in [20]. Moreover, in order to formally specify CPS along with their continuous aspects, a combination of formal methods Timed-CSP, ZimOO and differential (algebraic) equations is used in [32]. Even though such rigorous formal specifications allow us to catch bugs in the early stages of the design but they do not guarantee error-free analysis due to the informal nature of the analysis.

For formal verification of CPS, model-checking has been frequently explored. For example, Akella [2] proposed to discretize the events causing the change of flow and thus model the CPS as a deterministic state model with discrete values of flow within its physical components. This model is then used to formally verify insecure interactions between all possible behaviors of the given CPS using model checking. Similarly, Bu et al. [7] used hybrid model checking for verifying CPS. However, this verification is also not based on true continuous models of the system and instead a short-run behavior of the model is observed by providing numerical values of various parameters in order to reduce the state-space. A statistical model checker has been recently utilized to analyze some aspects of CPS [9]. However, this approach also suffers from the classical model checking issues, like the state-space explosion and inability to reason about generic mathematical relations. Thus the model checking approach, even though is capable of providing exact solutions, is quite limited in terms of handling true continuous models of CPS and thus various abstractions [30] have to be used for attaining meaningful results. The accuracy of the analysis is thus compromised, which is undesirable in the case of analyzing safety-critical applications of CPS.

Hybrid theorem provers, like KeYmaera [25], have also been used to verify CPS. However, these theorem provers use the support of computer algebra systems when it comes to solving differential equations and thus the solutions obtained cannot be completely trusted due to the presence of unverified symbolic manipulation algorithms in computer algebra systems.

Higher-order-logic theorem proving is capable of overcoming all the above mentioned problems. Atif et al. [22] used the HOL4 theorem prover for the probabilistic analysis of cyber-physical transportation systems. However, their focus was only on the formal verification of probabilistic aspects of CPS and they did not tackle the continuous aspects, especially the ones that require to be modeled by ODEs, which is the main focus of the current paper.

3   Derivatives in HOL4

In this section, we give a brief introduction to the formalization of the derivative function in HOL4 function to facilitate the understanding of the rest of the paper. Harrison [14] formalized the *real number theory* along with the fundamentals of calculus, such as real sequences, summation series, limits of a function and derivatives and verified most of their classical properties in HOL4. The limit of a function f, which takes a real number and returns a real number, is defined in HOL4 using the operator $\rightarrow$ as follows [14]:

Definition 1: ⊢ ∀ f y0 x0. (f → y0)(x0) = ∀e. 0 < e ⇒
  ∃d. 0 < d ∧ ∀x. 0 < |x - x0| ∧ |x - x0| < d ⇒
    |f(x) - y0| < e

where (f → y0)(x0) can be written mathematically as $lim_{(x \to x0)} f(x) = y0$, i.e., the function f approaches y0 as its real number argument approaches x0. Based on this definition, the derivative of a function f is defined as follows [14]:

Definition 2: ⊢ ∀ f l x.(f diffl l) x =
  ((λ h.(f (x + h) - f x) / h)→ l)(0)

Definition 2 provides the derivative of a function f at point x as the limit value of $\frac{f(x+h)-f(x)}{h}$ when h approaches 0, which is the standard mathematical definition of the derivative function. Now, the differentiability of a function f is defined as the existence of its derivative [14].

Definition 3: ⊢ ∀ f x. f differentiable x = ∃l. (f diffl l) (x)

A functional form of the derivative, which can be used as a binder, is also defined using the Hilbert choice operator @as follows [14]:

Definition 4: ⊢ ∀ f x. deriv f x = @l. (f diffl l) x

The function `deriv` accepts two parameters f and x and returns the derivative of function f at point x.

The above mentioned definitions associated with the derivative function have been accompanied by the formal verification of most of their classical properties, such as uniqueness, linearity and composition [14]. Moreover, the derivatives of some commonly used transcendental functions have also been verified. For example, the derivative of the Exponential function has been verified as follows:

Theorem 1: ⊢ ∀ g m x. ((g diffl m) x ⇒
  ((λx. exp (g x)) diffl (exp (g x) * m)) x)

where `exp x` represents the exponential function e^x and (λx.f(x)) represents the lambda abstraction function which accepts a variable x and returns $f(x)$. We build upon the above mentioned formalization to develop formal reasoning support for homogeneous linear differential equations and the details of our work are given in the next two sections.

4   Homogeneous Linear Differential Equations

An nth-order homogeneous linear ordinary differential equation can be mathematically expressed as follows:

$$p_n(x)\frac{d^n y(x)}{dx} + p_{n-1}(x)\frac{d^{n-1}y(x)}{dx} + \cdots + p_0(x)y(x) = 0 \qquad (1)$$

where $\frac{d^i f}{dx}$ denotes the ith ordinary derivative of the function f with respect to variable x and terms $p_i(x)$ represent the coefficients of the differential equation defined over a function y. The equation is linear because (i) the function y and its derivatives appear only in their first power and (ii) the products of y with its derivatives are also not present in the equation. By finding the solution of the above equation, we mean to find functions that can be used to replace the function y in Eq. (1) and satisfy it.

The first step in the proposed reasoning support framework is the ability to formalize homogeneous linear differential equation. We proceed in this direction by first formalizing an nth-order derivative function as follows:

Definition 5: ⊢ (∀ f x. n_order_deriv 0 f x = f x) ∧
   (∀f x n. n_order_deriv (n+1) f x = n_order_deriv n (deriv f x) x)

The function n_order_deriv accepts a positive integer n that represents the order of the derivative, the function f that represents the function that needs to be differentiated, and the variable x that is the variable with respect to which we want to differentiate the function f. It returns the nth-order derivative of f with respect to x. Now, based on this definition, we can formalize the left-hand-side (LHS) of Eq. (1) in HOL4 as the following definition.

Definition 6: ⊢ ∀ P y x. diff_eq_lhs P y x =
   sum (0,LENGTH P) (λn. (EL n P) x * (n_order_deriv n y x))

The function diff_eq_lhs accepts a list P of coefficient functions corresponding to the p_i's of Eq. (1), the differentiable function y, the order of differentiation n and the differentiation variable x. It utilizes the HOL4 functions sum (0,n) f, EL n L and LENGTH L, which correspond to the summation $(\sum_{i=0}^{n-1} f_i)$, the nth element of a list L_n, and the length of a list $|L|$, respectively. It generates the LHS of a differential equation of LENGTH(P)th order with coefficient list P. It is important to note that the order of the differential equation has been inferred from the number of its coefficients in the above definition.

The linearity property of derivatives play a very important role in our work. We verified this property for *class* C^n functions, i.e., the functions for which the first n derivatives exist for all x as the following higher-order-logic theorem:

Theorem 2: ⊢ ∀ f g x a b.
   (∀m x. m ≤ n⇒(λx. n_order_deriv m f x)differentiable x) ∧
   (∀m x. m ≤ n⇒(λx. n_order_deriv m g x)differentiable x) ⇒
      (n_order_deriv n (λx. a * f x + b * g x) x =
         a * n_order_deriv n f x + b * n_order_deriv n g x)

where variables a and b represent constants with respect to variable x. The formal reasoning about Theorem 2 involves induction on variable n, which represents the order of differentiation, and is primarily based on the linearity property of the first order derivative function [14].

5   Solution of Homogeneous Linear Differential Equations

It is a well-known mathematical fact that if $y_1(x), y_2(x), \cdots, y_n(x)$ are independent solutions of Eq. (1) then their linear combination

$$Y(x) = c_1 y_1(x) + c_2 y_2(x) + \cdots + c_n y_n(x) \tag{2}$$

also forms a solution of Eq. (1), where $c_1, c_2, \cdots, c_n$ are arbitrary constants [33]. This result plays a vital role in solving differential equations as it allows us to find the solution of a differential equation if its n independent solutions are known. A particular case of interest arises when the coefficients p_i's of Eq. (1) are constants in terms of the differentiation variable x. In this case, using the fact that the derivative of the exponential function $y = e^{rx}$ (with a constant r) is a constant multiple of itself $dy/dx = re^{rx}$, we can obtain the following solution:

$$Y(x) = c_1 e^{r_1 x} + c_2 e^{r_2 x} + \cdots + c_n e^{r_n x} \tag{3}$$

where $c_1, c_2, \cdots, c_n$ are arbitrary constants and $r_1, r_2, \cdots, r_n$ are the real and distinct roots of the characteristic equation

$$p_n r^n + p_{n-1} r^{n-1} + \cdots + p_0 = 0 \tag{4}$$

with constant p_i's [33]. The above mentioned results play a key role in solving homogeneous linear order differential equations and the main focus of this paper is the formal verification of these results, which in turn would facilitate formal reasoning about the correctness of solutions of differential equations in a higher-order-logic theorem prover.

We verified the first property, corresponding to Eq. (2), as follows:

Theorem 3: ⊢ ∀ Y C P x.
   (n_order_differentiable_fn_list Y (LENGTH P)) ∧
   (n_order_diff_eq_soln_list Y P x) ⇒
     (diff_eq_lhs P (λx. linear_sol C Y x) x = 0)

where Y represents the list of solutions $y_1(x), y_2(x), \cdots, y_n(x)$ of the given differential equation, C represents the list of arbitrary constants $c_1, c_2, \cdots, c_n$, P represents the list of functions corresponding to the coefficients $p_1(x), p_2(x), \cdots, p_n(x)$ of the differential equation and x is the variable of differentiation. The first predicate in the assumptions of Theorem 3, i.e., n_order_differentiable_fn_list, ensures that each element of the list Y is n^{th}-order differentiable, where n ranges from 0 to LENGTH P. It is defined in HOL4 recursively as follows:

Definition 7: ⊢ (∀ n. n_order_differentiable_fn_list [] n = True) ∧
   ∀ h t n. n_order_differentiable_fn_list (h::t) n =
   (∀m x. m ≤ n⇒(λx. n_order_deriv m h x)differentiable x) ∧
                    n_order_differentiable_fn_list t n

where :: represents the list *cons* operator in HOL4.

The second predicate in the assumptions of Theorem 3, i.e., n_order_diff_eq_soln_list, ensures that each element of the list Y is a solution of the given differential equation with coefficients P. This predicate is recursively defined in HOL4 as:

Definition 8: ⊢ (∀ P x. n_order_diff_eq_soln_list [] P x = True) ∧
    ∀ h t P x. n_order_diff_eq_soln_list (h::t) P x =
    (diff_eq_lhs P h x = 0) ∧ n_order_diff_eq_soln_list t L x

Finally the function linear_sol, used in the conclusion of Theorem 3, models the linear solution represented by Eq. (2) using the lists of solution functions Y and arbitrary constants C as follows:

Definition 9: ⊢ (∀ C x. linear_sol C [] x = 0) ∧
    ∀ C h t x. linear_sol C (h::t) x =
    EL (LENGTH C - LENGTH (h::t)) C * h x + linear_sol C t x

The recursive variable of Definition 9 is instantiated with the list Y in Theorem 3 and the expression EL (LENGTH C - LENGTH (h::t)) C picks the corresponding constant from list C for each y_i. Thus, using the functions linear_sol and diff_eq_lhs, we have formally verified the intended property in Theorem 3.

We verified Theorem 3 by performing induction on the variable Y. The proof is primarily based on the linearity properties of the nth-order derivative, (Theorem 2) and the summation function along with arithmetic reasoning.

The second property of interest, described using Eq. (3), can be expressed in HOL4 as the following theorem:

Theorem 4: ⊢ ∀ C P R x. (∀n. n < LENGTH R ⇒ EL n R <> r) ∧
    (ch_eq_roots_list R (const_fn_list P) x) ⇒
    (diff_eq_lhs (const_fn_list P)
               (λx. linear_sol C (exp_list R) x) x = 0)

where C represents the list of arbitrary constants $c_1, c_2, \cdots, c_n$, P represents the list of constants corresponding to the coefficients $p_1, p_2, \cdots, p_n$ of the differential equation, R represents the list of roots $r_1, r_2, \cdots, r_n$ of the characteristic equation, given in Eq. (4), and x is the variable of differentiation. The function const_fn_list used in the above theorem transforms a constant list to the corresponding constant function list recursively as follows:

Definition 10: ⊢ (const_fn_list [] = []) ∧
    (∀h t.const_fn_list (h::t) = (λ(x:real). h)::(const_fn_list t))

The function diff_eq_lhs permits coefficients that are functions of the variable of differentiation but Theorem 4 is valid only for constant coefficients. Thus, using const_fn_list we provide the required type for the coefficient list of the function diff_eq_lhs while fulfilling the requirement of Theorem 4.

The assumption predicate, i.e., ch_eq_roots_list, recursively ensures that each element of the list R is a valid root of the characteristic equation, like the one given in Eq. (4), with constant coefficients given by list P:

Definition 11: $\vdash \forall$ P r x. ch_eq_root P r x =
    (sum(0,LENGTH P)(λn.((EL n P x)) * (r pow n)) = 0) $\wedge$
    ($\forall$ P x. ch_eq_roots_list [] P x = True) $\wedge$
    ($\forall$ h t P x. ch_eq_roots_list (h::t) P x =
    (ch_eq_root P h x) $\wedge$ (ch_eq_roots_list t P x))

The first function ch_eq_root ensures that its argument r is a valid root of the characteristic equation formed by coefficients given in list P. The function ch_eq_roots_list recursively calls function ch_eq_root for each entry of the looping variable and thus ensures that all the entries of the looping list are valid roots of the characteristic equation formed by coefficients given in list P.

Finally, the function exp_list is used in Theorem 4 to model a list of exponential functions that are used to form the solution of the main differential equation, like the one given in Eq. (3). This function is defined as follows:

Definition 12: $\vdash$ (exp_list [] = []) $\wedge$
    (exp_list (h::t) = (λx. exp (h * x)) :: (exp_list t))

It is important to note that the function linear_sol is used to express the conclusion of Theorem 4 as has been then case for Theorem 3. This way, the formally verified result of Theorem 3 can be used in formally verifying Theorem 4. The formal reasoning about Theorem 4 is conducted by performing induction on variable Y and the reasoning is primarily based on Theorem 4 and the following lemma that allows us to express the left-hand-side of the step case of Theorem 4 in terms of real summation.

Lemma 1: $\vdash \forall$ P h x. (diff_eq_lhs P (λx. exp (h * x)) x =
    (exp (h * x)) * (sum (0,LENGTH P) (λn. EL n P x * h pow n))))

Now, If the roots of an characteristic equation are real and repeated then the solution of Eq. (1) can be written as

$$Y(x) = c_1 e^{rx} + c_2 x e^{rx} + \cdots + c_n x^{n-1} e^{rx} \tag{5}$$

where $c_1, c_2, \cdots, c_n$ are arbitrary constants and r is the real and repeated root of the characteristic equation given below

$$p_n r^n + p_{n-1} r^{n-1} + \cdots + p_0 = 0 \tag{6}$$

The solution of Eq. (1), described using Eq. (5), can be expressed in HOL4 as the following theorem:

Theorem 5: ⊢ ∀ C R r. (∀n. n < LENGTH R ⇒ EL n R = r) ∧
  (∀m. m < LENGTH R ⇒ (diff_eq_lhs
  (const_fn_list C) (λx. x pow m * exp (r * x)) x =0))
   ⇒ (diff_eq_lhs (const_fn_list C)
    (λx. linear_sol C (polynomial_function R) x) x = 0)

Where C and R are lists of constants and roots, respectively.

The assumptions of Theorem 5 ensure that the roots of the characteristic equation are the same and equal to r and $e^{rx}, xe^{rx}, x^2e^{rx}, \cdots, x^{LENGTH\ R\ -1}e^{rx}$ are all solutions of the given differential equation. The conclusion of the theorem specifies that Eq. 5 is a solution of the given differential equation using the functions `polynomial_function` and `linear_sol`. The function `linear_sol` is given in Definition 9 and the `polynomial_function` is defined as follows:

Definition 13: ⊢ (polynomial_function [] = []) ∧
  (polynomial_function (h::t) =
  (λx.(x pow (LENGTH t))*exp(h*x))::(polynomial_function t))

The formal reasoning about Theorem 5 is conducted by performing induction on variable R and the reasoning is primarily based on Theorem 3 and the following lemma that tells us that all derivatives of exponential with multiple of increasing power of x are differentiable.

Lemma 2: ⊢ ∀ R n h x. (λx. n_order_deriv n
  (λx. x pow LENGTH R * exp(h * x)) x) differentiable x

Besides the above mentioned key results, we also verified the famous quadratic formula, which plays a vital role in reasoning about the characteristic equations of second degree and also provides some support for reasoning about characteristic equations of higher order. The quadratic formula is verified as follows:

Theorem 6: ⊢ ∀ a b c x. (a ≠ 0) ∧ (4 * a * c < b pow 2) ⇒
  ch_eq_roots_list [((-b + sqrt (b pow 2 - 4 * a * c)) /
  (2 * a));((-b - sqrt (b pow 2 - 4 * a * c)) / (2 * a))]
  (const_fn_list [a; b; c]) x

where the functions `sqrt` and `pow` represent the square-root and square of a real number, respectively. The theorem essentially says that the roots of the characteristic equation $ax^2 + bx + c$ are given by the first list argument of the function `ch_eq_roots_list`. The assumption (4 * a * c < b pow 2) guarantees that the roots are always real.

The main benefit of the formalization presented above is that now building upon these results the formal verification of solutions of homogeneous linear differential equations would be done almost automatically as will be illustrated in the next section. It is worth while to point out that the major effort in our development was spent in finalizing the formal nomenclature, presented in the form of definitions in this paper, to represent homogeneous linear differential equations. The generic nature of these definitions allows us to represent almost all kinds of homogeneous linear differential equations. The formal verification of the theorems described in this section required human guidance but the simplifiers were a great help in this process. Our HOL proof script [28] is composed of over 1200 lines of code and the verification took about 300 man-hours.

6   Biomedical Applications

Biomedical applications are one of the most safety-critical applications of CPS as their bugs could eventually result in the loss of human lives. Differential equations form the core foundation of modeling almost all biomedical applications [11]. Due to a lack of formal reasoning support for differential equation solutions, most of the analysis of CPS used in biomedical applications with continuous components is done using informal analysis techniques so far. Our work tends to fill this gap and thus facilitates the usage of formal methods in this safety-critical domain. We present two case studies, i.e., the analysis of a heart pacemaker and a fluid-filled catheter, to illustrate the usefulness and effectiveness of our work.

6.1   Heart Pacemaker

Electronic heart pacemakers are widely used for supplementing or replacing heart's natural pacing mechanism in humans. The pacemaker specification has been proposed as a pilot project for the Verified Software Initiative [17].

Their main working principle is to store electrical energy in a capacitor and then discharge this energy in short pulses through the heart to provide it with the required sudden electrical stimulus. Besides the capacitor, they include a battery, which provides the energy source, and a switch to govern the charging and discharging of the capacitor. Figure 1 illustrates the connections between these main components and their working [11]. The capacitor is charged via the battery when the switch S is moved to position A, while the capacitor provides the short and intense pulses to the heart when the switch S is in position B.

Based on Fig. 1, the behavior of an electronic heart pacemaker can be described in terms of the following differential equation [11]:

$$\frac{dV}{dt} + \frac{1}{RC}V = 0, \ V(0) = E \tag{7}$$

since the current through the capacitor (CdV/dt) equals the current through the heart (V/R), which behaves as a resistor R, when the switch S is in position B. Moreover, the capacitor is allowed to charge to its full capacity when the switch is in position A and thus we obtain the initial condition $V(0) = E$. This simplistic but realistic mathematical model of a heart pacemaker has been extensively used in the literature to analyze the underlying properties of interest (See e.g., [11,31]. In this paper, we utilize our formalization described in the previous two sections to formally reason about the solution of Eq. (7). We proceed by specifying the theorem stating the solution $(Ee^{-\frac{t}{RC}})$ of Eq. (7) as follows:

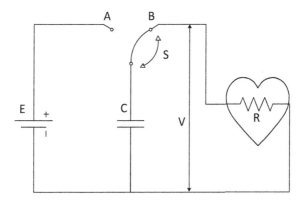

Fig. 1. Equivalent circuit of an electronic pacemaker

Theorem 7: ⊢ ∀ R C C1 V E t.
  (diff_eq_lhs (const_fn_list [(1/(R*C)); 1])
  (λx.linear_sol [C1] (exp_list [-(1/(R*C))]) x) t = 0)

The initial condition $V(0) = C1$ is implicitly contained in the above theorem as it is satisfied for the case $t = 0$. Thus, the theorem provides the general solution of the given differential equation and the value of the constant C for the particular solution.

Our formalized definitions facilitated the formal specification of the above theorem and the formally verified Theorem 4 allowed us to verify the above theorem in a few reasoning steps where we just had to provide the definitions of the functions used in Theorem 6 and some primitive list theory functions, like EL and LENGTH, along with invoking an automatic arithmetic simplifier. The straightforward reasoning process about the correctness of solution of the given differential equation in the sound environment of HOL4 clearly demonstrates the effectiveness of our work.

6.2 Fluid-Filled Catheter

As a second case study of our work, consider the dynamic analysis of a fluid-filled catheter, which allows physicians to measure the pressure of the internal organs and fluids of a human body without inserting a pressure transducer in the body. The main idea is to insert a long and small-bore fluid-filled tube or catheter in the body and thus bring the pressure of the pressure measuring site outside and then use a conventional pressure transducer to measure it. However, mechanical parameters like the mass of the catheter fluid and the friction of this fluid with the catheter wall may introduce some discrepancies in the pressure measurements. Therefore, it is very important to analyze the effects of such mechanical parameters on the pressure measurements as a wrong reading may endanger a patient's life. A number of studies, e.g. [12,18], have analyzed this aspect by considering the following second-order linear differential equation:

$$\frac{1}{\omega_n^2}\frac{d^2p}{dt^2} + \frac{2\zeta}{\omega_n}\frac{dp}{dt} + p = 0 \tag{8}$$

where p is the applied pressure, $\omega_n = \sqrt{k/\rho LA}$ represents the undamped natural angular frequency (radians per unit time) in terms of a constant k, catheter fluid density ρ, length L and cross-sectional area A, and $\zeta = c/2\sqrt{1/\rho kLA}$ is the damping factor with a constant c. Equation (8) allows us to find the pressure in response to any force function given that the coefficients ω_n and ζ are known. The solution of this equation can be formally verified as the following theorem:

Theorem 8: $\vdash \forall$ rho A L k c C1 C2.
```
(sqrt(4 * rho * L * A * k)<c ∧ 0<rho ∧ 0<L ∧ 0<A ∧ 0<k ⇒
(diff_eq_lhs (const_fn_list
            [k / (rho * L * A); c / (rho * L * A); 1])
            (λx. linear_sol [C1; C2]
(exp_list [(-(c / (rho * L * A)) +
           sqrt ((c / (rho * L * A)) pow 2
        - 4 * (k / (rho * L * A)))) / 2;(-(c / (rho * L * A)) -
           sqrt ((c / (rho * L * A)) pow 2 -
           4 * (k / (rho * L * A)))) / 2]) x) x = 0))
```

The assumptions of the above theorem declare the relationships between the various parameters that are required for the solution to hold. This is one of strengths of the proposed theorem proving based verification as all the assumptions have to be explicitly stated besides the theorem for its formal verification. Thus, there is no chance of missing a critical assumption which often occurs in paper-and-pencil proof methods where there is no such guarantee that the mathematician who worked out the proof has written down all the assumptions.

Formal reasoning about Theorem 8 is primarily based on Theorems 4 and 6 along with some arithmetic rewriting, which can be done in an automatic manner using the HOL arithmetic simplifiers. The straightforward proof scripts for of Theorems 7 and 8 clearly indicate the usefulness of our foundational formalization presented in Sects. 4 and 5 of this paper. Just like these case studies our formalization results can be utilized to formally reason about solution of any homogeneous linear differential equation and the results would be guaranteed to be correct due to the inherent soundness of theorem proving.

7   Conclusions

In this paper, we propose to use higher-order-logic theorem proving to analyze continuous aspects of CPS. Due to the high expressiveness of the underlying logic, we can formally model the continuous components of CPS while capturing their true behavior and the soundness of theorem proving guarantees correctness of results. To the best of our knowledge, these features are not shared by any other existing CPS analysis technique. The main challenge in the proposed approach is the enormous amount of user intervention required due to the undecidable nature of the logic. We propose to overcome this limitation by formalizing the foundational mathematical theories so that these available results can be built upon to minimize user interaction. As a first step towards this direction, we presented the formalization of the solutions of any homogeneous linear differential equation in this paper. Based on this work, we are able to formally analyze the CPS used in a couple of biomedical systems.

The proposed approach opens the doors to many new directions of research. We are working on developing reasoning support for non-homogeneous linear differential equations. Moreover, the calculus theories available in HOL-Light [15] are based on multivariate real numbers and thus can model complex numbers. Our formalization can be ported in a very straight-forward manner to this formalization of complex numbers in HOL-Light, which would enable handling the formal analysis of CPS that can be modeled in the complex plane only.

References

1. Abraham-Mumm, E., Steffen, M., Hannemann, U.: Verification of hybrid systems: formalization and proof rules in PVS. In: ICECCS, pp. 48–57 (2001)
2. Akella, R., McMillin, B.M.: Model-checking BNDC properties in cyber-physical systems. In: Computer Software and Applications Conference, pp. 660–663 (2009)
3. Platzer, A., Clarke, E.M.: Computing differential invariants of hybrid systems as fixedpoints. Formal Methods Syst. Des. **35**(1), 98–120 (2009)
4. Baier, C., Katoen, J.: Principles of Model Checking. MIT Press, Cambridge (2008)
5. Boca, P.P., Bowen, J.P., Siddiqi, J.I.: Formal Methods: State of the Art and New Directions. Springer, Heidelberg (2009)
6. Boldo, S., Clément, F., Filliâtre, J.-C., Mayero, M., Melquiond, G., Weis, P.: Formal proof of a wave equation resolution scheme: the method error. In: Kaufmann, M., Paulson, L.C. (eds.) ITP 2010. LNCS, vol. 6172, pp. 147–162. Springer, Heidelberg (2010)
7. Bu, L., Wang, Q., Chen, X., Wang, L., Zhang, T., Zhao, J., Li, X.: Towards online hybrid systems model checking of cyber-physical systems' time-bounded short-run behavior. SIGBED **2**, 7–10 (2011)
8. Butler, R.W.: Formalization of the integral calculus in the PVS theorem prover. J. Formalized Reasoning **2**(1), 1–26 (2009)
9. Clarke, E.M., Zuliani, P.: Statistical model checking for cyber-physical systems. In: Bultan, T., Hsiung, P.-A. (eds.) ATVA 2011. LNCS, vol. 6996, pp. 1–12. Springer, Heidelberg (2011)
10. Cruz-Filipe, L.: Constructive real analysis: a type-theoretical formalization and applications. Ph.D. thesis, University of Nijmegen, April 2004
11. Glantz, S.A.: Mathematics for Biomedical Applications. University of California Press, Berkeley (1979)
12. Glantz, S.A., Tyberg, J.V.: Determination of frequency response from step response: application to fluid-filled catheters. Am. J. Physiol. **236**, 376–378 (1979)
13. Gordon, M.J.C.: Mechanizing programming logics in higher-order logic. In: Birtwistle, G., Subrahmanyam, P.A. (eds.) Current Trends in Hardware Verification and Automated Theorem Proving, pp. 387–439. Springer, Heidelberg (1989)

14. Harrison, J.: Theorem Proving with the Real Numbers. Springer, Heidelberg (1998)
15. Harrison, J.V.: A HOL theory of euclidean space. In: Hurd, J., Melham, T. (eds.) TPHOLs 2005. LNCS, vol. 3603, pp. 114–129. Springer, Heidelberg (2005)
16. Harrison, J.: Handbook of Practical Logic and Automated Reasoning. Cambridge University Press, Cambridge (2009)
17. Hoare, C.A.R., Misra, J., Leavens, G.T., Shankar, N.: The verifed software initiative: a manifesto. ACM Comput. Surv. **41**(4), 1–8 (2009)
18. Hougen, J.O., Hougen, S.T., Hougen, T.J.: Dynamics of fluid-filled catheter systems by pulse testing. Ind. Eng. Chem. Fundam. **25**, 462–470 (1986)
19. Immler, F., Hölzl, J.: Numerical analysis of ordinary differential equations in Isabelle/HOL. In: Beringer, L., Felty, A. (eds.) ITP 2012. LNCS, vol. 7406, pp. 377–392. Springer, Heidelberg (2012)
20. Liu, J., Zhang, L.: QoS modeling for cyber-physical systems using aspect-oriented approach. In: 2011 Second International Conference on Networking and Distributed Computing (ICNDC), pp. 154–158 (2011)
21. Zhang, L., Hu, J., Yu, W.: Generating Test Cases for Cyber Physical Systems from Formal Specification, pp. 97–103. Springerl, Heidelberg (2011)
22. Mashkoor, A., Hasan, O.: Formal probabilistic analysis of cyber-physical transportation systems. In: Murgante, B., Gervasi, O., Misra, S., Nedjah, N., Rocha, A.M.A.C., Taniar, D., Apduhan, B.O. (eds.) ICCSA 2012, Part III. LNCS, vol. 7335, pp. 419–434. Springer, Heidelberg (2012)
23. Oduola, K., Sofimieari, I., Nwambo, P.: A method for solving higher order homogeneous ordinary differential equations with non-constant coefficients. J. Emerg. Trends Eng. Appl. Sci. **2**(1), 7–10 (2011)
24. Platzer, A.: Differential dynamic logics for hybrid systems. J. Autom. Reasoning **41**(2), 143–189 (2008)
25. Platzer, A., Quesel, J.-D.: KeYmaera: a hybrid theorem prover for hybrid systems (system description). In: Armando, A., Baumgartner, P., Dowek, G. (eds.) IJCAR 2008. LNCS (LNAI), vol. 5195, pp. 171–178. Springer, Heidelberg (2008)
26. Rajkumar, R., Lee, I., Sha, L., Stankovic, J.J.: Cyber-physical systems: the next computing revolution. In: 2010 47th ACM/IEEE Design Automation Conference (DAC), pp. 731–736 (2010)
27. Sanwal, M.U., Hasan, O.: Formal verification of cyber-physical systems: coping with continuous elements. In: Murgante, B., Misra, S., Carlini, M., Torre, C.M., Nguyen, H.-Q., Taniar, D., Apduhan, B.O., Gervasi, O. (eds.) ICCSA 2013, Part I. LNCS, vol. 7971, pp. 358–371. Springer, Heidelberg (2013)
28. Sanwal, M.U.: Formal Reasoning about Homogeneous Linear Differential Equations (2013). http://save.seecs.nust.edu.pk/students/usman/lde.html
29. Slind, K., Norrish, M.: A brief overview of HOL4. In: Mohamed, O.A., Muñoz, C., Tahar, S. (eds.) TPHOLs 2008. LNCS, vol. 5170, pp. 28–32. Springer, Heidelberg (2008)
30. Thacker, R.A., Jones, K.R., Myers, C.J., Zheng, H.: Automatic abstraction for verification of cyber-physical systems. In: Proceedings of the 1st ACM/IEEE International Conference on Cyber-Physical Systems, pp. 12–21. ACM (2010)
31. Zhang, H., Liu, J.H., Holden, A.V.: Computing the age-related dysfunction of cardiac pacemaker. Comput. Cardiol. **33**, 665–668 (2006)
32. Zhang, L.: Aspect oriented formal techniques for cyber physical systems. J. Softw. **7**(4), 823–834 (2012)
33. Zill, D.G., Wright, W.S., Cullen, M.R.: Advanced Engineering Mathematics, 4th edn. Jones and Bartlett Learning, London (2009)

Author Index

Printed in the United States
By Bookmasters